T0339830

Foreign Aid

Foreign Aid: Policy and Practice offers a complete overview of the basics of foreign aid. Who is it for? Who pays for it? Why does it exist? What is it spent on? How much is it? And most important, does it work?

The aid debate has been flooded by academic studies and popular books that either challenge or champion the effectiveness of aid. Most presume that the reader already knows the basic facts and characteristics of the aid industry. This book provides readers with a comprehensive summary of the background, actors, core principles and policies, and intended (and unintended) outcomes of foreign aid, followed by a more informed and balanced treatment of the key controversies and trends in aid today. Drawing on the author's 25 years' experience in development practice and 15 years in teaching, the book reflects on recent efforts to accelerate aid's impact and concludes by taking a look at the future of aid and the headwinds it will face in the first half of the 21st century.

Perfect for university teaching at advanced undergraduate and graduate levels, this book will also encourage development practitioners, policy makers, and members of the public to engage in more informed debates about aid and development finance.

Phyllis R. Pomerantz is Professor Emerita of the Practice of Public Policy at the Duke Center for International Development, Sanford School of Public Policy, Duke University, USA, where she has taught graduate students for over 15 years. Before this, she had a long career at the World Bank, including managerial appointments in agriculture, rural development, and infrastructure, and as a country director and the World Bank's first Chief Learning Officer.

Foreign Aid
Policy and Practice

Phyllis R. Pomerantz

 Routledge
Taylor & Francis Group

LONDON AND NEW YORK

Designed cover image: © Getty Images

First published 2024
by Routledge
4 Park Square, Milton Park, Abingdon, Oxon OX14 4RN

and by Routledge
605 Third Avenue, New York, NY 10158

*Routledge is an imprint of the Taylor & Francis Group,
an informa business*

© 2024 Phyllis R. Pomerantz

British Library Cataloguing-in-Publication Data
A catalogue record for this book is available from the British Library

ISBN: 978-1-032-20807-7 (hbk)
ISBN: 978-1-032-20806-0 (pbk)
ISBN: 978-1-003-26532-0 (ebk)

DOI: 10.4324/9781003265320

Typeset in Galliard Pro
by Apex CoVantage, LLC

Contents

Figures

Tables

Boxes and Classroom Vignettes

Boxes

Classroom Vignettes

Preface

I have been both a practitioner and a student of foreign aid for over 40 years. It was only after I began teaching graduate students at Duke University in the United States that I began to realize that I had learned a considerable amount over that time. My students encouraged me to write a book based on the Politics of International Aid course I taught for over 15 years at Duke. I began writing this book, both in my head and on paper, some years ago, but it was only when I stopped teaching that I had the time and energy to devote to this task.

I have realized over the years that complex issues seem to only get more complex. Nuances and exceptions abound. At the same time, there are tendencies and trends and even sometimes clarity and consensus on a particular subject. I hope that this book strikes the appropriate balance between the particular and the general. It was born out of years of practice but also shaped by the impressive aid literature generated by academia, think tanks, and aid organizations.

I would like to acknowledge first and foremost, my mostly international graduate students at Duke who were a true joy to work with, year after year. We laughed together and learned together; they had valuable experience and much to say about what had happened in their countries. The same is true for the many outstanding country officials I worked with over the years. Some of those conversations are engraved forever in my mind and also in my heart. I also want to thank my former colleagues at the World Bank and my colleagues at Duke and especially those at the Duke Center for International Development and the Sanford School of Public Policy. This book is the result of our work together. Both institutions provided a stimulating (and yes, also at times exasperating) environment and home base.

On this book especially, I want to thank my publications team at Routledge, especially Senior Editor Helena Hurd, who encouraged me from the start, and to the four anonymous reviewers who had many helpful comments on an early version of the book. I also want to thank Rosie Anderson, my first contact at Routledge and now an editor, Katerina

Lade, the editorial assistant who worked on this book, and Routledge's production staff.

Finally, I am grateful for Kiwi and Chico, who supervised the writing of this book. I am particularly indebted to Charles Hochman, my husband, who has no idea how much his "one day at a time" kept me going.

Part I

The Basics of Foreign Aid

1 Introduction

Economic and social development and "the end of poverty" are nearly universal aspirations. How best to achieve these is one of the greatest puzzles of our time. There is much discussion of resiliency and self-reliance. In reality, the nations of the world have been inextricably linked throughout history by war, trade, financial flows, contagious diseases, and the global ecosystem.

Among financial flows is foreign aid, when one nation decides to give money to another. Foreign aid is a controversial topic. It is tied to perspectives on nationalism and globalization as well as to policies and practices for economic, social, and political development. It has passionate defenders and equally passionate critics. Some credit aid with accelerating both economic growth and social welfare improvements. Others judge aid as harmful and an obstacle to achieving sustainable gains for the poor. Still others see aid as a necessary evil. It has been referred to as a "wicked problem" (Ramalingam, 2013) and a "black box" (Bourguignon & Sundberg, 2007), with the connotation that how, when, and why it succeeds is essentially unknowable.

Nor is it clear what success looks like; success means different things to different actors. Aid can be evaluated according to its ability to bolster the national security of the donor or its ability to promote economic and social development of the recipient. Aid can be judged according to its effect on gross national income per capita or its impact on incomes and living standards for the poorest. Even if successful aid is linked to development, what ultimately is development? Does it mean being richer or happier? Countries like Bhutan insist that Gross National Happiness is a more meaningful concept than Gross National Income (University of Oxford, n.d.).

Not surprisingly, given the complexity and controversy surrounding aid, there is a prolific literature explaining, analyzing, and critiquing it. That literature takes on many forms today: academic publications, official reports and documents, the popular press, and increasingly social media. There is an avalanche of words. Frequently, however, definitions and

DOI: 10.4324/9781003265320-2

sources of the information are unclear, and there is selective use of less-than-reliable data to support particular arguments and viewpoints. On top of this, aid and the objectives it supports are not static; who, what, when, how, and why are constantly in flux, even though major changes in the aid industry are painfully slow.

Why This Book?

So why add to the avalanche of words on foreign aid? There are several compelling reasons. The last 20 or so years have witnessed large changes in the amount of aid available and the number of donors. While private sector finance and other forms of development finance are growing and overshadowing aid in its strictest definition, aid is still critically important for low and middle-income countries and will remain so, especially in difficult times. And difficult times are upon us. The world is caught in the throes of multiple, interlinked crises: climate change, war, financial upheavals, pandemics. If astutely employed, aid can be useful in mitigating some of the worst effects of crises on developing countries. However, despite the changing face of aid over time, the debate over aid effectiveness has not diminished, and there is major emphasis on obtaining and measuring "results". Aid effectiveness, "getting the biggest bang for the buck", has to be central in a world where limited resources are facing more and more demands. Whether the way that results are being obtained and measured contribute to aid effectiveness is a question to be explored. Recent history, including the regime change in Afghanistan and the reversal of health and income gains due to the COVID-19 pandemic, strongly argue for the need to achieve more robust and sustainable results.

Another compelling reason to re-examine aid at this point is the changing international context. After the fall of the Soviet Union, the globe seemed to be headed towards a unipolar world led by the United States and Western Europe. Today, with the rise of China, the consolidation of the European Union, a revitalized and active Russia, and the wealth and power of the Gulf States in the Middle East, it is looking increasingly like a multi-polar world. What does this mean for low and middle-income countries and for the assistance they need? What does this mean for the world's ability to face global challenges? What are the implications for the world's poorest citizens?

The changing international context is straining the traditional international aid system. China, Turkey, and the United Arab Emirates have become significant donors, with aid practices that are different from those of Western Europe and the United States. While official aid has grown, the needs have grown even faster. Care for migrants and post-conflict reconstruction have emerged as important obligations for many donor countries. Multiple crises have landed many developing countries in debt distress, and debt relief is once again part of global aid discussions. The effects of global warming are already visible. More support for climate mitigation and adaptation is an urgent priority. Leveraging private sector resources has become a legitimate use of aid as recognition grows of the larger-than-ever funding gaps, especially given the ambition of global plans such as the Sustainable Development Goals approved by the United Nations in 2015. Aid discussions in this changing environment have broadened to include other sources of development finance and a focus on getting results. Yet, it is not apparent that the necessary steps have been taken for significant improvements in aid effectiveness. As donor countries experience financial difficulties at home, their generosity may wane. Given this context, it is a highly appropriate moment to review and critically examine both traditional aid practices and recent innovations.

Finally, and surprisingly given the amount written, there is a dearth of up-to-date textbooks for advanced undergraduate and graduate students interested in aid. There is a dizzying array of articles, documents, and specialized books, but few cover the basics of aid before going on to explore recent innovations and the debates and issues surrounding aid. Consequently, many aid and development courses focus on a few topics but leave students with a less-than-complete picture of the history and current state of the aid industry. This book aims to provide some measure of aid literacy so that afterwards students and practitioners confidently can go on to explore specialized topics in more detail. It's the kind of book I wish I had read early on in my career as a development practitioner and the kind of book I wish I had available when I was designing courses on aid and development as a professor.

No Grand Theories

Those who are looking for a "grand theory of aid" will be disappointed. Because aid is a "wicked problem" with many actors, no one theory can do it justice. This book uses fragments of theories from development economics, political science, international relations, and public policy to try and put together a coherent picture of aid. It strives to be evidence-based, so the theory is derived from the evidence and not vice versa. It is structured so that first the basics are covered regarding donors, recipients, and forms of aid before going deeply into issues of relationships, implementation, and effectiveness. At the end, there is speculation about the future of aid, but it is speculation born out of analysis of the past and present practices of aid, as well as analysis of the global context in which aid will likely be operating in the coming years.

The framework that is used, first developed by Bourguignon and Sundberg, is one that decomposes aid into three critical linkages (2007). The first is the relationship of policies to outcomes, in other words, technical knowledge. The second is the relationship of policymakers to policy; how exactly are decisions made? That connects aid to governance. The third linkage is the relationship of external aid donors to policymakers. Do aid donors influence policymakers and vice versa? How so? While some evidence has been accumulated on technical knowledge, evidence on the role of governance is mixed, and evidence on the role of aid relationships is largely missing. In the end, this means that aid continues to be a "wicked problem", one that is best dealt with by trial and error and with a large dose of humility.

A Definitional Note

What is aid? As it turns out, that is not an easy question to answer, and Chapter 4 will delve further into the various definitions. For the purpose of this book, aid is mainly defined as official aid that is given to countries and organizations on concessional terms for improving incomes and living conditions for people living in relatively poor countries. While humanitarian aid is included in that definition, the book focuses mostly on developmental aid. While many of the issues with humanitarian aid are similar, that kind of aid has some unique characteristics that deserve a careful treatment of its own. The book does cover, although not extensively, aid provided by private foundations for developmental purposes, although this type of assistance is not official aid. What is not covered in this book is military aid, even though foreign troops have been instrumental in many conflict and post-conflict settings.

As noted earlier, aid effectiveness is also a complex concept, and as the book will show the presumed characteristics and the very definition of aid effectiveness have changed over time. In this book, aid effectiveness is defined as aid that reduces poverty and improves the welfare and well-being of people. It is important to keep that definition in mind while sorting through the complexity associated with the aid industry today.

A Note on Language

Language is a powerful tool that can convey meaning far beyond words. Today the official language of aid has changed. Countries that provide aid and countries that receive aid are "development partners". In some contexts, countries that provide aid are "financing partners" and only the recipient countries are "development partners". Aid itself is frequently referred to as "development cooperation". Countries like China see their assistance as "South-South cooperation" rather than aid. The official language is meant to convey partnership and cooperation; more often than not, it is aspirational or at best only partially true. To avoid confusion, this text deliberately uses the old-fashioned terms *donor*, *recipient*, and *aid provider* because they are clear and unambiguous. Most low and middle-income countries (sometimes collectively referred to as *developing countries* in this book – another old-fashioned term) see the countries and organizations that give or lend them money on concessional terms (i.e., significantly below market rates) as "donors" regardless of their geographical or political affiliation. The choice of language was made for clarity's sake, but also as a reminder of both the history and the power dynamics of aid from post-World War II until today.

Outline of the Book

The book has two parts. Part I, The Basics of Foreign Aid, aims to give everyone a common understanding of the context, actors, amounts, and mechanics of aid. Part II, Effective Aid: Debates and Trends, delves into the main issues and arguments concerning aid and aid effectiveness. It then reviews recent trends, and it ends by conjecturing about key features of aid in the future.

After this Introduction, Chapter 2 sets out the overall context for aid, briefly reviewing its history from the end of colonialism until today. It recounts the concerns with aid effectiveness beginning in the 1990s, brought on by "aid fatigue" accompanied by diminishing amounts of aid, and the change in motivations resulting from the end of the competition with the Soviet Union. The chapter concludes by focusing on the overall situation of low and middle-income countries today and some the challenges they face in using aid to bolster economic and social development.

Chapter 3 looks at the main actors who receive and provide aid. It discusses the motivations of both recipients and donors and shows who is receiving the most aid. It goes on to review the key characteristics of four types of donors: traditional bilateral donors who belong to the Development Assistance Committee of the Organization for Economic Cooperation and Development (OECD-DAC); "new" or "emerging" donors who are not part of OECD-DAC; multilateral organizations and banks, like the United Nations and the World Bank, that are heavily involved in development; and foundations and non-governmental organizations (NGOs). This last group works with both official and private sources of finance. The chapter also mentions private citizens and the importance of the funds they provide to relatives and friends in other countries. Remittances are not counted as official development finance or aid, but they pay for many private goods and community-level public goods that contribute to incomes and well-being.

The next chapter, which is the concluding chapter of Part I, is all about official aid. It discusses definitions of aid and the differences between what the public thinks of as aid and Overseas Development Assistance (ODA), the more formal and limited definition of aid. The chapter covers broader development finance as well as other important terms and definitions, and it analyzes the relative importance of ODA. It then outlines how aid is packaged, explaining the types (along with examples), modalities, and channels of aid, and the basis on which decisions about packaging aid are made. The chapter concludes with a look at the amount of overall aid and how it is distributed by major purpose, region, and income group.

Part II, Effective Aid: Debates and Trends, begins with a chapter on judging donor performance. The chapter asks what makes a good donor. It reviews the various theories and indices that have been developed over the years to judge donor quality. The emphasis is not on how individual donors scored but on identifying indicators that are considered fundamental for satisfactory donor performance. While the efforts to identify donor quality are only a couple of decades old, the variation among indices and across time is striking. There is little consensus on indicators or results, although there is a tendency for multilateral agencies to be judged more favorably. Nonetheless, the indicators tell a powerful story about how the meaning of good donor performance has changed over time within the donor community and how this diverges from the recipients' point of view.

Chapter 6 reviews the vigorous debate on aid effectiveness by public intellectuals that began in the first decade of this century. It succinctly describes the differences of opinion between Jeffrey Sachs, an aid enthusiast, and William Easterly, an aid skeptic. This debate was accompanied by serious critiques of aid by Dambisa Moyo, a Zambian economist, and Angus Deaton, a Nobel Laureate. In response, others pointed to aid's positive accomplishments. Bill Gates, for example, said that funding health delivery was "the best investment I've ever made" (Gates, 2019). More recently, Abhijit Banerjee and Esther Duflo, two more Nobel economists, have argued for moving away from the great debate on aid effectiveness. Instead, they prioritize a more focused approach, conducting randomized controlled trials (RCTs) to learn what works in specific circumstances. The widely differing views of prominent intellectuals lead to a concluding discussion on the confounding issues in evaluating aid effectiveness.

Chapter 7 analyzes aid effectiveness through the framework first developed by Francois Bourguignon and Mark Sundberg (2007). The workings of aid consist of three linkages involved with knowledge, governance, and aid relationships. The chapter then turns to the evidence on aid effectiveness, which is plentiful but often contradictory. The evidence at the macro level indicates that at least some aid is effective even though the widely held belief that "aid works best in a good policy environment" likely overstates the impact of policy. At the micro level, more rigorous project evaluations and the emphasis on RCTs have yielded a great deal of site-specific and project-specific knowledge on "what works" but tell relatively little about how and why results are achieved. Focusing primarily on technical aspects is unlikely to be sufficient to guarantee improved aid effectiveness. The chapter concludes by returning to the other two linkages, governance and aid relationships, to review what is known about how these contribute to aid effectiveness. More understanding of both is needed to finally open the "black box".

Chapter 8 traces the efforts towards improving aid over the last decade or so. The vigorous process that culminated in the Busan High-Level Meeting in 2011 has been far more modest in the last decade, as threats to peace, pandemics, climate change, and economic disruptions have preoccupied donors and recipient countries alike. Despite maintaining aid levels, creating new organizations such as the Global Partnership for Effective Development Cooperation (GPEDC) and approving an ambitious agenda codified in the Sustainable Development Goals (SDGs), overall development and poverty results have been disappointing. The multiple crises have even reversed some of the previous gains. Despite this, there are some hopeful signs on the horizon, with new project types, more flexible disbursement mechanisms, new financing vehicles, and a focus on innovation, resilience, and recovery along with increased emphasis on underinvested areas such as climate and gender. There are also some new ways that donors are doing business, with more attention paid to the local context and the hiring of local staff. Nonetheless, global pressures and some of the new mechanisms may evoke or at least reflect a growing trust deficit between donors and recipients, creating new barriers to aid effectiveness.

Chapter 9 is the concluding chapter, summing up and looking ahead. It points to a new age of pragmatism, where aid is expected to bear tangible results over the short-term and is viewed as an integral part of the foreign policy "toolbox". Despite earlier thoughts that aid was a dying industry, aid is here to stay. While there is much discussion and disagreement as to aid priorities, the differing agendas and the resulting tensions provide a certain stability for aid. That stability also means that aid policies and practices in reality are quite slow to change, and the rhetoric of partnership far outstrips the reality. In terms of the future, the aid effectiveness discussion will not return to prominence, while aid amounts may grow slowly. Because of pandemics and natural disasters, most traditional donors will continue heavy support for social sectors and humanitarian aid. The need to fund global public goods will likely mean more global programs and considerable amounts of aid flowing to middle-income countries, limiting the amount directed to the poor in poor states. Aid fragmentation will continue until recipient countries can adroitly manage their aid. Africa will continue to lag behind unless special efforts are made.

In short, aid is very much alive, but the future of aid is decidedly mixed. The following pages will provide evidence and analysis to show why this is the case. The first step on this journey is a brief look at the history and context in which aid is provided.

Bibliography

Bourguignon, F., & Sundberg, M. (2007). Aid effectiveness: Opening the black box. *American Economics Review*, *97*(2), 316–321.

Gates, B. (2019, January 16). *Bill Gates: The best investment I've ever made*. Retrieved from Wall Street Journal online: www.wsj.com/articles/bill-gates-the-best-investment-ive-ever-made-11547683309

Ramalingam, B. (2013). *Aid on the edge of chaos*. Oxford: Oxford University Press.

University of Oxford. (n.d.). *Bhutan's gross national happiness index*. Retrieved from Oxford Poverty and Human Development Initiative: https://ophi.org.uk/policy/gross-national-happiness-index/

2 Setting the Context

Foreign aid or foreign assistance from one nation to another has been around for a long time, reaching as far back as the Greek and Roman empires, if not earlier. In the last century, foreign aid can be traced back to late colonialism and the aftermath of World War II. After the war, there was a need to reconstruct both the victorious and vanquished countries and to aid newly established nation states. The relatively quick recovery of Europe, after a massive injection of funds from the Marshall Plan and other sources, increased both the visibility and popularity of foreign aid. As successful as aid was in post-war Europe, its results have been much less obvious in the poor countries that became independent after World War II. The many reasons for this will be discussed in this and subsequent chapters.

In the public's mind, all foreign aid is lumped together. However, officially, there is a distinction between foreign aid provided for military or other purposes and foreign aid that is specifically earmarked for economic and social development. Chapter 4 will further discuss the various forms of foreign aid, including the differences between humanitarian and developmental aid. First, however, it is important to understand the context in which aid is being given. This chapter will begin with a brief history of the broad developments over the last 60 years that affected aid recipients, before focusing more closely on some key challenges facing aid recipients today.

The End of Colonialism

The post-World War II period bore witness to important changes in the world's governance structure. While many countries in Latin America had achieved independence in the first half of the 19th century, the countries of the Middle East, Asia, and Africa were ruled by a small group of colonizing nations led by Great Britain and France. Figure 2.1 shows a map of the colonies and their affiliations before 1945. The map changed quite rapidly after the war. Self-determination was embedded in the United Nations Charter, a sign of the times (United Nations, 1945). Newly independent nations sprung up around the globe, first in the Middle East and

DOI: 10.4324/9781003265320-3

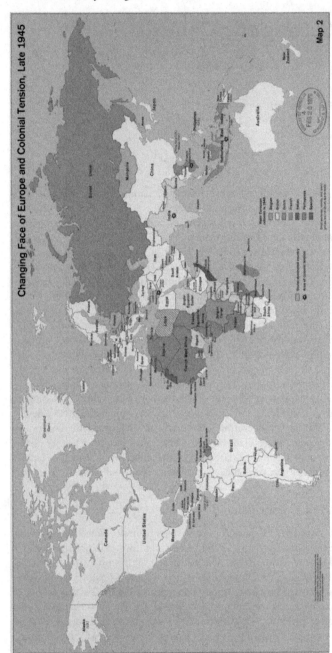

Figure 2.1 Colonization In Late 1945

Source: United States Central Intelligency Agency 1945

Asia, followed rapidly by most African nations in the 1960s. Although there were exceptions, many of the new states were ill prepared to govern themselves. In addition to setting up new legal and political systems and the corresponding institutions, the new governments were also responsible for the welfare of their citizens. Colonialism had done little to build the needed capacities.

The newly independent countries were convinced that throwing off the chains of colonialism would mean an exciting array of new opportunities (Cooper, 2002). Despite early optimism and some achievements, few of the countries were able to remain on an economically sustainable growth path. While in need of basic infrastructure, a functioning public service, and the means to attend to the basic needs of their citizens, many of the nations faced enormous challenges.

Among the challenges, several stand out. First was a series of external events. Cold War politics produced conflict in some cases and aid that rewarded loyalty as opposed to economic development. In addition, the oil crises of the 1970s, coupled with cyclical declines in prices for other primary commodities, crippled the budgets of many of the new states, leading to poor services and mounting foreign debt. There were also governance challenges. The developmental state model in vogue at the time led new governments – and foreign aid donors – to place almost exclusive reliance on the public sector as the engine of economic growth. At the same time, colonialism, by example, had taught many of the new leaders a "command and control" system of government and a "gatekeeper" model that led to a concentration of power and resources. This was accompanied by a distrust of wider democratic movements. Many of the new leaders were the beneficiaries of those movements in the colonial era, and they understood their potential power (Cooper, 2002). Finally, there was a dearth of well-trained civil servants, especially in the more recent colonial states. The educational system in the colonies, when it existed, was geared towards teaching basic writing and math. Those who received further education were trained to be clerks as opposed to high-level bureaucrats and managers. The external and internal challenges combined to stymie progress and eventually led to crisis through out much of what came to be known as the Third World.

The 1980s and 1990s – Painful Transitions

The 1980s and 1990s turned out to be a period of radical change. International financial institutions, primarily the World Bank and the International Monetary Fund (IMF), supported by foreign aid donors, pushed for broad changes in the way that developing country economies were managed. Structural adjustment, as the package of economic reforms came to be called, attempted to bring some order into what was an inevitably messy, and at times chaotic, change process. The basic thrust of the reforms was to reignite growth by introducing a set of policies and principles aimed at strengthening the market and decreasing the role of government in the control and management of the economy. Those policies, which had been adopted in some Latin American countries such as Chile, were also known as the *Washington Consensus*, a term dubbed by the economist John Williamson (Williamson, 2000; Williamson, 2003)[1] (Box 2.1). While having a different intellectual origin, the policies also echoed developments in some more-advanced economies. It was the age of Reagan in the United States and Thatcher in the United Kingdom.

Box 2.1 Structural Adjustment and the Washington Consensus

"Stabilize, Liberalize, and Privatize"

- **Economic Stabilization**

  - Competitive exchange rates
  - Smaller fiscal deficits linked to budget discipline and tax reform
  - Lower inflation
  - Financial sector reform, including interest rate stabilization

- **Structural Reforms**

  - Privatization of state-owned enterprises
  - Trade liberalization, eliminating non-tariff barriers and reducing tariffs
  - Deregulation of the private sector to remove obstacles to entry or competition
  - Removing barriers to foreign direct investment
  - Redirecting spending to sectors with high economic returns, such as education and health
  - Secure property rights

Other sectoral reforms such as agricultural sector reform and energy sector reform, civil service reform, and policy reforms associated with "good governance" were also frequently included in structural adjustment operations, while not strictly part of the so-called Washington Consensus.

Source: Adapted from Williamson (2003)

The merits of structural adjustment are still being debated today. There were concerns about the theory behind the reform. Others questioned the rapid pace, depth of reform, and sequencing, feeling that it was too much too soon. Many worried about the ultimate impact on the poor and the economy in general. There were others, however, with almost the opposite views. They thought the reforms in many countries were not fast or deep enough and that the quality of implementation muted the impact of the reforms. Certainly, the reforms did not work as intended and did not lead to an immediate resumption of sustained economic growth in most countries. The few exceptions, such as Uganda and Tanzania, where growth accelerated became "aid darlings", receiving much attention from the donors.

The 1980s became known as the "lost decade" in both Latin America and Africa, the two continents where structural adjustment efforts were the greatest. Latin America suffered a series of commercial debt crises, while in Africa, official foreign debt piled up while trade receipts fell. In the 1990s, Africa, for the most part, continued to decline. Latin America recovered slightly and then plateaued. Poverty stagnated or grew worse.

As growth failed to materialize, aid donors expanded the reform agenda, increasingly focused on the need for "sound institutions" and "good governance". There was, however, no consensus on what exactly those meant. Poor countries were subject to a long list of conditions, some of which were decidedly political in nature. Many aid recipients and observers grew cynical, as few of those issues had come up as part of aid discussions during the Cold War when the US and other Western countries were competing with the Soviet Union for countries' support. However, with the changing global circumstances and the dissolution of the Soviet Union, many donors felt pressed to show that their aid was resulting in positive change. Disillusion set in among aid donors and recipients alike, with a corrosive effect on relationships and trust. "Aid fatigue" became a familiar phrase in the 1990s, with aid totals falling in US dollar terms, as well as in share of national income (ODA as a share of GNI) (OECD, 2018).

The reasons for Africa's poor economic performance in the 1990s are manifold. The long-term effects of colonialism, the Cold War competition and its aftermath, mounting external debt, and the world's attention drawn elsewhere to Latin America and Eastern Europe all resulted in an unfavorable external environment that contributed substantially to poor economic performance.

In addition, both external and internal factors led to a high level of conflict involving African states. At the peak in 1993, over 40 percent of the region's countries were involved in some type of conflict (Marshall, 2005). Among the most tragic was the Rwandan mass genocide. From April to July 1994, members of the Hutu ethnic group murdered about 800,000 people, mostly of the Tutsi minority, while the international community more or less stood by. During the 1990s, there were also serious conflicts in Angola, Sierra Leone, Liberia, Somalia, Sudan, and the Congo, to name a few of the most prominent ones. These conflicts caused much human tragedy, including large numbers of displaced populations. Serious conflict obviously impedes economic growth; it also creates humanitarian crises that place additional financial demands on international aid donors, neighboring countries, and the countries in conflict.

At the same time, Africa was suffering from a burgeoning health crisis. HIV/AIDs spread quickly throughout Eastern and Southern Africa especially, and aid donors were slow to realize the extent of the crisis and to respond. By the end of the 1990s, over 25 million people were living with HIV/AIDs in Africa. The disease hit prosperous and poor countries alike. In Botswana, by 2000, life expectancy at birth had plunged from 69 to 44. More than one out of three adults was infected there. In Zambia, one out of every four adults living in cities was HIV-positive. South Africa had the largest number of people living with HIV/AIDs in the world (United Nations, April 2001). In heavily affected countries, the disease created a serious drag on economic productivity and incomes. It also created major demands on weak and underfunded public health systems. It was clear by the end of the 1990s that spending on HIV/AIDs had to be ramped up dramatically.

The second half of the 1990s was also a bleak time in Eastern Europe and Central Asia. The radical economic transformation resulted in steep declines in national income for most of the countries, along with increased poverty and inequality. Russia's income loss (as measured by Gross National Product – GNP) was greater in the 1990–1998 transition years than during the World War II period. It was accompanied by a big drop in industrial production (42.9 percent) (Stiglitz, 2003, p. 143). Poverty rose from 2 percent in 1989 to almost 24 percent in 1998 (p. 153).

Economic news was more hopeful in Asia. Both South Asia, led by India, and East Asia, led by China, experienced rapid growth in the 1980s and 1990s. This contributed to a significant decline in poverty (World Bank, 2005). Although the Asian countries pursued economic reform, they did so at a gradual pace and in a fairly piecemeal fashion (p. 39), in many ways challenging the conventional orthodoxy on structural adjustment. Their developmental state models, rooted in local context, acknowledged the market as a necessary economic tool while recognizing that the state was a powerful and essential actor in promoting economic development. An intense financial crisis disrupted East Asian progress in the late 1990s. While painful, recovery was relatively rapid.

The 1980s and 1990s also were a time of great political change. A "third wave" of democratization took place in the late 1980s and 1990s. In Africa, 34 out of 47 states held multi-party elections. For many, it was the first time in well over a decade that contested elections were being held (van de Walle, 2001). This is remarkable given that at the end of the 1980s, not one African head of state had been removed from office through elections (Meredith, 2005). South Africa, against all odds, made a peaceful transition, abolishing apartheid and electing Nelson Mandela as president. Similarly, in Latin America, there was a return to democratic government in a number of countries. The fall of the Soviet Union led to rapid, albeit uncertain, political transformation in many Eastern European and Central Asian countries. The Cold War ended, and in places like Mozambique, proxy wars were allowed to subside.

The 2000s – A New Millennium Gets Underway

The global economic picture at the start of the century was not without a certain irony. While a general consensus had emerged (more or less) on the need to adopt at least parts of a market-based economic model, the results were widely divergent. Conventional economic wisdom had postulated that developing countries' income would eventually catch up to that of industrial countries. Instead, the picture was one of "divergence big time" as Lant Pritchett put it in a widely read article (Pritchett, 1997; World Bank, 2005). The gap was not only widening between industrial and developing countries, but among developing countries. East Asia was doing particularly well, while Latin America struggled. In South Asia and Africa, there were some countries managing to sustain high growth rates, others were stagnating, and still others were falling further and further behind.

Confronted by pressure from a vibrant civil society in industrialized countries and a felt need to reverse a trend that could affect world peace and eventually well-being in industrial countries, aid donors decided to renew their efforts. One of the first new programs was the Heavily Indebted Poor Country (HIPC) Initiative approved in 1996 with the objective of alleviating the crushing debt burden on the poorest countries. However, the initial set of requirements was so rigorous that few countries even started the analysis required to fulfill the conditions. In 1999 the Enhanced HIPC Initative was approved, with 39 countries theoretically eligible for debt relief from multilateral, bilateral, and participating private creditors. By the end of 2005, 18 of the countries had completed the requirements and were relieved of their unsustainable debt burdens. By the end of the decade they were joined by 14 more, with 6 more completing the program after 2010. Somalia reached the completion point in March 2020, and Sudan in June 2021. Eritrea is the only country left that is theoretically eligible for debt relief under this initiative. In addition, 2005 saw the approval of the Multilateral Debt Relief Initiative (MDRI), which eliminated the remaining multilateral debt (as of end 2003) for the countries that reached the final stage under the HIPC debt relief. Of those 38 countries receiving debt relief under the HIPC and MDRI initiatives, 32 were African nations (International

Development Association (IDA), 2005; International Monetary Fund, 2013, pp. 20–22, 2021, 2022a, pp. 25–26).

As the new century started, poverty reduction, following two decades of structural adjustment, was back on the agenda, and poor countries were required to complete poverty reduction strategy papers (PRSPs) as a requirement for debt relief. In 2000, the United Nations embraced the Millennium Development Goals (MDGs), which mainly targeted poverty and social issues (Box 2.2). On the one hand, the MDGs' focus on poverty and social welfare was laudable and understandable given the economic disruptions of the earlier two decades. In retrospect, the MDGs seem quite narrow with little mention of infrastructure, productive sectors, employment, and overall economic performance.

Box 2.2   The Millennium Development Goals

In 2000, world leaders came to United Nations Headquarters in New York and adopted the UN Nations Millennium Declaration. This Declaration formed the basis for eight Millennium Development Goals.

The Eight Millennium Development Goals are:

1 **Eradicate extreme poverty and hunger**
2 **Achieve universal primary education**
3 **Promote gender equality**
4 **Reduce child mortality**
5 **Improve maternal health**
6 **Combat HIV/AIDs, malaria, and other diseases**
7 **Ensure environmental sustainability**
8 **Develop a global partnership for development**

Each of the goals had specific targets that were to be achieved by 2015. These targets included, among others: halving the number of people living in extreme poverty between 1990 and 2015; eliminating gender disparity at all levels of education by 2015; reducing by two-thirds the under-five mortality rate between 1990 and 2015; reducing by three-quarters the maternal mortality rate by 2015; and halting and starting to reverse the spread of HIV/AIDs by 2015.

Source: UN-NGLS (n.d.)

Renewed international attention, debt relief, stronger commodity prices, better-functioning governments (with noted exceptions), and increased aid brought with them a welcome renewal of growth for many middle and low-income countries in the late 1990s and the 2000s. However, the disappointments and setbacks of the 1980s and 1990s were not forgotten, and criticism of the effects of globalization abounded. Donor and recipient countries intensified a discussion that started in the 1990s about aid effectiveness. After all, significant aid had been disbursed during those decades with seemingly little to show for it, particularly in Africa. Questions swirled around the conditions and types of aid, recipient government effectiveness, and donor behavior (Figure 2.2).

The adoption of the MDGs, along with those concerns, led a series of extraordinary high-level international meetings. Many of the issues brought up in the meetings were not new, but their discussion in public and at the highest levels was far from common practice. The first meeting was the Conference on Financing for Development held in Monterrey, Mexico in March 2002. The Monterrey Consensus document called for greater financial support to developing countries. Much of the conference was "business as usual"; the spotlight was on the actions needed to be taken by developing countries to absorb and use those resources effectively. However, there was also an explicit call for more partnership among donors and recipients, and for donors to facilitate more recipient ownership of aid projects. Limiting tied aid (the practice of allowing aid only to be used for goods and services from the donor country) and moving towards increased harmonization of policies and practices among aid donors were also highlighted (United Nations, 2003). This conference was followed the next year by the Rome Conference on Harmonization. That Conference was notable in that the participants publicly recognized, many for the first time, that diverse donor practices could decrease aid effectiveness.

> We in the donor community have been concerned with the growing evidence that, over time, the totality and wide variety of donor requirements and processes for preparing, delivering and monitoring development assistance are generating unproductive transaction costs for, and drawing down the limited capacity of, partner countries. We are also aware of partner country concerns that donors' practices do not always fit well with national development priorities and systems. . . . We recognize that these issues require urgent, coordinated, and sustained action to improve our effectiveness on the ground.
> (Rome Conference on Harmonization, 2003, p. 1)

Stressing the need for greater harmonization among donors, the conference also called for donor coordination at the national level to be led by the recipient government.

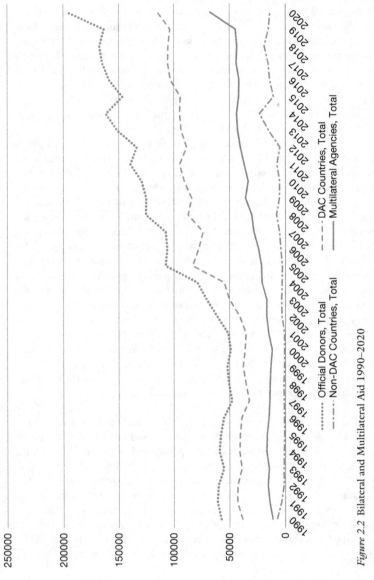

Figure 2.2 Bilateral and Multilateral Aid 1990–2020

Source: (OECD, 2022a)

The major aid conference of the 2000s was the High-Level Conference on Aid Effectiveness held in Paris in 2005. It established five principles for enhanced aid effectiveness, covering both donor and recipient, that became widely known as the Paris Principles. (Paris Declaration on Aid Effectiveness and the Accra Agenda for Action, 2005, 2008). The five principles are:

Ownership – Recipient countries were to develop their own national development strategies, while donors were to respect country leadership and help strengthen country capacity to lead aid coordinaton.

Alignment – Donors were to align their aid with country strategies and systems and to streamline conditionality, help strengthen capacity and systems, avoid creating separate project management units, and make progress on untying aid.

Harmonization – Donor actions were to be better coordinated, including in fragile states and in addressing environmental issues, with common arrrangements and/or division of labor, where possible.

Managing for Results – Donors were to link country programs and resources to results, based on better information and monitoring, with performance indicators consistent with the national development strategies of the recipient.

Mutual Accountability – Donors and partner countries were *both* accountable for development results, including broader consultations and more involvement of parliaments by recipient countries as appropriate, as well as more timely and complete information on aid flows by donors.

The Paris meeting also led to a specific monitoring framework with key indicators used to assess progress. In 2008, the Third High-Level Forum on Aid Effectiveness was held in Accra, Ghana. Progressively, with each international meeting, there were more and more participants; there were over 800 in Accra. The Accra Agenda for Action, building on the Paris Declaration, emphasized the need for more predictability and forward planning for aid flows, a greater use of country systems, conditionality based on a country's own objectives and plans, and untying of aid.

So the first decade of the century held promise for strengthening country ownership and moving away from donor-dominated development policies. That promise was only partially kept. Although some progress was made, most of the targets set for 2010 were not met. Looking back, it is hardly surprising that many of the ambitious targets set in Paris and Accra were not achieved. The challenge of providing more aid did not automatically translate into providing more effective aid. Growing security concerns, wars in Afghanistan and Iraq, and the financial crisis in the second half of the decade distracted donors' attention from the aid agenda.

Most recipient countries fared better than in the 1990s. it was a relatively good decade for most of South Asia and East Asia in terms of growth. Eastern Europe recovered from the transition and began to do reasonably well. Progress in Latin America also occurred, although growth was uneven, with some countries flourishing while others languished. Peru and Chile, based on mineral exports, did well up until the financial crisis in the late 2000s. On the other hand, Mexico's growth performance was below the average for the continent (Moreno-Brid & Garry, 2016). The expectation was that Latin America as a whole would continue to do well; aid to the continent declined, with the need for domestic resource mobilization becoming more urgent.

Africa went from being the "hopeless continent" to the "hopeful continent", recording average growth around 5.7 percent from 2001–2010 (*The Economist*, 2000, 2013; World Bank, 2018). This strong economic growth performance masked several continuing challenges. Perhaps the most serious and varied challenge concerned governance. While some long-standing conflicts (e.g., Sierra Leone and Liberia) wound down, there were still serious conflicts in the Democratic Republic of the Congo, Ethiopia, Kenya, Sudan, and Somalia, with a series of other incidents. Even in countries that had emerged from conflict and held elections in the 1990s, there were a host of governance issues. Some, despite the façade of elections, remained one-party or "one-man" states. Democratic or not, many took on the trappings of a "hybrid" state: one that had modern western-style institutions and processes, but where clientelism and neopatrimonial arrangements dictated real power and decisions (van de Walle, 2001). Instability and corruption were other signs of weak governments. While individual capacity grew quickly, institutional capacity remained weak. Political rivalries meant that some existing capacity was sidelined and not fully utilized. Few of the "aid darlings" of the 1990s were able to keep their image burnished and bright during the 2000s, despite more stable economies and better economic prospects (Table 2.1).

Those brightening economic prospects were by no means certain. African countries had difficulties in accelerating trade due to poor infrastructure and logistical support systems, as well as continuing trade barriers. Transit and trade among African nations was still fraught with difficulties. Countries whose economies were driven by primary commodity exports enjoyed relatively high prices and many put needed diversification on a back burner. Consequently, agriculture, a crucial sector for sustainable growth and poverty reduction, continued its weak performance. It was clear, almost from the start of the decade, that even with increased aid from both traditional donors as well as from China, most countries in Africa, and the continent as a whole, would fail to meet many of the MDG goals.

Table 2.1 Developing Country Average Annual Growth Rates by Region and Decade*

REGION	1990–2000	2001–2010	2011–2020	2011–2019**
Sub-Saharan Africa	2.1	5.7	2.7	3.2
South Asia	5.3	7	5.0	6.1
Middle East and North Africa	4.6	4.5	1.4	1.9
Latin America and the Caribbean	2.9	3.3	1.0	1.8
Europe and Central Asia	–2.8	4.8	2.7	3.2
East Asia and Pacific	7.9	9.1	6.4	7.0
HIPC Countries	3.1	5.3	4.0	4.4

Source: Calculated from World Bank, World Development Indicators, 2022

* IDA and IBRD countries only, i.e., excludes high-income countries in region
** For comparison purposes, the growth rates are without 2020, the starting year of the COVID-19 pandemic

The 2008–2009 financial crisis came as a blow to the world economy, and developing countries also were affected. Most managed to withstand the crisis better than expected, but the crisis ushered in another period of lower growth. China's lower demand for commodities after 2010 led to falling prices and new economic woes for the countries dependent on primary products for their income.

The 2010s – Progress for Some

The state of affairs following the global financial crisis was complex for both aid donors and recipients, with far more diversity in their respective circumstances. During the decade that followed, Asia recovered relatively quickly and grew rapidly, but Latin America and the Middle East did not fare as well. Political and economic issues affecting Venezuela, Argentina, and Brazil, the uncertainty created by the Arab Spring, and the economic and social repercussions of the war in Syria were drags on overall economic performance in those regions. European, Central Asian, and

African low and middle-income countries had widely variable economic performance, with some growing well while others virtually stagnated.

The donors were faced with this unfolding scenario as the Fourth High Level Meeting on Aid Effectiveness convened in Busan, South Korea in 2011. The donors themselves had also grown far more diverse. On the donor side, there were the traditional aid donors who belonged to the Development Assistance Committee (DAC) of the Organization for Economic Cooperation and Development (OECD). There were also "new" or "emerging" providers whose significance had grown rapidly over the last few years. Several were former and current aid recipients. China was one of those; Saudi Arabia, Turkey, and the United Arab Emirates (UAE) were also included in this group. Then there were the multilateral organizations and funds; many of these were created after World War II as part of the UN system (the various UN agencies and the World Bank and the IMF). Over the last 20 years, new ones had emerged such as the Global Fund for Aids, Malaria, and Tuberculosis (GFATM) and, more recently, after Busan, the New Development Bank and the Asia Infrastructure Investment Bank (AIIB). Finally, there was an explosion of NGOs and foundations involved in aid at both the national and international levels. The next chapter paints a more complete picture of today's aid providers.

The Busan Conference recognized this new donor diversity in its carefully worded statement:

> While North-South co-operation remains the main form of development co-operation, South-South co-operation continues to evolve. . . . We now all form an integral part of a new and more inclusive development agenda, in which these actors participate on the basis of common goals, shared principles and *differential commitments*. On this same basis, we welcome the inclusion of civil society, the private sector and other actors.
>
> *(Italics added)* (Busan Partnership for Effective Development Co-operation, 2011, p. 4)

The statement clearly recognized the emergence of China as one of the two largest economies in the world and a major aid provider, while underscoring China's need to differentiate itself from traditional aid donors. The aid environment was becoming even more complex.

After Busan, both optimism and pessimism prevailed in almost equal measure. On the one hand, there was optimism that the gains made in the previous decade would continue with further reductions in poverty. The Arab Spring gave hope that a new generation would pursue political, social, and economic reform in the Middle East. Gender equity and girls' education efforts were given a boost when Malala Yousafzail from Pakistan won the Nobel Peace Prize in 2014, some two years after she was viciously attacked by the Taliban for her desire to go to school. Progress towards the MDGs was judged sufficient in most countries to begin the planning of a whole new set of goals for post-2015. The main goal of halving extreme poverty was met, thanks mainly to Asia. Despite the fact that the MDGs were not met in the poorest countries, the feeling was that the development goals needed to be more comprehensive and ambitious. In 2015, the Sustainable Development Goals (SDGs), a set of 169 goals, were adopted by the United Nations General Assembly. The SDGs combined previous work on the environment and development, and they set the overarching goal of eliminating extreme poverty by 2030. Also in 2015, 195 countries and the European Union signed the Paris Agreement, a legally binding United Nations treaty on climate action.

By mid-decade, however, a number of events had turned the international environment in which foreign aid operates less hospitable. The wars in Syria and Libya created a refugee crisis in Europe and new demands on aid budgets. ISIS (the Islamic State organization) was fighting for control over Iraq and Syria and was increasingly active in other countries. Food prices had spiked in 2012, so food security became once again a major topic. Despite the Paris Agreement, not nearly enough was being done on climate mitigation and adaptation, as the effects of global warming became alarmingly more evident. The election of Donald Trump in the United States and Great Britain's exit from the European Union were viewed with alarm by foreign aid proponents. Those events also highlighted the growing inequality *within* countries even though inequality had lessened between countries in the preceding decade. The slowing pace of poverty reduction brought worries that both kinds of inequality would worsen. In the 1990s and 2000s, democracies were taking hold in a number of countries, but the 2010s saw a retreat from liberal democratic ideals and processes in both rich and poorer countries. Many believed that authoritarian government was a viable alternative and might even be better at tackling problems like violence, terrorism, corruption, and economic mismanagement. This went hand in hand with a renewal of nationalism, a reaction against globalization that had increased the interdependency of all nations over the last several decades. Given this environment, it is noteworthy that aid totals continued to increase, albeit at a modest pace (Figure 2.2). At the same time, high-level global attention was directed elsewhere, away from discussions of aid effectiveness.

The Roaring 2020s

Although the decade is still far from over, so far, it has been eventful. The COVID-19 pandemic, almost inconceivable despite experts' warnings, showed how poorly prepared the world was for major health crises (Mahroum, Seida, Esirgun, & Bragazzi, 2022). As of mid-Decembr 2022, there had been over 6.6 million deaths and over 645 million cases worldwide.[2] Europe and the Americas were the regions most affected (or most accurately reported), with the US, India, France, Germany, and Brazil reporting the most cases (World Health Organization, 2022). The pandemic led to a worldwide economic crisis as productive activities slowed significantly and supply chains were crippled. Recovery efforts were stalled shortly after they began to take effect by a new set of world crises: the Taliban takeover of Afghanistan and the war in Ukraine. The Ukraine war brought with it inflation worldwide and food shortages in low-income countries. Efforts to curb inflation through higher interest rates edged many countries into economic recession. Meanwhile, many countries were not living up to the climate targets they had set under the Paris Agreement. Severe weather was becoming more damaging and widespread, with major hurricane losses in the United States and the Caribbean, drought in Brazil, and catastrophic flooding in South Asia and elsewhere.

The effects on low and middle-income countries were disastrous. Gains made in previous years were reversed. Extreme poverty increased in 2020, and income losses were greatest in the poor countries, leading to a rise in global inequality for the first time in decades (World Bank, 2022a). Eliminating extreme poverty by 2030, already an ambitious goal, now looked unrealistic. Food insecurity was worsening. Funding for climate mitigation and adaption had not reached anywhere near the levels required. Another debt crisis loomed as low and middle-income countries fell into debt distress and default. As a result, all countries faced an uncertain future. However, it is the poorest countries that were least able to bear the brunt of what many have termed the 2020s global "polycrisis".[3]

A Recap of the Challenges for Developing Countries

A major stumbling block for low-income countries is that they are besieged by multiple challenges that make it difficult for them to use aid effectively for economic growth and poverty reduction (Commission for Africa, 2005, pp. 101–118; Collier, 2007; Gertz, 2018). As Tolstoy famously wrote in *Anna Karenina*: "Every unhappy family is unhappy in its own way." Nonetheless, there are several types of challenges that show up in the history of these countries time after time. Some of these problems are internal in origin; others are the result of external actors or circumstances such as those described in this chapter.

The challenges are related to weak governments, war and serious conflicts, the lack of a dynamic private sector leading a vibrant formal economy, a lagging agricultural sector, inadequate health systems leading to serious health crises, recurrent natural disasters along with climate change, improper management of natural resources, and aid and debt dependency. Not every country suffers from each and every challenge, but most LDCs suffer from at least two of these. These challenges cast a long shadow over low-income countries, making it difficult for aid donors, the private sector, and even the governments themselves to believe they can catch up and advance.

Weak governments are perhaps one of the most important reasons why poor countries have fallen behind and remained so. Weak governments are defined in a number of ways. Many continue to exhibit the characteristics of a hybrid state, i.e., the formal processes and rules do not match how things actually work. Weak governments generally are unable to provide public goods (e.g., education, health, infrastructure, safety) in sufficient quantity and quality on a day-to-day basis, let alone in an emergency situation. Lack of funds may be part of the equation, but there are other factors. Among those are inadequate and/or cumbersome bureaucratic procedures and safeguards, major policy disagreements leading sometimes to abrupt shifts in policy, outright corruption, poorly trained and motivated civil servants, and frequently changing officials and leadership. The last can be the product of coups or changing forms of government but can also be present in one-party or one-man states. The result is endemic instability, uncertainty, and a clear time preference for the short-term.

War and other types of serious conflicts are another major obstacle to progress. Conservatively, at least 23 of the 48 countries currently considered to be the poorest countries have experienced war or serious civil strife since independence. War is quite possibly the opposite of growth and poverty reduction. Particularly in cases of internal conflict, major public assets are destroyed, and people are left bereft and displaced. Even for countries not directly involved in a conflict, close proximity can lead to new, burdensome obligations (e.g., refugee camps in Kenya, Tanzania, or Zambia). Countries that settle wars can enjoy a major "peace dividend" in the form of a few years of high growth rates; generally speaking, this is not enough to make up for lost ground. The memory of conflict and the constant threat of its return also add to a climate of uncertainty that can undermine progress.

Some countries lack a clear "engine of growth". The overall environment is not conducive to the establishment of a dynamic private sector. A combination of infrastructure deficits, adverse or ambivalent policies towards the private sector, a lack of specialized staff, and a highly constrained financial sector combine in many countries to stifle entrepreneurs. A robust, formal private sector, with influential spokespeople, can also help a government become more efficient by keeping up the pressure for better performance. This is not the case with the informal sector that has flourished in many poor countries. The urban informal economy satisfies subsistence needs for many, but many small enterprises fail to grow. Banerjee and Duflo labelled informal business owners "Reluctant

Entrepreneurs" because participating in the informal economy is largely a default option due to the scarcity of jobs in the formal sector (Banerjee & Duflo, 2011, p. 205).

Agriculture, which employs the majority of people in many low-income countries, has traditionally been the sector that underpinned the early stages of more dynamic growth in advanced economies. Africa, especially, suffers significant lags in agricultural productivity, although there have been some gains in the last decade and visible pockets of success (e.g., grain production in Ethiopia) (African Agriculture: A green evolution, 2016). Added to the usual woes of small farmers (insecure land tenure, lack of credit and modern agricultural inputs, marketing issues, among others) comes the difficulty of adapting to the volume, quality, and packaging requirements of national and global value chains in today's marketplace. Despite public pronouncements on the importance of agriculture, few governments have adopted policies conducive to stimulating increased agricultural production and productivity among small-scale farmers (Barrett, Christiaensen, Sheahan, & Shimeles, 2017; Mellor, 2017; Otsuka & Fan, 2021). As the war in Ukraine showed, stimulating domestic agricultural production is an urgent matter for many countries since global food production and marketing chains cannot always be relied on.

Low-income countries have a heavy disease burden. It is costly not only in terms of longevity and quality of life, but also in terms of economic impact. The disease burden manifests itself in four ways. First, there are preventable common diseases that show the need for basic improvements in water, sanitation, and health services. For example, gastrointestinal diseases are prevalent throughout low-income countries. Second, there are tropical diseases like malaria and dengue fever that can be controlled but require concerted public health campaigns. The third burden comes from regional and worldwide epidemics and pandemics – HIV/AIDs, Ebola, and COVID-19 – that have brought suffering to millions of people in low-income countries. Finally, as low-income countries begin to move closer to middle and higher-income status, they begin to have higher incidences of "rich country" diseases such as heart disease and diabetes. While aid and spending on health have increased substantially in the last two decades, new challenges continue to emerge. Many countries require a stronger general health system that would allow them to successfully meet multiple burdens.

Natural disasters and climate change risks are another obstacle for low-income countries. Natural disasters happen to rich and poor countries alike. However, the devastating effects linger much longer in low-income countries because they have not yet acquired much resiliency, that is, the sufficient financial and human capacity required to recover rapidly from a disaster. Consequently, earthquakes, hurricanes, and major floods and droughts become events that set countries back years. Climate change has already made flooding and drought cycles more prominent in recent years, hurting agricultural production, endangering lives and livelihoods, and destroying infrastructure. Being able to adapt to climate change and mitigate its more damaging effects is a tall order for countries struggling to achieve sustainable growth. Poor countries also maintain that they are owed assistance from richer countries since richer countries are largely responsible for causing climate change.

The challenge of managing natural resources in a sustainable manner is another problem area. For many countries that are richly endowed with natural resources, having the resources has been a mixed blessing at best. Having a particular resource in demand (e.g., oil or minerals) can make an economy over-reliant on a particular export commodity and therefore extremely vulnerable to international price fluctuations. This can lead to a cycle of over-confidence and over-spending in the boom times and depression and over-borrowing when prices go down. Managing this cycle well has been difficult for many developing countries, leading economists to speak of "a resource curse" or "a resource trap". This is not inevitable: both Chile and Botswana show that, if managed wisely, natural resources can be the foundation for diversified rapid growth rather than a curse.

Aid dependency and the proper management of aid are significant challenges for low-income countries. Although aid dependency in general (as measured by aid as a percentage of GNI) has fallen over two decades, low-income countries are still quite aid dependent with aid equal to at least 5 percent of GNI. The average aid dependency percentage for the 28 countries defined by the World Bank as low-income was 11.6 percent in 2020 (World Bank, 2022b) and has been increasing since 2010. For the larger list of 48 Least Developed Countries (LDCs) maintained by the United Nations, the percentage was lower, 4.9 percent in 2019, better reflecting the general trend towards a reduction in aid dependency since 2005 (World Bank, 2022b). While the ultimate impact of aid dependency is still the subject of debate, heavily aid-dependent countries are subject to intense donor interaction. This taxes governments tremendously and involves heavy transaction costs. Governments that fail to manage aid well are in danger of falling victim to donor-driven development ideas and strategies that may or may not be appropriate. Governments that succeed in managing aid fairly well understand that the effort involved is substantial and constitutes an additional burden on already-limited resources. Most governments, even while recognizing its necessity, are genuine in their desire to limit aid. For some, aid dependency has become just one more challenge to overcome.

In addition to aid dependency, there is also the problem of debt dependency. During the first two years of the COVID-19 pandemic, the G-20, a global economic cooperation group of 19 countries plus the European Union, suspended official debt payments for 73 low and lower-middle income countries. Even so, in 2022, 41 of those countries were at high risk for or already in debt distress. Of those 41 countries, 19 had already received debt relief under the HIPC-MDRI initiatives in the 2000s or later. Under the earlier initiatives, much of the debt had been held by Paris Club creditors or multilateral institutions. Today, the creditors are more varied: the Paris Club and multilateral institutions are still important, but others, including China, non-Paris Club members, and private creditors have become significantly more important. This is particularly true of China, the largest official bilateral creditor in over half of the countries (Chabert, Cerisola, & Hakura, 2022; International Monetary Fund, 2022b). External circumstances are important in this debt story, and certain low-income countries are hard-pressed to live within their means. However, significant debt relief brings with it both a heavy burden of coordination and negotiations among creditors and an enhanced risk of moral hazard, especially among repeat debtor nations. For countries that are not consistently growing at a reasonable pace, debt dependency can become a bad habit, a symptom of weak government and a drag on achieving sustainable growth.

The final challenge for low-income countries is about attitudes. In many countries, there are bouts of optimism interspersed with doubt that things could really change. Evidence for both points of view abounds in both newspapers and scholarly journals. There are also international skepticism and mood swings. During Africa's growth run in the 2000s and beyond, there were a plethora of hopeful titles: "Africa Rising", "Emerging Africa", "Lions on the Move" (Radelet, 2010; Roxburgh et al., 2010; August, 2013). As growth rates slowed, the titles became more doubtful or pessimistic: "Africa Still Rising?"; "'Africa Rising'? 'Africa Reeling' May Be More Fitting Now"; "The Myth of Africa Rising" (Coulibaly, 2017; Gettleman, 2016; Rowden, 2013). For a recipient government, donor, or private investor, it is difficult to keep making tremendous efforts when doubt is constantly present and public opinion is subject to substantial swings (Classroom Vignette 2.1).

Can low-income countries get on and stay on a sustainable growth path? The progress made by countries like China, Vietnam, and India, among others, makes it clear that it is possible to overcome the considerable challenges and climb up the path to prosperity. However, the setbacks experienced in the 2020s, especially by the poorest nations, highlight the difficulties. What role aid has played and will play – as help or a hindrance – is explored in the following chapters.

Classroom Vignette 2.1 The History of Poor Countries

After listening to short accounts of the recent history of a selection of low-income countries, graduate students were asked to summarize recurring themes in the stories. To make it more challenging, they were asked to do this using only words that begin with the letter "c". Here is a list of words frequently cited by graduate students from 2009 to 2019*:

Colonization
Cold war
Civil war
Coups
Conflict
Corruption
Commodities
Catastrophes
Climate change
Currency problems
China
Contagious diseases
Child trafficking
Charity
Crowding
Christianity
Communism
Crime
Communications
Connectivity
Civil Society
Centralization
Camps

*No doubt after 2020 COVID-19 would be on this list.

Notes

1 Of course, there actually was no consensus, and to this day, controversy swirls around the effects – both positive and negative – of structural adjustment/Washington Consensus type policies. See, among many others, Summers and Pritchett (1993); Birdsall, de la Torre, and Valencia Caicedo (2010); and Easterly (2019).

2 Both numbers are likely understated.
3 The definition of a polycrisis is: "A polycrisis is not just a situation where you face multiple crises. It is a situation . . . where the whole is even more dangerous than the sum of the parts" (Tooze, 2022).

Bibliography

African agriculture: A green evolution. (2016, March 12). *The Economist.*

Africa rising a hopeful continent. (2013, March 3). *The Economist.*

Africa the hopeless continent. (2000, May 13). *The Economist*, p. Cover.

August, O. (2013, March 2). *Africa rising: A hopeful continent.* Retrieved from The Economist: www.economist.com/news/special-report/21572377-african-lives-have-already-greatly-improved-over-past-decade-says-oliver-august

Banerjee, A. V., & Duflo, E. (2011). *Poor economics.* New York: Public Affairs.

Barrett, C. B., Christiaensen, L., Sheahan, M., & Shimeles, A. (2017). *On the structural transformation of Rural Africa.* Washington, DC: World Bank.

Birdsall, N., de la Torre, A., & Valencia Caicedo, F. (2010). *The Washington consensus: Assessing a damaged brand.* Washington, DC: Center for Global Development.

Busan Partnership for Effective Development Co-operation. (2011). *4th high level forum on aid effectiveness.* Busan, Korea.

Chabert, G., Cerisola, M., & Hakura, D. (2022, April 7). *Restructuring debt of poorer nations requires more efficient coordination.* Retrieved from IMF Website: www.imf.org/en/Blogs/Articles/2022/04/07/restructuring-debt-of-poorer-nations-requires-more-efficient-coordination

Collier, P. (2007). *The bottom billion.* Oxford: Oxford University Press.

Commission for Africa. (2005). *Our common interest.* Retrieved from: https://reliefweb.int/report/world/our-common-interest-report-commission-africa

Cooper, F. (2002). *Africa since 1940: The past of the present.* Cambridge: Cambridge University Press.

Coulibaly, B. (2017, October 4). *Is Africa still rising?* Retrieved from Project Syndicate: www.project-syndicate.org/commentary/africa-economic-growth-2017-by-brahima-coulibaly-2017

Easterly, W. (2019). *In search of reforms for growth: New stylized facts on policy and growth outcomes.* Cambridge, MA: National Bureau of Economic Research.

Gertz, G. A. (2018). *Leave no country behind: Ending poverty in the toughest places.* Washington, DC: Brookings.

Gettleman, J. (2016, October 16). "Africa rising"? "Africa reeling" may be more fitting now. *The New York Times*, p. A5.

International Development Association (IDA). (2005). *The multilateral debt relief initiative: Implementation modalities for IDA.* Washington, DC: World Bank.

International Monetary Fund. (2013). *Heavily indebted poor country (HIPC) initiative and multilateral debt relief initiative (MDRI) – Statistical update.* Washington, DC: IMF.

International Monetary Fund. (2021, February 18). *Factsheet: Debt relief under the heavily indebted poor country (HIPC) initiative.* Retrieved from IMF: www.imf.org/en/About/Factsheets/Sheets/2016/08/01/16/11/Debt-Relief-Under-the-Heavily-Indebted-Poor-Countries-Initiative

International Monetary Fund. (2022a). *2022 review of adequacy of poverty reduction and growth trust finances.* Washington, DC: IMF.

International Monetary Fund. (2022b, August 29). *List of LIC DSAs for PRGT eligible countries*. Retrieved from IMF: www.imf.org/external/Pubs/ft/dsa/DSAlist.pdf

Mahroum, N., Seida, I., Esirgun, S. N., & Bragazzi, N. L. (2022). The COVID-19 pandemic – how many times were we warned before? *European Journal of Internal Medicine, 105,* 8–14.

Marshall, M. G. (2005). *Conflict trends in Africa, 1946–2004: A macro-comparative perspective*. Report prepared for the Africa Conflict Prevention Pool, https://www.systemicpeace.org/vlibrary/ConflictTrendsAfrica2006MGMarshall.pdf

Mellor, J. W. (2017). *Agricultural development and economic transformation: Promoting growth with poverty reduction*. New York: Palgrave MacMillan.

Meredith, M. (2005). *The fate of Africa*. New York: Public Affairs.

Moreno-Brid, J. C., & Garry, S. (2016). Economic performance in Latin America in the 2000s: Recession, recovery, and resilience? *Oxford Development Studies, 44*(4), 384–400.

OECD. (1996). *The DAC list of ODA recipients used for 1996 flows*. Retrieved from DAC List of ODA Recipients: www.oecd.org/dac/financing-sustainable-development/development-finance-standards/1809431.htm

OECD. (2018). *Net ODA*. Retrieved January 24, 2018, from OECD Data: https://data.oecd.org/oda/net-oda.htm

OECD. (2021a). *DAC list of ODA recipients effective for reporting on 2021 flows*. Retrieved from OECD DAC: www.oecd.org/dac/financing-sustainable-development/development-finance-standards/DAC-List-ODA-Recipients-for-reporting-2021-flows.pdf

OECD. (2021b, May). *ODA to developing countries -summary*. Retrieved from ODA Website: www.oecd.org/dac/financing-sustainable-development/development-finance-topics/Developing-World-Development-Aid-at-a-Glance-2021.pdf

OECD. (2022a, October 11). *Aid (ODA) disbursements to countries and regions [DAC2a]*. Retrieved from Query Wizard for International Development Statistics (QWIDS): statistics.oecd.org/qwids

OECD. (2022b). *DAC list of ODA recipients effective for reporting on 2022 and 2023 flows*. Retrieved from OECD website: www.oecd.org/dac/financing-sustainable-development/development-finance-standards/DAC-List-of-ODA-Recipients-for-reporting-2022-23-flows.pdf

OECD. (2022c, May). *ODA receipts and selected indicators for developing countries and territories table 25 2020*. Retrieved from DAC: website www.oecd.org/dac/financing-sustainable-development/development-finance-data/

Otsuka, K., & Fan, S. (2021). *Agricultural development: New perspectives in a changing world*. Washington, DC: IFPRI.

Paris Declaration on Aid Effectiveness and the Accra Agenda for Action. (2005 and 2008). Paris: OECD.

Pritchett, L. (1997). Divergence, big time. *Journal of Economic Perspectives, 11*(3), 3–17.

Radelet, S. (2010). *Emerging Africa: How 17 countries are leading the way*. Washington, DC: Center for Global Development.

Rome Conference on Harmonization. (2003). *Rome declaration on harmonization*. Rome.

Rowden, R. (2013, January 4). *The myth of Africa's rise*. Retrieved from Foreign Policy: foreignpolicy.com/2013/01/04the-myth-of-africa-rise/

Roxburgh, C., Dorr, N., Leke, A., Tazi-Riffi, A., van Wamelen, A., Lund, S., . . . & Zeino-Mahmalat, T. (2010). *Lions on the move: The progress and potential of African economies.* McKinsey Global Institute. Retrieved from: https://www. mckinsey.com/featured-insights/middle-east-and-africa/lions-on-the-move

Stiglitz, J. E. (2003). *Globalization and its discontents.* New York: Norton.

Summers, L. H., & Pritchett, L. H. (1993). The structural-adjustment debate. *American Economic Review*, 383–389.

Tooze, A. (2022, June 24). *Defining polycrisis – from crisis pictures to the crisis matrix.* Retrieved from Chartbook: https://adamtooze.substack.com/p/ chartbook-130-defining-polycrisis

United Nations. (1945, June 26). *United Nations charter.* Retrieved from United Nations web site: www.un.org/en/about-us/un-charter/full-text

United Nations. (2001, April). *HIV/AIDs in Africa.* New York: UN Department of Public Information/UNAIDS.

United Nations. (2003). Financing for development. In *Monterrey consensus of the international conference on financing for development.* New York: UN.

United Nations. (2021). *LDC identification criteria & indicators.* Retrieved from Development Policy and Analysis Division: www.un.org/development/desa/ dpad/least-developed-country-category/ldc-criteria.html

United Nations Non-Governmental Liaison Service (UN-NGLS). (n.d.). *MDG targets and indicators.* Retrieved from United Nations Non-Governmental Liaison Service: www.un-ngls.org/index.php/background-mgd10/1386-mdg-targets-and-indicators

United States Central Intelligence Agency. (1945). Changing face of Europe and colonial tension, late. [Washington, D.C: Central Intelligence Agency] [Map] Retrieved from the Library of Congress: https://www.loc.gov/item/81690522/

van de Walle, N. (2001). *African economies and the politics of permanent crisis, 1979–1999.* Cambridge: Cambridge University Press.

Williamson, J. (2000). What should the world bank think about the Washington consensus? *The World Bank Research Observer*, *15*(2), 251–264.

Williamson, J. (2003). Our agenda and the Washington consensus. In P.-P. A. Kuczynski (Ed.), *After the Washington consensus: Restarting growth and reform in Latin America* (pp. 323–331). Washington, DC: Institute for International Economics.

World Bank. (2005). *Economic growth in the 1990s: Learning from a decade of reform.* Washington, DC: The World Bank.

World Bank. (2018, February 15). *Data Bank.* Retrieved from World Development Indicators: https://databank.worldbank.org/source/world-development-indicators

World Bank. (2022a). *Poverty and shared prosperity 2022: Correcting course.* Washington, DC: World Bank.

World Bank. (2022b, October 18). *World development indicators.* Retrieved from Net ODA as a Percentage of GNI: https://data.worldbank.org/indicator/ DT.ODA.ODAT.GN.ZS?view=chart&locations=XM

World Bank/IDA. (2020, July). *IDA graduates.* Retrieved from IDA: http://ida. worldbank.org/about/ida-graduates

World Bank/IDA. (2022). *Borrowing countries.* Retrieved from IDA: http://ida. worldbank.org/about/borrowing-countries

World Health Organization. (2022, December 13). *WHO Coronavirus (COVID-19) dashboard.* Retrieved from WHO website: https://covid19.who.int/

3 The Main Actors
Recipients and Donors

Chapter 4 will review the different types of aid, explain how aid is packaged and delivered, and discuss how much aid is provided, where, and to whom. First, it is important to meet the main actors: aid recipients and aid donors. While it is not possible to have an exhaustive treatment of each recipient and donor, this chapter will provide a snapshot of each group and some of the differences within the group.

Aid Recipients

Both the UN and the World Bank categorize developing countries by income group. Many other types of categorizations of countries exist, such as the United Nations Development Program's (UNDP) Human Development Index (HDI) or the Institute for Economics and Peace's (IEP) World Peace Index (WPI). However, in today's world of foreign aid, GNI per capita is the measure that is most frequently used. While there are minor differences between the UN and World Bank classifications, aid recipients are in the low and middle-income groups. Box 3.1 explains the classifications.

Box 3.1 Country Classification Criteria

The UN and OECD use the following definitions and categories to classify developing countries that are aid recipients:

Least-Developed Countries: Defined as countries with per capita Gross National Income (GNI) below US$1,045 in 2020, as well as low levels of human capital (as measured by five health and education indicators) and high levels of economic vulnerability (as measured by a composite index

---

DOI: 10.4324/9781003265320-4

including size, location, economic structure, and vulnerability to trade shocks, natural shocks, and environmental degradation).

Other Low-Income Countries: Countries that meet the income criteria for Least-Developed Countries, but have better health and education indicators and lower degrees of economic vulnerability.

Lower Middle-Income Countries: Countries with GNI per capita between US$1,046 and US$4,095 in 2020.

Upper Middle-Income Countries: Countries with GNI per capita between US$4,096 and US$12,695 in 2020.

These categories are similar to those used by the World Bank and the International Development Association (IDA) except that:

- IDA makes no distinction between LDCs and other low-income countries.
- The cut-off point for eligibility for IDA's subsidized credits for low-income countries is updated each year and was US$1,255 as of July 2022. Above that threshold, countries are eligible for IBRD loans until their income per capita reaches levels above those for Upper Middle-Income Countries.
- IDA provides credits to some countries above the IDA threshold because of an exception made for small island and country states. IDA also provides some support on less favorable, but still subsidized, terms to countries transitioning from low-income to middle-income status.

Sources: (United Nations, 2021; World Bank/IDA, 2022a; OECD, 2022d)

Progress and Stagnation

Over the last 25 years, there has been tremendous progress moving up the country income ladder. Leaving aside the United Nations' category of Least Developed Countries (LDC) for the moment, almost all of the 24 countries classified as other low-income countries in 1995 (per capita income less than US$765 in 1995) have moved to middle-income status, with one moving to high-income (China), 6 moving to upper middle-income, and 16 moving to lower middle-income status. Only one country moved back to the LDC category (Senegal). Of 45 countries classified as lower middle-income in 1995,[1] 27 have moved to upper middle-income status, while 15 have remained in the lower middle-income group. Two have regressed into the low income grouping (North Korea and Syria), and one has moved back to LDC status (East Timor). There has also been movement among those classified as upper middle-income in 1995. While Brazil, Mexico, and South Africa have stayed upper middle-income countries (along with 14 others on the 1995 list), 11 countries (Chile, Croatia, and Uruguay, along with 8 others) have transitioned to high income countries (OECD, 2022d, 2021b, 1996).

Many developing countries have succeeded in "moving up the ladder", resulting in growth and at least better *average* incomes and living conditions in their countries. Nonetheless, a group of countries has made less progress over the past 25 years. Despite all the other changes, strikingly, the list of Least Developed Countries has remained stagnant. Only 4 countries (Maldives, Equatorial Guinea, Cabo Verde, and Vanuatu) listed as LDCs in 1995 are now classified as middle-income countries, while 2 additional countries (Senegal and Timor Leste) have been added to the LDC list. Of the 48 countries classified as LDCs or other low-income countries today, 33 are in Africa (OECD, 2022d). There are a few poor countries left in Asia and Oceania, along with Yemen, Syria, and Haiti (the outliers for the Middle East and Latin America). European and Central Asian aid recipients are all classified as middle-income countries. The challenge of moving out of extreme poverty now appears to be centered on the African continent. Table 3.1 provides a list of aid recipients by country income and region.

IDA graduation data (i.e., becoming ineligible for IDA credits because of higher income) tell the same story. Since IDA was created in the mid-1960s, 36 countries have graduated for good. Only 5 of those are from Sub-Saharan Africa (World Bank/IDA, 2022b). That is why, when looking at the present and future of aid, Africa needs to remain "front and center" in the analysis. Good development progress has been made over the past 75 years, but Africa, for the most part, has not enjoyed the same level of progress. It may well be that the weight of colonialism as well as the other challenges described in Chapter 2 have fallen more heavily on Africa.

Who Receives Most Aid Today?

Who typically receives aid today? Every country in Table 3.1 receives some aid or is eligible to receive it. Typically, however, by the time a country gets to upper middle-income status, the level of highly subsidized credits or grants (what is officially known as aid) falls off, although there are some important exceptions that will be discussed later. Today, a good portion of aid is channelled towards low-income countries and lower middle-income countries. Table 3.2 tells an interesting story about the top 20 recipients of Official Development Assistance (ODA) in 2020.

Table 3.1 List of Aid Recipients by Country Income Grouping and Region

LDCs	Other Low-Income	Lower Middle-Income	Upper Middle-Income
Africa	**East Asia**	**Africa**	**Africa**
Angola	North Korea	Cabo Verde	Botswana
Benin		Cameroon	Equatorial Guinea
Burkina Faso	**Middle East**	Congo	Gabon
Burundi	**and North**	Cote d'Ivoire	Mauritius
Central African	**Africa**	Ghana	Namibia
Republic	Syria	Kenya	South Africa
Chad		Nigeria	
Comoros		Swaziland	**South Asia**
Democratic		Zimbabwe	Maldives
Republic of the			
Congo		**South Asia**	**East Asia and**
Djibouti		India	**Pacific**
Eritrea		Pakistan	China
Ethiopia		Sri Lanka	Malaysia
Gambia			Thailand
Guinea		**East Asia and**	
Guinea-Bissau		**Pacific**	Cook Islands
Lesotho		Indonesia	Fiji
Liberia		Mongolia	Marshall Islands
Madagascar		Philippines	Nauru
Malawi		Vietnam	Niue
Mali			Palau
Mauritania		Micronesia	Tonga
Mozambique		Papua New Guinea	
Niger		Samoa	**Middle East and**
Rwanda			**North Africa**
Sao Tome and		**Middle East and**	Iraq
Principe		**North Africa**	Lebanon
Senegal		Algeria	Libya
Sierra Leone		Egypt	
Somalia		Iran	**Latin America**
South Sudan		Jordan	**and the**
Sudan		Morocco	**Caribbean**
Tanzania		Tunisia	Argentina
Togo		West Bank and	Brazil
Uganda		Gaza	Colombia
Zambia			Costa Rica
		Latin America	Ecuador
South Asia		**and the**	Guatemala
Afghanistan		**Caribbean**	Guyana
Bangladesh		Belize	Mexico
Bhutan		Bolivia	Panama
Nepal		El Salvador	Paraguay
		Honduras	Peru
		Nicaragua	Suriname
			Venezuela

LDCs	Other Low-Income	Lower Middle-Income	Upper Middle-Income
East Asia and Pacific Cambodia Lao People's Democratic Republic Myanmar Timor-Leste Kiribati Solomon Islands Tuvalu Vanuatu **Middle East and North Africa** Yemen **Latin America and the Caribbean** Haiti		**Europe and Central Asia** Armenia Kyrgyzstan Tajikistan Ukraine Uzbekistan	Antigua and Barbuda Cuba Dominica Dominican Republic Grenada Jamaica Saint Lucia Saint Vincent and the Grenadines **Europe and Central Asia** Albania Azerbaijan Belarus Bosnia & Herzegovina F.Y.R. of Macedonia Georgia Kazakhstan Kosovo Moldova Montenegro Serbia Turkey Turkmenistan

Source: (OECD, 2022d)

Table 3.2 Top 20 Official Aid Recipients in 2020*

Aid (ODA) Recipients	US$ Millions	Country Income Status
Syrian Arab Republic	10,006	Low-Income
Bangladesh	5,374	LDC
Ethiopia	5,302	LDC
Afghanistan	4,207	LDC
Kenya	3,988	Lower Middle
Democratic Republic of the Congo	3,377	LDC
Nigeria	3,375	Lower Middle
Jordan	3,114	Upper Middle
Uganda	3,083	LDC

(*Continued*)

Table 3.2 (Continued)

Aid (ODA) Recipients	US$ Millions	Country Income Status
Somalia	3,040	LDC
Myanmar	2,870	LDC
Pakistan	2,591	Lower Middle
Mozambique	2,547	LDC
Yemen	2,544	LDC
Iraq	2,359	Upper Middle
Sudan	2,348	LDC
Ukraine	2,335	Lower Middle
Tanzania	2,275	LDC
Ghana	2,204	Lower Middle
West Bank and Gaza	2,030	Lower Middle

Source: (OECD, 2022f)

* ODA from OECD, Multilateral Organizations, and OECD reporting donors only

The list seems to be aligned with the principle of giving to the poorest countries: only 2 out of 20 countries are upper middle-income countries: Jordan and Iraq. Aid to Jordan has increased in recent years to deal with the influx of migrants from Syria's war, and Iraq is recovering from war as well. Of the rest, 11 countries are LDCs and low-income, and 7 countries are lower middle-income. Half of the top recipients are from Sub-Saharan Africa, as might be expected. Beyond the question of poverty, the driving principle in this list seems to be the presence of conflict: at least 14 of the recipients are countries recovering from, engaged in, or on the brink of serious conflict situations or wars.

From the donors' viewpoint, aid is meant to serve many purposes and is not only directed towards poverty reduction and development. The need to tackle global problems such as pandemics, climate change, and conflict can lead to different priorities in terms of which countries receive aid. Another reason is the imperative that aid agencies have to show results. As discussed earlier, the LDCs as a group have stagnated while better off countries, as measured by both income and social indicators, have shown more progress. It is easier to argue the case for aid when there is tangible "success" to show. The next section will delve more deeply into donor motivations.

The macro-data on aid reinforces the point that donors look beyond income levels when providing aid. When looking at Official Development

Assistance (ODA), there is a gap between those that arguably need aid the most (LDCs) and where a good portion of the aid money is going. In OECD's most recent summary of ODA to developing countries, one-third went to low-income countries, one-third went to middle-income countries, and one-third is unspecified. The unspecified amount could include donor administration costs charged to the aid budget, regional programs that benefit multiple income groups, global program budgets, and multi-country trust funds. How much more than one-third of the aid budget is going to the poorest countries is an open question (OECD, 2021d). Chapter 4 will have more aggregate information on aid recipients by income, region, and sector. Box 3.2 has some definitions that may be helpful in reading the rest of this chapter as well as Chapter 4.

Box 3.2 Helpful Definitions

These definitions may help in reading this chapter and Chapter 4.

Official Development Assistance (ODA)

Official Development Assistance is aid that is provided in accordance with the stipulations of OECD's Development Assistance Committee (DAC). To be ODA, public funds must be given outright (a grant) or loaned on concessional terms (below commercial market rates) and used to support the welfare or development of low or middle-income countries. Loans provided at market rates (non-concessional) or with an insufficient amount of concessionality, even if they are used to support welfare or development, are not considered ODA, although they are a form of development finance. Loans and grants provided to countries that are not on OECD's official list of developing countries and territories are *not* considered ODA, and loans and grants to developing countries that do not support welfare or development (e.g., military aid) are *not* considered ODA (OECDa, n.d.). Chapter 4 has more detail on ODA.

Net ODA is ODA given in a year, minus any repayments of the principal of concessional loans previously counted as ODA.
Gross ODA is ODA given in a year without any deductions for repayments. Starting in 2018, loans are counted on a "grant equivalent basis" so eventually the difference between net and gross ODA will disappear.

Bilateral aid is official (government) funds or other assets given by a country's government to another country's government or an NGO. The organization or country that provides this aid is referred to as a "bilateral donor" or simply "a bilateral".

Multilateral aid is official (government) funds given to multilateral agencies that are then used to finance the multilateral agencies' own programs (OECDb, n.d.).

Multi-Bi aid or Bi-Multi aid is aid that has been given to a multilateral agency by a bilateral donor for a specific program and/or country (i.e., earmarked). These funds are typically counted as bilateral flows (OECDb, n.d.).

Country Programmable Aid (CPA) is a measure of the amount of aid that official donors program for individual countries or regions and over which recipient countries have or could have a significant say. This measure has been in use since 2007 (OECDc, n.d.).

Tied aid is aid provided to a recipient country that must be used to purchase goods and services originating in the donor country only.

Commitments are the amount of aid pledged firmly in writing to be given within a certain timeframe.

Disbursements are the amount of aid delivered within a certain timeframe.

Sources: Author and OECD (a, b, c, n.d.)

Before discussing donor motivations for providing aid, it is pertinent to ask what the recipients' motivations are for *accepting* aid. Obviously, there is the imperative of need: low-income countries require aid even to provide basic services and infrastructure. However, need is not the only motivation. In the case of countries undertaking reform programs, some recipients value the advice and technical support that come along with the money. Some governments may also see international donors as important allies when domestic opposition to government policies is strong. Educated technical staff regard aid agencies and projects as potential sources of stable and decent employment. Some forms of aid convey legitimacy: an IMF program supported by a loan and/or a large Development Policy Credit from IDA/World Bank provide comfort to other · donors as well as to private sector investors. For upper middle-income countries who are commercial borrowers, any grants or concessional loans they receive are generally welcome as an inexpensive source of capital, provided the bureaucracy or conditions are not overly burdensome and the funds are directed towards something beneficial for the country. This list of recipient motivations would not be complete without mentioning corruption. It is not as strong or frequent a motivation as is generally thought by the public. However, it is true that some government officials and others see aid as "rich people's money" and welcome it as an avenue to personal enrichment.

Aid Donors

Each donor has a set of distinct interests that guide the type of aid it provides and to whom it provides that aid. This chapter gives a picture of donor motivations generally, describes broad tendencies in groups of donors, and provides a "snapshot" of some of the most important donors. While the Paris Declaration called for increased harmonization, what has happened over the last 20 years is increased heterogeneity – with donors committed to broad goals such as the Sustainable Development Goals, but with very different ways of joining the effort. This is not only the case globally, but at the recipient country level as well.

Motivations for Developmental Aid

Not all aid is the same. Military aid and aid given to relatively well-off allies have purposes other than improving the incomes and welfare of a country's population. However, even with developmental aid, there are many different motivations for providing aid. While there may be some donors who see aid as a form of charity or "doing good", this is more likely to be the case when humanitarian or emergency aid is being provided. In non-emergency situations, official donors generally have more self-interest in mind. Aid, like diplomacy, is a tool of statecraft (Lancaster, 2007; Yanguas, 2018; Radelet, 2006). Perhaps this seemed most clear during the Cold War Era when both the Soviet Union and the United States attempted to use aid to block the other's influence on newly independent states. The United States and China may be engaging in some of the same behavior today, and Russia revitalized its aid program to seek friends for its unpopular war in Ukraine. Not all aid is provided in the context of competition for power, but self-interest and the desire for influence still predominate.

Not surprisingly, historical ties are an important factor in motivating aid. This is especially true of donors and their former colonies. The British may have seen aid as a way of maintaining strong influence over former colonies in Africa and Asia without having the full responsibilities that colonialism demanded after the mid-20th century. The French have also maintained close ties with their former colonies in West Africa through aid as well as other mechanisms. The "Francophonie" (nations and territories that speak French) is one way France is able to maintain its international profile. Religious and cultural concerns have also motivated some donors who view the spread of Western ideas and values as important to global progress (Classroom Vignette 3.1).

Proximity is important in many aid decisions. While it may seem like "neighbors helping neighbors", it is more about ensuring that the neighborhood stays friendly and the donor's interests (and borders) are protected.

Many observers have tied aid to commercial interests, whether it be access to minerals, oil, and other raw materials or fertile ground for foreign direct investment taking advantage of cheap labor and proximity to other inputs. Aid contracts have been a lucrative business for some countries. The international left has historically seen aid as little more than another mechanism that allows the Global North to exploit the Global South. Today, in an era where the market and private sector seem the predominant route to prosperity, there is an open association between official aid and private finance in the former of public-private partnerships and blended finance arrangements.

The need to demonstrate the ability to lead in international affairs is also an important motivation. Today, providing aid is a signal of "having made it" (even while some countries continue at the same time to receive aid from even richer countries). Giving aid is now an accepted international norm, a sign of growing prestige on the world stage. In addition, an entire industry has grown up around aid with its own career tracks and rules for advancement. The staff, contractors, and companies involved in aid have become some of its most ardent supporters.

Finally, the need to mitigate global problems is becoming an increasingly important motivation for aid. Preventing the spread of infectious diseases, containing conflict, slowing down environmental damage and global warming, and stopping the flood of migration are near the top of each official donor's agenda. While there are benefits from these actions that accrue to developing countries, many of the benefits are also critical to maintaining the welfare of donor countries. Two recent examples include the aid provided for the COVID-19 pandemic as well as for outbreaks of Ebola disease in the Democratic Republic of the Congo and elsewhere.

The specific reasons for providing aid and the historical context do change over time. However, for the most part, the motivations for aid continue to be centered around self-interest. Whether explicitly stated or not, providing aid is a tool linked to national security and reflects the way in which a country wishes to portray itself on the international stage.

Classroom Vignette 3.1   The Link Between Colonialism and Foreign Aid

When graduate students were asked about motivations for aid, they put up the following list:

- Historical ties
- Commercial ties
- Diplomatic, geopolitical, and security concerns
- Capitalism and the need for new markets and cheap inputs
- Humanitarian and social concerns
- Cultural and religious goals
- Moral obligation
- Accepted international norm (To be a leader, you need to do it.)

When asked if this list reminded them of another list earlier in the semester, the reply was: "It looks just like the list we put up for the motivations of colonialism!"

The following pages describe the key characteristics of four types of donors: those in the traditional "OECD-DAC Club", "new" or "emerging" providers who are not part of the club, multilateral organizations and banks involved in development, and foundations and non-governmental organizations (NGOs). Many NGOs are, in fact, working at least partially with aid provided by donor governments. Foundations' resources and a portion of NGOs' resources originate with private citizens and corporations and are not considered official aid, but they are part of the overall "aid effort". Foundations and NGOs have been increasingly involved, and at times influential, in the overall aid and development dialog. Finally, expatriate citizens, friends, and relatives who live abroad send money home through remittances. They are a significant source of development finance although not aid providers in a strict sense. The chapter ends by highlighting their importance.

The Traditional OECD-DAC Donors

There are currently 31 members of OECD's Development Assistance Committee, DAC.[2] What unites the group is a common commitment to use DAC guidelines and recommendations in formulating their aid programs, report their aid in detail to the OECD, undergo a peer review from time to time of their development cooperation, and participate in regular meetings. Members also share an understanding of the role DAC has played in establishing aid and development norms and a desire to belong to what some have seen as the Global North's "Rich Man's Club" ("A question of definition", 2006). Many of the norms discussed in this and subsequent chapters have in fact evolved from DAC decisions, and DAC data and statistics are widely used by the aid community. The key players within the group, not surprisingly, are the most prominent donors, either by amount or percentage of GNI.

Notwithstanding their membership in "the club", there are clear differences among groups of donors within DAC. The Nordic countries share a number of common characteristics that are not universal within the DAC. For example, Norway, Sweden, and Denmark all reached the 0.7 percent of GNI benchmark for their aid programs years ago and continue to provide aid on that basis. All three countries (plus Finland) focus on Africa, low-income and fragile states, and provide their aid in the form of grants. Traditionally, these countries have formed the core of a "like-minded" group that is sympathetic to recipient country ownership of aid programs and places high priority on poverty reduction and climate action. Gender and governance concerns also figure prominently (Denmark, Ministry of Foreign Affairs, 2022; OECD, 2022a, 2022b; Donor Tracker, 2022).

The next group of donors are the European members of the European Union (EU). Of the 31 DAC members, 21 belong to the EU. This group is very diverse. Aside from the three Nordic members (Finland, Sweden, and Denmark), there are the G7 members who are traditionally large aid providers: Germany, the United Kingdom, France, and Italy.[3] Germany and the UK have been especially active in establishing DAC rules and reporting requirements. The UK met the 0.7 percent benchmark until 2021, when its aid dropped significantly to 0.5 percent. Germany met the 0.7 percent target in 2021. Both donors are still well above the average for DAC country donors of .033 percent (OECD, 2022a). The UK provides all of its aid in the form of grants, while Germany provides some of its aid in concessional loans (about 12 percent), with the rest as grants (OECD, 2022b). Germany is now the second largest bilateral donor and has been a leader on environmental and agricultural issues. The UK has also been a leader over many years in championing aid's poverty-reduction objectives, although British commercial and diplomatic interests have always played a role and have become more prominent in recent years. In 2020, Britain's aid agency, DFID (Department for International Development) was merged into the foreign affairs ministry, which was renamed the Foreign, Commonwealth, and Development Office (FCDO). There has been concern that foreign aid is becoming less a priority for the British government.

France provides considerable support mainly to its former colonies in Africa and Haiti. France has increased its aid in recent years and is now at 0.51 percent of GNI; it provides about one-quarter of its aid in the form of concessional loans. Italy provides only 0.28 percent of its GNI for aid mostly through bilateral channels. The last few years have seen all these donors focusing first on the migration crisis in Europe and, more recently, on the COVID-19 pandemic and the consequences of the war in Ukraine (OECD, 2020, 2022b).

The rest of the group of Europeans (Austria, Belgium, Czech Republic, Greece, Hungary, Lithuania, Luxembourg, Poland, Portugal, Slovak Republic, Slovenia, and Spain) are relatively small aid providers, some of whom are relatively new members of the EU. Their impact on overall aid policy, either at the country level or at the global level, is relatively small. Two exceptions, not included in that list, or in the other groups, are the Netherlands and Ireland. The Netherlands has traditionally been a strong aid provider, with a focus on Africa and low-income countries, and its aid has been delivered as grants. While its aid effort has been reduced in recent years, it still provides over 0.5 percent of its GNI as aid and is overall the ninth largest donor in the DAC, and it is likely to increase its aid again in the coming years. At times, the Netherlands has been part of the "like-minded" group; at other times, it pursues its policies and programs independently. Ireland, while a small donor, in terms of amounts and effort, has had considerable influence because of favorable ratings from recipient countries because of its emphasis on country ownership and long-standing focus on low-income countries, mainly in Sub-Saharan Africa (Donor Tracker, 2022; OECD, 2022b).

Another small group within the DAC are the members that are not major donors nor members of the EU. These countries are Canada, Australia, New Zealand, and Switzerland. Canada is the sixth largest donor but provides only about 0.32 of its GNI as aid (OECD, 2022a). Just over half of its aid is channeled through and to multilateral institutions. Its focus is increasingly on low-income and fragile states (Donor Tracker, 2022). Gender and environment are also important areas, and Canada spent over 12 percent of its ODA on refugees and asylum seekers in 2020 (OECD, 2022b). Australia and New Zealand are prominent donors in Oceania primarily, with Australia also providing aid to some of the poorer countries in East Asia. Much of their aid is bilateral. Australia's aid steadily reduced from 2012 until 2021, when even with a small increase it constituted only about 0.2 percent of its GNI. Switzerland is a relatively small donor, regarded positively by recipient countries for its neutral stance in global politics. Its level of effort, now averaging 0.5 percent of GNI, is above the OECD average but is unlikely to rise much further in the near term (OECD, 2022a, 2022b).

Finally, that leaves the United States and Japan, two big, but quite different, DAC donors. The United States views aid as part of its overall national security and foreign affairs effort. It is an active donor in many countries, providing grants for a wide range of projects and technical assistance. Countries where the US has major military or strategic interests (e.g., Syria, Jordan, Iraq, Afghanistan until 2022) tend to receive the most aid. The US provides aid in the form of grants, and in recent years it has had a big focus on global health. The US is the largest donor of food aid, and humanitarian assistance is a substantial part of its aid program. About two-thirds of US aid is provided bilaterally. Even so, the US is the largest provider of financial contributions to multilateral organizations. Less than half of its contribution is without restriction, with the rest earmarked for specific programs (Donor Tracker, 2022; OECD, 2018a, 2022b). Despite the large sums provided by the US, it has the lowest official aid to GNI percentage among major donors, around 18 percent.

For a long time Japan was the only Asian donor in the DAC until South Korea joined in 2010. Currently, Japan is the third largest donor in amount, following the US and Germany. Underlying Japan's aid program is a concern for global and regional issues and its own commercial interests. Countries in Asia receive most of its aid, but it also provides funds to sub-Saharan Africa. Japan is providing about 0.34 percent of its GNI as aid, and like the US, it provides most of its aid (about 70 percent) as purely bilateral aid. Unlike most of the other DAC donors (except for France and South Korea), Japan is committed to providing aid as concessional loans, and the majority of its aid is provided in the form of loans. It sees this as important for recipient ownership of the programs. Unlike many DAC donors, infrastructure is a priority sector (OECD, 2022a, 2022b; Donor Tracker, 2022).

Because of the heterogenity of the DAC group, it is difficult to provide a coherent snapshot of the group's aid efforts. While there are clear DAC recommendations and targets, including eliminating tied aid and the 0.7 percent of GNI benchmark for aid, not all DAC members adhere to the guidelines. In order to provide a skeletal picture of the DAC group, Table 3.3 characterizes some of the major DAC donors (those providing $1 billion or more in aid annually) using selected criteria and indicators.

As can be seen from the table, there is wide variation in individual members' efforts. For example, for countries such as Italy, Spain, Austria, and Finland, multilateral aid forms an important part of their overall aid effort. In contrast, others, including the largest donors (US, Japan, and Germany), prioritize bilateral aid; their multilateral aid contributions, as a percentage of their total aid, fall below the DAC country average. While some individual donors (e.g., Norway and Canada) use multilaterals for earmarked programs over which they retain some control, others (e.g., France and Japan) shy away from multi-bilateral aid.

There is similar diversity in DAC donor support for NGOs. There are two different types of funds channeled to NGOs. The first type includes funds that go to NGOs for direct support of their organizations' work (core contributions). The second type, by far the most popular, are funds provided to NGOs to act as implementing agencies for donor programs. In that type, the donor defines objectives and strategy and retains control over important aspects of the program. The DAC country average for both types of support for NGOs is about 14 percent of the bilateral portion of their aid programs. However, as seen in Table 3.3, there are different strategies with regard to NGOs. A number of countries channel over 25 percent of their bilateral aid through NGOs. That means that about 15 to 18 percent of each country's aid is being channeled either to or through NGOs. Other donors, such as Germany, Japan, France, and Korea channel less than 7 percent of their bilateral aid through and to NGOs.

Clearly, there are divergent views about NGO partnerships. Some donors see their aid as a means to strengthen civil society both at home and in recipient countries. Others use NGOs to avoid further build-up of government aid bureaucracies and to attempt to keep down the costs of delivering aid. In some countries, such as the US, large NGOs compete with private firms for the government's aid business. Donors also use NGOs in situations where they believe the recipient government is incapable of implementing the program properly because of lack of capacity or ingrained corruption.

Donors who channel only small amounts to NGOs are also a mixed group. Some, including some of the newer donors, do not have a tradition of public support to NGOs, or else see it as inappropriate or inefficient to provide public funds to them or to use them as implementors. Others limit using NGOs as implementing agencies because they want the recipient government to be the key decision-maker. In their view, the recipient government should decide on implementing agencies for their programs, and it is best to have NGOs accountable to recipient governments.

The percentages of CPA (country programmable aid) also show variation among OECD-DAC donors. In Table 3.3, the overall DAC country average for CPA (50 percent of bilateral aid) is considerably higher than the overall country average for the larger donors (42 percent) shown in the table. Furthermore, among the largest donors, CPA ranges from 14 percent (Austria) and 19 percent (Belgium) to 82 percent (Japan and Korea). While the actual percentages reflect many different situations regarding the use of aid funds (e.g., first-year migrant costs, administrative costs, COVID-19, and other global expenditures), lower percentages of CPA mean less recipient government involvement in and control of the aid.

Table 3.3 "Snapshot" of DAC Donors (providing US$1 billion or above in 2021)

Donor	.7% of GNI (2021)	Grants Over 86%* (2020)	Untied Aid Over 90%* (2020)	Focus on SSA	Overall Aid Profile (%)			CPA 2020 (% of Bilateral)	Support to NGOS 2020 % of Bilateral		Separate Aid Agency (2022)
					Bilateral Aid	Multi-Bi (2020)	Multi-lateral		TOTAL - "to" and "thru"	Just "to"	
Australia		XX	XX		57	24	19	65	11	2	X
Austria		X			31	12	57	14	12	<1	X
Belgium		X	X	X	42	7	51	19	25	18	X
Canada		X	XX	X	49	28	23	23	28	7	
Denmark	X	XX	X	X	38	26	36	38	28	3	
Finland		XX		X	34	17	49	37	22	4	
France		X	X	X	65	5	30	66	5	<1	X
Germany	X	X		X	62	18	20	46	7	3	X
Italy		X			21	10	69	47	15	6	X
Ireland		XX	XX	X	39	14	47	35	41	19	
Japan			XX		75	8	17	82	1	1	X
Korea		X			64	15	21	24	3	0	X
Netherlands		XX	XX	X	52	17	31	32	26	3	
Norway	X	XX	X	X	41	34	25	24	28	8	X
Spain		X	X		29	5	66	44	56	0	X
Sweden	X	XX		X	34	23	43	38	32	6	X
Switzerland		X	XX	X	58	19	23	38	40	10	X
UK		X	XX	X	46	18	36	34	17	4	
US		XX		X	64	20	16	45	22	0	X
AVERAGE GROUP					47	17	36	42	22	5	
AVERAGE DAC					57	16	27	50	14	2	

*XX = 100% grants
*XX = 100% untied

Source: OECD (2022a, 2022b, 2022c), Donor Tracker (2022)

Figures in yellow are those donors who provide less than the country average of multilateral aid.
Figures in yellow are those donors who provide NGOs with above average support.

Table 3.3 also shows that the majority of the largest DAC donors in dollar terms have a clear focus on Sub-Saharan Africa (OECD, 2022b). This is an evolving, positive trend. Just five years ago, only half of the largest DAC donors had aid programs focused on Sub-Saharan Africa (OECD, 2018a).

The last indicator in Table 3.3 is whether or not the country has a specialized aid agency. Although both Canada and Australia, and more recently, the UK, have moved to close their aid agencies and fold them into ministries of foreign affairs, many of the larger donors still maintain separate aid agencies. Nonethless, this indicator is misleading, since the level of autonomy and authority of aid agencies varies significantly. Increasingly, overall aid policy is set at the ministerial level, with aid channeled through a variety of agencies and ministries, including the aid agency where one exists. Some aid agencies disburse a significant portion of the country's aid (e.g., the US's Agency for International Development – USAID – and France's Agence Francaise de Developpement – AFD). Others, including the aid agencies in Belgium, Austria, and Italy, disburse only a small portion of the government's aid. When the British aid agency DFID existed, it had overall responsibility for policy, strategy, and implementation and disbursed a large portion of the United Kingdom's aid, a fairly unique situation among DAC donors.

The picture that emerges from this snapshot of the OECD-DAC donors is one of heterogeneity. Nonetheless, these donors are important in that collectively they set directions for aid and provide definitions for what is considered aid "best practice". They also have a commitment to be forthcoming and relatively transparent in reporting their aid on an annual basis, and DAC's aid statistics are invaluable for understanding ODA. Further, in DAC meetings and working groups, there is continuous discussion among the various donors. This, along with the DAC Peer Reviews, allows for good information exchanges and the evolution of aid practice. Also, although there are other large individual donors, DAC donors as a group provide the largest share of aid by far to low and middle-income countries and many multilateral institutions.

The "New" Providers

The "new" or "emerging" aid donors are not exactly new. Socialist countries – most prominently the USSR and China – began providing aid in the 1950s. For the USSR, this was part of the Cold War competition with the United States. With the dissolution of the USSR, Soviet aid disappeared. In this century, Russia is once again taking up the mantle of aid, albeit in a much smaller way. China's aid activities began with providing grain, medicine, and industrial inputs to North Korea during the Korean War, but its assistance spread rapidly to other parts of Asia, the Middle

East, and Africa. In the initial period, China's motivations were a mixture of diplomacy (to support newly independent states and displace Taiwan from the United Nations) and commercial interests. In the late 1970s and 1980s, Chinese aid (especially to Africa) declined, with China focusing on its own development. This changed again, beginning in the 1990s, when the Chinese, following the Tiananmen Square uprising, sought to bolster their international reputation and gain new friends. China's aid programs increased and have kept increasing until the recent economic downturn. Since the beginning of this century, Chinese aid has been a sign of China's rapid economic development, where aid, along with trade and investment, have been hallmarks of China's growing international presence (Mawdsley, 2012). More recently, aid has become a symbol of China's global power and a challenge to the West's presence and its aid policies and practices.

Russia and China are joined by other BRICS countries (Brazil, India, and South Africa) as emerging donors. Middle-Eastern countries such as the United Arab Emirates (UAE), Saudi Arabia, Qatar, and Kuwait have also emerged as important donors, as has Turkey. In 2021, Turkey was the only non-DAC country to meet the 0.7 percent of GNI guideline for aid. There are also a number of smaller donors from Europe, Central Asia, and Latin America. In all, there are 29 emerging donors (Luijkx & Benn, 2017; OECD, 2022b). Some 23 of these countries report aid spending to OECD (with varying detail), and 7 of these countries (Azerbaijan, Bulgaria, Romania, Kuwait, Qatar, Saudi Arabia, and UAE) are now participants in (but not members of) DAC, while Lithuania was admitted to the DAC in 2022. Seven donors (China, India, Indonesia, Brazil, Peru, Argentina, and South Africa) do not report aid data to OECD. Although Russia provides aid, it has stopped reporting its aid. The last available estimate was for 2017, when it provided US$1.2 billion (World Bank, n.d.).

Many of the emerging providers have been slow to develop an official aid database (Asmus, Fuchs, & Muller, 2017); for some, accurate, detailed data is hard to come by. In one estimate from OECD from almost a decade ago, in 2014 non-DAC donors provided about 17 percent of total aid (gross disbursements), or about US$32 billion (Luijkx & Benn, 2017, p. 4). As Table 3.4 shows, in 2020–2021, non-DAC donors provided about US$18 billion, or about 9 percent of total concessional flows (OECD, 2022b, 2022a). Because 2020 and 2021 were pandemic years, it is not surprising that contributions from emerging donors declined. However, as the next chapter will show, aid totals from DAC donors have also increased substantially over that time period. In general, less is known about emerging aid donors' individual aid projects and practices, and even overall aid totals are estimates in some cases.

Of the emerging donors, China is the most noticed and closely watched, although it is not the largest. Saudi Arabia, UAE, Turkey, and

Table 3.4 Bilateral Concessional Finance

Country	US$ Billions	Percent of Total	Country		US$ Billions	Percent of Total
DAC DONORS			**Non-DAC Donors Who Report to OECD/DAC**			
Germany	32.23		Turkey		7.61	
Japan	17.62		Saudi Arabia		2.12	
UK	15.81		UAE		1.49	
France	15.45		Qatar	2020	0.59	
Canada	6.27		Kuwait	2020	0.39	
Italy	6.02		Israel		0.39	
Sweden	5.93		China Taipei		0.33	
Netherlands	5.29		Romania		0.33	
Norway	4.67		Croatia		0.09	
Switzerland	3.93		Bulgaria		0.09	
Spain	3.54		Lithuania		0.08	
Australia	3.44		Thailand		0.06	
Denmark	2.87		Estonia		0.06	
Korea	2.86		Latvia		0.05	
Belgium	2.57		Azerbaijan		0.04	
Austria	1.46		Kazakhstan		0.04	
Finland	1.44		Mexico	2019	0.02	
Ireland	1.17		Lichtenstein		0.02	
Poland	0.95		Cyprus	2020	0.01	
New Zealand	0.68		Colombia	2020	0	
Luxembourg	0.54		Malta		0	
Hungary	0.46		Chile	2020	0	
Portugal	0.45		Costa Rica	2020		
Czech Republic	0.36		**TOTAL NON-**			
Greece	0.26		**DAC Reporting**		**13.81**	**7%**
Slovak Republic	0.15					
Slovenia	0.11		**Estimates for Non-DAC Donors Who Do Not Report**			
Iceland	0.07		China	2020	2.94	
TOTAL DAC	**178.91**	**91%**	India	2020	1.01	
			Brazil	2020	0.03	
			South Africa	2020	0.03	
			Argentina	2020	0	
			Indonesia	2020	0	
			Peru	n/a	0	
			Total Non-DAC Estimated Only		**4.01**	**2%**
			Total Non-DAC		**17.82**	**9%**
		TOTAL Con-cessional Flows	**196.73**			**100%**

Source: OECD (2022a, 2022b)

Note: Countries with 0 have ODA reported or estimated at less than US$5 million or estimates are not available.

Year is 2021 unless indicated.

China have all been within the top 20 aid providers in recent years (Luijkx & Benn, 2017, p. 5), and in some years the others have provided more aid than China; in 2021 Turkey led the group. While each "new" donor has a different profile, what unites them is that they are not aligned (to a greater or lesser degree) with DAC ODA principles. For some, like the BRICS countries, this is because they reject being seen as donors. They see themselves as providing South-South cooperation, more in tune with developing country needs than is the case for traditional donors. Many of them were once aid recipients or are still receiving aid. Emerging donors are generally more likely to use tied aid and provide aid in the form of concessional loans rather than grants. Some also provide general budget support and, in certain circumstances, can be more agile than some of the larger traditional donors. As a group, they are less likely than DAC donors to have country development strategies, and several, including China, structure their programs by responding to recipient country requests, although China's way of operating is changing. Other emerging donors have more in common with the way that DAC members provide aid (Luijkx & Benn, 2017). In short, the emerging donors are as diverse as the DAC donors themselves.

For Middle Eastern countries providing aid, a considerable portion is devoted to humanitarian aid, given the difficult circumstances in several countries in the region. For example, Saudi Arabia spent more than 32 billion dollars over a ten-year period from 2007 to 2017. Although it financed projects in 78 countries, over half of that amount was spent on its top three recipients – Yemen, Syria, and Egypt (Government of Saudi Arabia, 2017). In the last decade, UAE made a conscious decision to raise its international profile and become one of the largest aid donors. The amount it spends on aid met the 0.7 percent benchmark that DAC endorses from 2013 to 2018. Since 2018, it has reduced its aid to around 0.4 percent. Like Saudi Arabia, its biggest recipients are in the region, although it has a number of small aid programs in Sub-Saharan Africa. Turkey's aid has grown in the last few years, in light of both the refugee crisis in the nearby region and the need for humanitarian assistance. Most, but not all, of its aid is given to predominantly Muslim countries, with the majority going to Syria.

China is the emerging donor that has been subject to the most scrutiny, especially since its aid program expanded significantly in Africa over the last 20 years. China maintains that its assistance to other countries is driven by several key principles. These include:

- No imposition of political conditions
- Non-interference in the affairs of recipient countries
- Respecting recipients' rights to choose own paths and models of development

- Mutual respect
- Mutual benefit and "win-win"
- Honoring commitments ("Keeping promises")
      (China, People's Republic of, 2014)

In fact, the first principle has not strictly been met, since China conditions its aid on a country's decision to no longer recognize Taiwan as an independent, sovereign state. Critics of Chinese aid believe that China's principle of non-interference is a "double-edged sword" since it allows Chinese aid to prop up regimes considered unacceptable by other donors (e.g., Sudan under al-Bashir, Zimbabwe under Mugabe) (Naim, 2007). Recent studies indicate that Chinese aid does not seem to take into account the quality of institutions in a country. However, there is also no evidence that it provides aid in a substantially different pattern than other donors (Dreher, Fuchs, Strange, & Tierney, 2015; Petrikova, 2016). Selectivity is relatively weak in both instances. There continue to be ongoing concerns, however, that aid from China is undermining the objectives and impact of traditional donors, mainly in the governance and environmental spheres (Brautigam, 2009; Li, 2017; Kelly, Brazys, & Elkink, 2016; Hernandez, 2017). In contrast, others report that Chinese aid had had little direct impact on the funding decisions of traditional donors. The reasoning is that Chinese aid is concentrated in sectors that receive less attention from more traditional donors (e.g., agriculture and infrastructure), and poorer countries still rely heavily on DAC donor aid as well as welcoming Chinese aid (Swedlund, 2017). It may also be that because of domestic pressure at home traditional donors are somewhat slow in responding to new stimuli and circumstances in recipient countries. Finally, there are concerns that China may be trying to "buy" its way into African natural resources through aid, and that aid, along with China's massive investment program, is paving the way for Chinese dominance or "neo-colonialism" in the region (Larmer, 2017). Researchers have found many of these concerns to be exaggerated.

> To be sure, increased Chinese engagement comes with significant and very real challenges for many Africans. Traders complain about competition from Chinese migrants. . . . We've interviewed African workers who now have jobs but complain about Chinese bosses who expect long hours at low pay. Chinese demand for African ivory, abalone, rhinoceros tusk and materials from other endangered species have taken a significant toll on conservation efforts. . . . China is often lambasted as a nefarious actor in its African dealings, but the evidence tells a more complicated story. Chinese loans are powering Africa, and Chinese firms are creating jobs. China's agricultural investment is far more modest than reported and welcomed by some Africans. China may

boost Africa's economic transformation, or they may get it wrong – just as American development efforts often go awry.

(Brautigam, 2018, p. 3)

China does not dispute that it is benefiting from its aid efforts. Frequently, its aid projects use Chinese materials and management, and sometimes, Chinese labor. Aid may be packaged along with investment loans and export credits as well. Chinese aid may also pave the way for more robust Chinese commercial investment in the future, and repayments can take the form of resource export commitments. China sees this as upholding the principle of "mutual benefit" and does not see itself as a classic "donor" but rather a partner in development with each of the parties on an equal footing. Chinese aid is likely to continue in coming years. It created a dedicated aid agency, the State International Development Cooperation Agency (SIDCA) in 2018, and in early 2021, issued a new White Paper detailing more of its principles and plans (Cornish, 2018; China, People's Republic of, 2021). While the White Paper mainly recaps China's recent programs, it also emphasizes China's approach to international development cooperation. Among the important concepts are promoting a global community; balancing the greater good and shared interests, with emphasis on the greater good; "repaying kindness with kindness"; fostering South-South cooperation as a form of mutual assistance (as opposed to "North-South cooperation"); and focusing on both its own Silk Belt and Road programs (harmonizing infrastructure for greater connectivity and trade) and its commitment to the UN 2030 Agenda for Sustainable Development (the SDGs) (China, People's Republic of, 2021, Sections I 1, 2).

Multilateral Organizations and Banks

International organizations and multilateral banks and funds are important entities in the aid architecture. Core multilateral aid has remained stable, hovering around 30 percent (27 percent in 2021) of ODA. Ear-marked bilateral aid channeled through multilateral organizations is a type of aid that has increased markedly in recent years. Consequently, the total figure for aid flowing to and through multilateral organizations is now over 40 percent (OECD, 2015, 2022c). There are a number of reasons why donor countries choose to spread their available aid funds over both bilateral and multilateral organizations. First, it is a way of diversifying their portfolios and lowering the risks associated with implementing agencies. Second, providing aid through a multilateral organization can mean a lower profile for the donor country, particularly attractive when dealing with sensitive economic and social issues. Conversely, for smaller donors, it can be a way to magnify their influence. Third, this is a good way to provide more aid without increasing donor administrative costs and can be a mechanism to complement a donor's own "in-house" skill set and areas of expertise.

There are at least three kinds of multilateral organizations to whom donor countries provide aid so that these organizations, in turn, provide assistance to developing countries:

- United Nations organizations including, among others, the United Nations' Children's Fund (UNICEF), the United Nations Relief and Works Agency (UNRWA), the World Health Organization (WHO), the United Nations Development Program (UNDP), the United Nations Population Fund (UNFPA), and the United Nations Aids Agency (UNAIDS).
- International Financial Institutions (IFIs) including, among others, the World Bank/IDA, the IMF, the Asia Development Bank (AsDb), the African Development Bank (AfDB), the Interamerican Development Bank (IDB), and the Islamic Development Bank (IsDB).
- A variety of single-purpose funds in health, environment, and agriculture including among others, the Global Fund for Aids, Tuberculosis, and Malaria (GFATM or the Global Fund); the Global Alliance for Vaccines and Immunization (GAVI); the Global Environmental Facility (GEF); the Green Climate Fund (GCF); and the International Fund for Agricultural Development (IFAD).

UN agencies and funds fulfill a variety of global development objectives. There are 30 agencies, funds, and programs along with six related organizations. While some agencies are clustered in New York and Geneva, many others are headquartered in a variety of capitals including Rome and Nairobi. Their mandates vary but frequently involve agenda-setting, establishing global norms (e.g., the International Health Regulations spearheaded by WHO), and advocacy (campaigns by UNAIDS), in addition to carrying out projects. The entire UN organization serves member states including developing countries. Box 3.3 provides brief descriptions of the UN agencies, funds, and programs that are most involved in development activities. Some of them have their own budgets and budget processes, while others depend on contributions from bilateral donors. One of the issues for UN organizations is the scarcity of core funds. Currently, many of the programs and agencies operate mainly through earmarked funds provided by individual or groups of donors. As the UN itself says:

> Core or unrestricted aid is generally seen as the most efficient way of building relevant and effective partnerships with programme countries in the delivery of operational activities for development. . . . Restricted aid in the form of non-core resources, on the other hand, is often seen as potentially distorting programme priorities by limiting the proportion of funding that is directly regulated by intergovernmental governing

Box 3.3   UN Funds, Agencies, and Programs Most Involved in Development Activities

UNDP – The United Nations Development Program was established in 1965 as the lead agency on international development. It works in 170 countries and territories to reduce poverty and inequality and has about 7,500 staff. UNDP designs, funds, and implements technical cooperation and capacity-building projects working with developing countries to improve policies, leadership skills, and institutions. Its work is focused on three areas: sustainable development, democratic governance, and climate and disaster resilience. The UNDP Resident Representative is usually the UN System Resident Coordinator for all the UN agencies operating in a country.

UNICEF – The United Nations Children Fund was founded in 1946 to provide emergency food and health care to children and mothers in countries affected by World War II. In 1950, its mandate was expanded to include assistance to children in developing countries, Today, UNICEF works in over 190 countries on a broad range of topics (e.g., education, health, nutrition, gender, water supply, and sanitation) related to children's protection, survival, and well-being. It engages in both long-term development projects and emergency assistance, as well as advocating for children worldwide. It has over 14,400 staff.

WFP – The World Food Program was created in 1961 as an experiment to provide food aid through the UN system. Today it provides food assistance in emergency and conflict situations, while also working to improve nutrition and resilience through school feeding programs, cash transfers, and other mechanisms. Two-thirds of its staff work in conflict-afflicted countries, and most are recruited locally. In 2020, it was awarded the Nobel Peace Prize for its efforts to combat hunger, especially in conflict situations. In 2021, it assisted more than 128 million people in 120 countries. WFP has just over 9,000 staff.

UNHCR – The United Nations High Commissioner for Refugees has grown into the UN's refugee agency. The office was founded in 1950 to help post-World War II refugees. At the end of 2021, there were over 89 million people forcibly displaced from their homes. UNHCR is responsible for over 21 million refugees who have crossed borders and are being hosted in low and middle-income countries. It provides emergency assistance, protection, health care, and shelter for refugees, helps with the journey for those who return home, and funds income-generating projects for those who have resettled. In addition to direct field action, UNHCR establishes norms, implements international standards and laws, and advocates for refugees. It has over 18,800 staff, with more than 90 percent in the field.

FAO – The United Nations Food and Agriculture Organization is the lead agency for food, food security, and agriculture to make sure that all people have access to enough high-quality food. In addition to implementing programs on the ground in a host of areas related to food and agriculture, it collects and makes available statistics and research on a broad range of related topics. It works in over 130 countries worldwide. It has over 3,200 staff.

WHO – The United Nations' World Health Organization has become more well-known because of the COVID-19 pandemic. Founded in 1948, the organization's mandate is to ensure global health and safety working with its member states. In addition to proposing international health regulations and norms, it works to expand universal health coverage, prevent and mitigate health emergencies, strengthen ongoing programs for communicable and non-communicable diseases, improve access to medicines, and provide research and statistics to monitor and improve health outcomes. It has over 8,800 staff.

There are many other agencies, funds, and programs in the UN system that do important work in and on behalf of developing countries. These include, among others, the International Fund for Agricultural Development (IFAD); the International Labour Organization (ILO); the International Organization for Migration (IOM); the United Nations Educational, Scientific, and Cultural Organization (UNESCO); the United Nations Population Fund (UNFPA); the Joint United Nations Programme on HIV-AIDs (UNAIDS); the United Nations Environment Programme (UNEP); the United Nations Relief and Works Agency for Palestine Refugees in the Near East (UNRWA); UN-Women; and the United Nations Human Settlement Program (UN-HABITAT).

Sources: UNDP (2022), UNICEF (2022a, 2022b) World Food Program (2022), UNHCR (2022), FAO (2022), World Health Organization (2022); United Nations System Chief Executive Boards for Coordination – UNSCEB (2022).

bodies and processes. Restricted aid is further seen as contributing to fragmentation, competition and overlap among entities and providing a disincentive for pursuing United Nations system-wide focus.

(United Nations, 2013)

Despite the concerns, well over half of all of the UN's revenue is earmarked, and for some agencies, it is much higher (OECD, 2020, p. 7). For example, over 80 percent of UNICEF's 2021 US$8.1 billion budget was earmarked, and 88 percent of the UNDP's US$5.3 billion budget was earmarked (UNDP, 2022; UNICEF, 2022b).

International Financial Institutions (IFIs) provide loans to developing countries at close to market rates. They also frequently provide policy and technical advice and carry out research. Their broader development finance lending (not "aid" in the official sense) generally accounts for most of their financial disbursements and institutional priorities. However, the older IFIs, like the World Bank, the African Development Bank, the International Monetary Fund (IMF), and the Asian Development ment Bank, have significant programs that provide grants and loans at concessional rates and qualify as ODA providers. In recent years, new commitments for the World Bank's concessional arm, the International Development Association (IDA), have sometimes run ahead of new lending commitments by the bank. The newer IFIs, like the Asia Infrastructure Investment Bank and the New Development Bank, are not substantially involved in grants and other types of concessional financing; their role is mostly aimed at mobilizing much-needed additional finance for middle-income countries. Within the IFIs, project and program design and processes tend to be similar, regardless of the degree of concessionality. Box 3.4 provides a snapshot of the World Bank and the International Monetary Fund, two of the most influential institutions in development finance.

Box 3.4   The World Bank and the IMF – Sister Institutions

The World Bank and the IMF were created in 1944 at the Bretton Woods Conference in New Hampshire, United States. Formally UN specialized agencies, each has its own management and funding apart from the UN system. The World Bank has 189 member states and the IMF, 190.* The IMF was created in the aftermath of World War II to promote foreign exchange stability, trade, and international monetary cooperation and to make funds available to members with balance of payments difficulties. Similarly, the World

Bank was created to help fund post-war European reconstruction and the needs of developing countries.

Today the World Bank Group consists of five different organizations; its mission is to end extreme poverty and promote shared prosperity. The International Bank for Reconstruction and Development (IBRD) lends money to middle-income countries at near market rates. The International Development Association (IDA) provides credits and grants to the poorest nations on highly concessional terms; it is an important aid provider. The International Finance Corporation (IFC) provides loans and equity to the private sector in developing countries, while the Multilateral Guarantee Agency (MIGA) provides guarantees to investors against risks, and the International Center for the Settlement of Investment Disputes (ICSID) mediates conflicts between foreign investors and developing countries.

IBRD and IDA help finance investment projects in many different areas (e.g., health, education, infrastructure, agriculture). In addition, they provide funds to promote policy reforms and provide advice and studies to developing countries on a host of macroeconomic and sectoral issues. The World Bank also provides knowledge and research to the development community at large. Headquartered in Washington DC, it has about 13,000 staff plus more than 6,000 consultants and offices in over 130 locations. About 48 percent of its staff are located in country offices. There is growing pressure from G7 countries for the World Bank to do more to provide global public goods and help solve global issues, especially those related to health and climate change.

The IMF is a smaller institution, with about 2,900 staff. It has country representatives, but decision-making is still centralized in its headquarters across the street from the World Bank in Washington, DC. The IMF lends to poor countries and countries in short-term financial crises, alongside policy advice and conditions. It provides surveillance at the country, regional, and global levels to be able to detect and, where possible, deter new challenges to financial stability. Finally, the IMF is building capacity within countries to improve statistics and macroeconomic management. The IMF is critical because donors and lenders are reluctant to provide funds to countries that do not have a satisfactory macroeconomic policy framework in place as determined by the IMF. In developing countries, the IMF and the World Bank work together closely on macroeconomic and sector policy issues, with the IMF taking the lead on the former and the World Bank on the latter.

Source: World Bank (2022b, n.d.; International Monetary Fund (2022b)

Note: * Andorra is a member of the IMF but not the World Bank.

Single-purpose funds have mostly emerged over the last 20 years. They allow bilateral (and in some cases, private) donors to put funds into specialized institutions that concentrate on specific priorities. Originally conceived as a vehicle for global public goods (goods that cross national boundaries and are non-rivalrous and non-excludable), these funds have proliferated in recent years across the development landscape. Objectives are set globally but implemented at the country level. By keeping the mandates simpler and focused on specific goals, the funds were expected to be more agile than the IFIs or UN agencies, with results that are easier to monitor. Global funds have been especially helpful in galvanizing additional support for health. GAVI and the Global Fund are the two largest global funds. The Global Environment Facility (GEF), the Global Program for Education (GPE), the Green Climate Fund, and the Climate Investment Funds (CIF) are some of the other global programs and funds that provide significant funding.

As noted earlier in the chapter, the bilateral donors – along with academics and others – have varying views and levels of support for the multilateral institutions as aid providers. While multilateral institutions are sometimes seen as less partisan than bilateral donors, many of them have evolved into routinely slow bureaucracies with cumbersome procedures and a high degree of risk aversion. Furthermore, some of the more powerful ones have acquired a "life of their own" and espouse independent views that can differ markedly from the governments that sit on their boards (Barnett & Finnemore, 2004). At the same time, there is a feeling that many of the multilateral organizations have been dominated for too long by the United States, European governments, and Japan. Given today's global landscape, there is a sense that the governance, funding arrangements, and operating procedures of multilateral institutions need to change and reflect more of the concerns and lessons of the Global South. Some of the frustration is because the availability of multilateral funds pales in comparison to the needs, particularly in sectors such as infrastructure. This, coupled with mounting concern over the slow pace of governance changes, led China to create the AIIB as well as the New Development Bank (Strand, Flores, & Trevathan, 2016). Some of these same issues – the desire to retain control and policy influence, as well as to increase funding in certain areas – explain the growth of earmarked funds within agencies (multi-bilateral aid) as well as the proliferation of new global funds. This has led some to proclaim that this is the "Age of Choice" (Prizzon, Greenhill, & Mustapha, 2017). Undoubtedly, the new sources of funding are welcome, but it is also the age of fragmentation and confusion for providers and recipients alike.

Table 3.5 provides a snapshot of annual disbursements and expenditures by some of the prominent multilateral organizations. If the European Institutions were included as a source of multilateral funding (the EU's funding is considered bilateral funding), they would be one of the

Table 3.5 Disbursements/Program Expenditures – Select Multilateral Organizations

Agency	Concessional	Non-Concessional
	Gross Disbursements US$Millions	
Multilateral Banks and IMF		
World Bank *(FY2022)*	21,214	28,168
IMF*	5,739	105,740
Asia Development Bank	3,310	14,726
African Development Bank**	1,898	2,347
Inter-American Bank	169	12,425
Islamic Development Bank *(approvals)*	61	2,293
Asia Infrastructure Investment Bank		4,620
New Bank		7,600
European Bank for Reconstruction and Development		7,300
Single Purpose/Vertical Funds		
GAVI	8,500	
Global Fund	5,200	
Green Climate Fund	792	
GEF	675	
Climate Investment Funds***		274
UN Organizations		
WFP *(expenditures)*	8,300	
UNICEF *(expenditures)*	8,100	
WHO (2-year *expenses – 2020–2021*)	6,640	
UNHCR *(expenditures)*	4,918	
UNDP (program expenditures)	4,800	
UNAIDS *(expenditures)****	254	
Year is 2021 unless noted		

Sources: (Asian Development Bank, 2022) (African Development Bank, 2022) (Inter-American Development Bank, 2022) (European Bank for Reconstruction and Development, 2022) (GAVI, 2022) (Global Fund, 2022) (Green Climate Fund, 2022) (UNICEF, 2022a, 2022b) (UNHCR, 2022) (World Food Program, 2022) (World Health Organization, 2022) (Global Environment Facility, 2021) (Islamic Development Bank, 2022) (UNAIDs, 2022) (Asia Infrastructure Investment Bank) (New Development Bank, 2022) (World Bank, 2022a, 2022b, n.d.) (International Monetary Fund, 2022a, 2022b)

*converted to US$; exchange rate June 30, 2022
**converted to US$; exchange rate December 31, 2021
***cumulative; includes some concessional funding
****includes US$87m in transfers and grants

largest. In 2021, they disbursed over US$19 billion in concessional funding (OECD, 2022a). As can be seen, the World Bank, the regional development banks, GFATM, GAVI, and some leading UN agencies have large programs. Most UN agencies have much smaller financial capabilities.

Table 3.5 is meant to show the relative importance of some of the multilaterals in the delivery of aid. It is good to remember, however, that many of these multilaterals receive most of their funding for aid from bilateral sources, although some funds come from other multilateral sources (funding each other on specific programs) and from corporate or private sources. So in terms of total aid, most of the funds have already been counted as bilateral aid and are not additional. Also, while the multilateral banks and single-purpose funds show disbursements in the table, the UN organizations show total expenditures. That means that those figures include staff costs and other overhead. Since most UN organizations execute their own programs, most expendures are not disbursements to the recipient countries. Finally to be noted is that non-concessional funding by the IFIs is far greater than the aid they provide. For them, development finance is not just about aid, and they are highly influential actors.

NGOs and Foundations

NGOs

The last set of aid providers are NGOs and foundations. As noted earlier in the chapter, NGOs work with both privately raised funds and with official aid. While some donors contribute to NGOs' core funding, most of the aid funds they receive are for specific programs or projects where they act essentially as contractors for an aid agency or a recipient government.

There are many different types of NGOs and many different views of their place in society. There are NGOs that are formed to support specific causes or political issues. There are NGOs that provide services or sponsor activities, some because of gaps in private or public provision or to diversify the types of providers. Development and humanitarian NGOs are usually characterized by their service provision and advocacy on behalf of the poor. Large international NGOs are influential on a global scale, while national NGOs, especially in developing countries, vary greatly in size. Many are underfunded, with one or two full-time staff only. National NGOs in developing countries partner with and receive the bulk of their funding from three sources: international NGOs, donor governments, or their own government. Most of those funds are ODA but not all. International NGOs receive funds from private donations, and sometimes developing country governments contract with them to provide services using their own budget funds.

Using NGOs as executing agencies for aid programs stems from many different motivations. First are cost-saving considerations; in some instances, NGOs can deliver aid at a lower cost than either donor agencies or recipient governments. For donors, subcontracting to NGOs can also lower their overhead and direct administrative costs. Funding donor country NGOs can also broaden the constituency in favor of aid and show some benefit "at home". NGOs are also used to implement projects in difficult circumstances or where there is mistrust in local governments or a clear lack of capacity. Recipient governments themselves have subcontracted NGOs to augment their ability to reach certain populations, especially in the education and health sectors. Third, there may be instances where NGOs are deemed more effective because they are more knowledgeable about the ultimate beneficiaries' wants and needs and can adapt project inputs and outputs and innovate accordingly (Banks & Hulme, 2012).

Whatever the case, the number of NGOs has expanded exponentially. Until the late 1970s, they were mainly located in the United States and Europe. Many had a religious affiliation or dealt primarily with humanitarian crises. Beginning in the late 1970s through the mid-1990s, NGOs came to be seen as attractive service providers, especially in light of shrinking public mandates and capacity, in part a result of structural reforms. By the late 1990s, with increased focus on governance and the state, questions emerged about both NGOs' efficiency and independence, given that a close relationship with their funders was necessary for many of them to survive. In the first decade of the 2000s, following from the NGOs' prominent role in successfully arguing for debt relief for heavily indebted poor countries and the renewed emphasis on partnership, prominent NGOs were invited into "the big tent" of development, and the high-level aid meetings in Ethiopia and South Korea emphasized their inclusion (Banks & Hulme, 2012).

Today there is a mixed picture, with a number of unresolved concerns regarding NGOs as aid providers. There are questions as to whether NGOs can faithfully advocate for the poor and criticize shortcomings in development policy and strategy, given their dependency on official aid sources for their funds (Edwards & Hulme, 1996; Banks, Hulme & Edwards, 2015). There are also questions as to whether NGOs are, in fact, superior service providers and better at targeting the poor than other types of aid channels. Evidence has called these assumptions into question (Aldashev & Navarra, 2018). Over the last few years, a number of developing country governments have attempted to sharply curtail NGO advocacy and other activities and have placed additional restrictions or registration requirements upon them. On the one hand, this could stem from a view that a course correction is needed: NGOs have been overemphasized and over-estimated, given their track record in many countries. At the same time, public service provision has improved in a number of countries. On the other hand, it may be the case that despite the funding dependency, NGOs are powerful independent voices that can destabilize weak regimes. In reality, given the explosion in the number of NGOs in developing countries, with varied sources of funding and purposes, the backlash is probably the result of both types of views.

To make life even more difficult for NGOs, in 2018, beginning with OXFAM, a number of international NGOs have suffered reputational crises, stemming from inappropriate and sometimes illegal relationships between male staff members and local women in countries where they are working (OXFAM International, 2018; Reuters, 2018). This led to a decline in both public and private funding, while disrupting normal work programs. For some international NGOs, this ushered in an era of slower growth, while others continue to expand at a rapid pace. With the growing number of refugees and migrants, the NGOs who deal with those populations have become more prominent.

NGOs are an important piece of the aid architecture. As noted earlier in this chapter, on average, about 14 percent of OECD-DAC bilateral aid is now flowing to and through NGOs, with some countries reaching as high as 40 to 50 percent of their bilateral aid channeled to NGOs (Table 3.3). The numbers of NGOs are in the tens of thousands. It is estimated however that a handful of the largest international NGOs account for more than half of total NGO revenue. A similar picture emerges at the recipient country level as well. A handful of national NGOs capture the bulk of the revenue.

Table 3.6 provides a look at the current structure of some of the largest international NGOs. As can be noted, the biggest and most powerful international NGOs are "big business" operating in many countries, with thousands of staff members and a spending capacity that outstrips many of the smaller bilateral agencies. The amount of private versus public money (aid funds, mostly) that they operate with varies quite markedly from NGO to NGO, but all have worked diligently to diversify their sources of funding in recent years. As a group, they have increased their use of locally hired staff. The increased use of local staff and local NGOs – the "localization" agenda – is very much on the minds of both private and public funders of NGOs. International NGOs have also been working hard to reassure their funders on the use of donations by increasing their transparency and accountability. Most large NGOs now publish on their websites annual reports or "accountability" reports that include either excerpts from or full versions of their annual audit reports.

Foundations

Not all foundations are involved with international development, but some of the largest ones are part of the donor cohort. Technically, private foundations do not work with official aid, and their funds are not counted as ODA. However, they have become an important source of financial assistance (aid in the broader sense) in a number of countries and

Table 3.6 A Snapshot of Large International Development and Humanitarian NGOs

Name	Income	Fiscal Year	% Private	Staffing	# Of Countries
	(millions US$)				
WORLD VISION (WV)	3,150	2021	63	34,000+	100
MEDICINS SANS FRONTIERES (MSF)	1,935	2021	>98	46,148	>85
SAVE THE CHILDREN INTL (SCI)*	1,335	2021	<48	17,441	61
BRAC	1,218	2021	85	107,259	11
CATHOLIC RELIEF SERVICES (CRS)	1,191	2021	21	5,200	116
PLAN INTERNATIONAL (PI)	1,188	2021	61	9,498	75
OXFAM INTERNATIONAL	1,069	2020	54	9,000	93
INTERNATIONAL RESCUE COMMITTEE (IRC)	980	2021	30	13,000	40+
CARE INTERNATIONAL (CARE)	808	2020	n/a	11,507	102
FHI 360	798	2021	11	4,000+	>60
MERCY CORPS	564	2021	>13<32	5,400+	>40
DANISH REFUGEE COUNCIL (DRC)	471	2021	>6<44	7,532	40
PATH	343	2021	53	1,600	70+
PARTNERS IN HEALTH (PIH)	313	2021	52	18,000	12
ACTIONAID	255	2021	61	2,506	45

Sources: World Vision International (2022a, 2022b), Medicins San Frontieres (2022a, 2022b), Save the Children International (2022), BRAC (2022), Catholic Relief Serves (2022), Plan International (2022), Oxfam International (2021, 2022), International Rescue Committee (2022), Care International (2021), FHI 360 (2021, 2022), Mercy Corps (2021, 2022), Danish Refugee Council (2022), PATH (2022), Partners in Health (2022), Action Aid (2022a, 2022b), TheDotGood (n.d.), Humanitarian Quality Assurance Initiative (2020, 2022a, 2022b, 2022c), BOX (2022)

Notes: % private are estimates calculated by author based on the information available.

Currency conversions into US$ where needed were based on the exchange rate at the end of the organization's fiscal year.

CRS and World Vision staffing from Linked In and Wikipedia

*With affiliates, the total income is over US$2.2 billion working in 128 countries.

multilateral institutions. Many of them work in partnership with NGOs, governments, and bilateral and multilateral donors on specific projects and programs. They provide grants to NGOs, universities, other foundations, private enterprises, and governments.

Foundations differ from NGOs in that the source of their funds are private individuals and companies. Foundations engaged in international development – what OECD termed as "global private philanthropy for development" (OECD, 2017) – are essentially private actors providing public goods. Their accountability is not to the public, but to a board of directors appointed by the source of funds. While many of the larger foundations have improved their transparency in recent years, there is still room for improvement (OECD, 2018b, 2018a, 2021a). This is particularly important since foundations have been catalysts for innovation as well as influential in policy formulation in certain instances.

It is hard to arrive at arrive at reliable figures on aggregate global foundation spending in developing countries. OECD launched a groundbreaking survey in 2016 that aimed to provide better data on foundations to the development community (OECD, 2018b). That survey found that "ODA-like" philanthropic flows over the three-year period 2013–2015 were relatively modest, averaging about US$8 billion a year or about 5 percent of ODA. However, in some sectors, notably health and productive health, foundations were major sources of funding (p. 29). The survey also found that sources of philanthropic funding were highly concentrated. Of the 143 foundations in the survey, the Bill and Melinda Gates Foundation was by far the largest, providing 49 percent of total giving. Further, 81 percent of total giving during the survey period was provided by only 20 foundations (OECD, 2018b, p. 30). The report also showed that about two-thirds of philanthropy allocated to specific countries was targeted to middle-income countries with less than one-third of the total directly targeted to LDCs (p. 30).

Since 2018 when the OECD survey came out, foundations have been much more forthcoming with information, and OECD published a second edition. There are now over 40 foundations that report their development spending to OECD. Figure 3.1 shows the top 20 foundations and the amount of money they provided to developing countries and other development institutions in 2020 as reported by OECD.[4] Just over half are US-based, and the rest are based in Europe. As in the 2018 survey, most tend to give the largest share of their funds to middle-income countries. Many also provide finance to regional and global programs, multilateral institutions, and NGOs; a large portion of their total is unallocated by country. The Gates Foundation continues to dominate the field, with 43 percent of the total funding reported and 45 percent of the total funding of the top 20 foundations. While it started its philanthropy in global health, over the last decade it has expanded rapidly to other

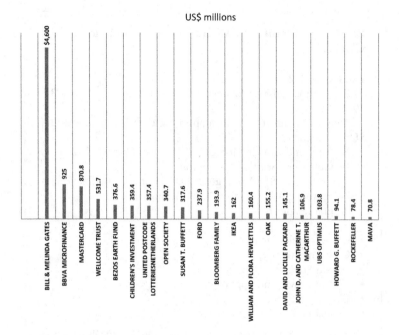

Figure 3.1 Large Foundation Development Flows in 2020

Source: OECD, 2022b

Note: Besos Earth Fund only commenced in 2020 so the amount shown is for commitments, not disbursements.

sectors, including agriculture, water, and sanitation. While many of the smaller foundations work on their own or partner with other foundations and non-governmental agencies, the Gates Foundation often partners with bilateral and multilateral aid agencies and governments. It is essentially a funder, but like other larger providers of aid, it is active in both priority-setting and strategy formulation. Box 3.5 provides a brief snapshot of the Gates Foundation.

As a group, the total that large foundations reported to OECD in 2020 was about US$10.8 billion. To put this number in perspective, this is equivalent to 6.6 percent of the total ODA provided by OECD-DAC members in 2020. The largest foundation, the Gates Foundation, provided more funding than 21 of the individual country members of OECD-DAC (author's calculations based on OECD, 2022a and 2022b). Clearly, that has earned the Gates Foundation "a seat at the table". But even without the Gates Foundation, foundations have a greater influence than the numbers suggest because they can be catalytic: funding experiments, moving quickly, and strategically filling gaps.

Box 3.5   The Bill and Melinda Gates Foundation – At a Glance

Year founded: 2000

Foundation trust endowment: US$54 billion (December 31, 2021)

Total 2021 direct grantee support for global programs 2021: $US5.2 billion

No. of foundation employees: 1,736 (December 31, 2021)

Headquarters: Seattle, Washington

Other offices (8): Washington, D.C.; London; Berlin; Johannesburg; Abuja; Addis Ababa; Delhi; Beijing

Programmatic areas:

- Global development
- Global health
- United States program
- Global growth and opportunity
- Global policy and advocacy
- Gender equality

Sources: Bill and Melinda Gates Foundation (2022a, 2022b); Bill and Melinda Gates Foundation Trust (2022)

Private Individuals

While not officially aid, private individuals who have migrated from or have relatives in low and middle-income countries provide substantial resources to those still living in developing countries. Remittances in 2019, the year before the COVID-19 pandemic, reached over US$554 billion, much larger than the total amount of ODA and *all* development finance from official sources. Remittances to lower and middle-income countries grew to be larger than foreign direct investment to developing countries, as Figure 3.2 shows. While these funds are not counted as official development finance, the substantial sums pay for many private goods and contribute to community-level public goods. With the COVID-19 pandemic, remittances were projected to decline sharply, by as much as 20 percent overall (World Bank, 2020). However, this has not been the case. In 2020, remittances declined by only 1.7 percent, followed by an impressive increase of 8.6 percent in 2021 and another increase of over 4 percent in 2022 (Ratha et al., 2021; World Bank, 2022c).

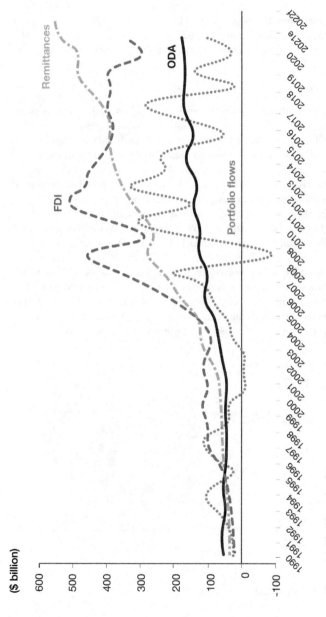

Figure 3.2 The Growth of Remittances to Low and Middle-Income Countries (excluding China)

Source: Ratha, et.al., 2021

Development specialists believe that, given the right environment, remittances can be instrumental in funding entrepreneurial activity and private sector development. There have also been attempts by governments, such as Mexico, to harness remittances to finance public goods through matching funds programs (Duquette-Rury, 2014). Finally, in conflict situations like Ukraine in 2022 and 2023, remittances present a lifeline to many, complementing the official resources available.

Conclusion

As can be seen, there is a rich assortment of aid and other development finance providers. While many are from the Global North, there are also providers from the Global South. While the DAC bilateral donors still dominate official aid, they are by no means alone, joined by an increasing number of "emerging" countries, multilateral agencies, NGOs, foundations, and private individuals. Figure 3.3 provides a simplified version of the "aid ecosystem", which has grown increasingly more complex.

Despite the complexity, individuals are the driving force of the system because they are the ultimate funders: they provide bilateral governments with funds for aid through taxes, and they provide donations for NGOs and foundations, as well as their direct giving through remittances. The complex system that has evolved has provided more choice to some recipient countries, but the sheer number of actors has also created confusion and additional transaction costs. The relationships among all these actors and between them and the recipient governments will be explored in subsequent chapters. The costs of development cooperation are worth

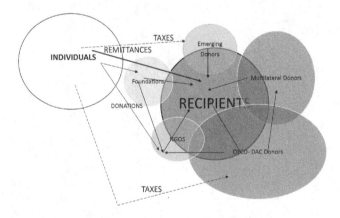

Figure 3.3 The Simplified Ecosystem of Aid

bearing when donors are supporting activities that lead to increased growth and equity (and a lessening of the need for aid). In other words, doing the right thing. That is the crux of the aid debate. However, it is also important that donor practices and behaviors contribute to efficient and effective aid – essentially, doing things the right way. We will return to the question of donor quality in Chapter 5 after reviewing what aid is, where it goes, and what it actually does.

Notes

1 Excludes territories and Venezuela temporarily not classified.
2 Lithuania was the latest state to join and is not included in 2020 and 2021 data.
3 The G7 is a group of seven industrialized democratic countries that meet on a regular basis to coordinate policy on issues of global interest. The G7 countries are Canada, France, Germany, Italy, Japan, the United Kingdom, and the United States.
4 There are other large foundations based in developing countries that are reporting to OECD.

Bibliography

Action Aid. (2022a). *Annual report 2021.* Retrieved from ActionAid website: https://actionaid.org/sites/default/files/publications/annual_report_2021_online.pdf

Action Aid. (2022b). *Aggregated financial statements for the year ending December 31, 2021.* Retrieved from ActionAid website: https://actionaid.org/sites/default/files/publications/Action%20Aid%20Federation%20Aggregated%20Accounts%202021.pdf

African Development Bank. (2022, May 26). *Financial report 2021.* Retrieved from African Development Bank website: www.afdb.org/en/documents/financial-report-2021

Aldashev, G., & Navarra, C. (2018). Development NGOs: Basic facts. *Annals of Public and Cooperative Economics, 89*(1), 125–156.

Asia Infrastructure Investment Bank. (n.d.). *2021 AIIB annual report.* Retrieved from AIIB website: www.aiib.org/en/news-events/annual-report/2021/_common/pdf/2021_AIIBAnnualReport_web-reduced.pdf

Asian Development Bank. (2022, April 25). *Annual report 2021: Toward a green and inclusive recovery.* Retrieved from Asian Development Bank website: www.adb.org/sites/default/files/institutional-document/814476/adb-annual-report-2021.pdf

Asian Infrastructure Investment Bank. (2021). *Financing operations.* Retrieved from AIIB website: www.aiib.org/en/about-aiib/who-we-are/financing-operations/index.html

Asmus, G., Fuchs, A., & Muller, A. (2017). *BRICS and foreign aid.* Williamsburg, VA: AIDDATA.

Banks, N., & Hulme, D. (2012). *The role of NGOs and civil society in development and poverty reduction.* Manchester: Brooks World Poverty Institute.

Banks, N., Hulme, D., & Edwards, M. (2015). NGOs, states and donors revisited: Still too close for comfort? *World Development, 66,* 707–718.

Barnett, M., & Finnemore, M. (2004). *Rules for the world: International organizations in global politics.* Ithaca, NY: Cornell University Press.

Bill and Melinda Gates Foundation. (2022a). *About.* Retrieved from Bill and Melinda Gates Foundation website: www.gatesfoundation.org/about

Bill and Melinda Gates Foundation. (2022b). *Annual report 2021.* Retrieved from Bill and Melinda Gates Foundation website: www.gatesfoundation.org/about/financials/annual-reports/annual-report-2021

Bill and Melinda Gates Foundation Trust. (2022). *Financial Statements December 31, 2021 and 2020.* Retrieved from Bill and Melinda Gates Foundation website: https://docs.gatesfoundation.org/documents/f_292755d-1b_billmelindagatesfoundationtrust_fs.pdf

BOX. (2022). *International rescue committee.* Retrieved from Box website: www.box.com/customers/international-rescue-committee

BRAC. (2022). *Annual report 2021.* Retrieved from BRAC website: www.brac.net/downloads/ar2021/BRAC.pdf

Brautigam, D. (2009). *The dragon's gift.* Oxford: Oxford University Press.

Brautigam, D. (2018, April 12). *U.S. politicians get China in Africa all wrong.* Retrieved from Washington Post website: www.washingtonpost.com/news/theworldpost/wp/2018/04/12/china-africa/?utm_term=.c125978f2b4b

Care International. (2021). *Financial overview FY2020.* Retrieved from CARE International website: www.care-international.org/resources/care-financial-overview-fy2020

Catholic Relief Services. (2022). *Persevering for change: 2021 annual report.* Retrieved from CRS website: www.crs.org/sites/default/files/22mk-649957_annual_report_2021_web.pdf

China, People's Republic of. (2014, July 10). *China's foreign aid (2014).* Retrieved from Government website: http://english.gov.cn/archive/white_paper/2014/08/23/content_281474982986592.htm

China, People's Republic of. (2021, January 10). *China's international development cooperation in the new era.* Retrieved from: www.xinhuanet.com/english/2021-01/10/c_139655400.htm

Cornish, L. (2018, April 20). *China's new aid agency: What we know.* Retrieved from DEVEX: www.devex.com/news/china-s-new-aid-agency-what-we-know-92553

Danish Refugee Council. (2022). *Annual report 2021.* Retrieved from Danish Refugee Council website: https://drc.ngo/media/sp0jv3mj/2021-drc-annual-report_2021_uk.pdf

Denmark, Ministry of Foreign Affairs. (2022). *Danida.* Retrieved from Denmark Ministry of Foreign Affairs: https://um.dk/en/danida

Donor Tracker. (2022). *Donor profiles.* Retrieved from DonorTracker: https://donortracker.org/

Dreher, A., Fuchs, A., Strange, A. M., & Tierney, M. J. (2015). *Apples and dragon fruits: The determinants of aid and other forms of state financing from China to Africa.* AidData.

Duquette-Rury, L. (2014). Collective remittances and transnational coproduction: The 3X1 program for migrants and household access to public goods in Mexico. *Studies in Comparative International Development, 49*(1), 112–139.

Edwards, M., & Hulme, D. (1996, June). Too close for comfort? The impact of official aid on nongovernmental organizations. *World Development*, 24(6), 961–973.

Ernst and Young. (2021). *Family health international consolidated financial statements years ended September 30, 2021 and 2020*. Retrieved from FHI360 website: www.fhi360.org/sites/default/files/media/documents/fhi-360-audited-financials-fy2021.pdf

European Bank for Reconstruction and Development. (2022). *Financial report 2021*. London: EBRD.

FAO (Food and Agriculture Organization). (2022). About FAO. Retrieved from FAO website: https://www.fao.org/home/en/.

FHI 360. (2022). *FHI annual impact report 2021–2022*. Retrieved from FHI360 website: www.fhi360.org/sites/default/files/media/documents/fhi-360-impact-report-2021-22.pdf

GAVI. (2022, June 25). *GAVI annual financial report 2022*. Retrieved from GAVI website: www.gavi.org/sites/default/files/2022-06/GAVI-Alliance-2021-Annual-Financial-Report.pdf

Global Environment Facility. (2021). *The GEF monitoring report 2021*. Washington: GEF.

Global Fund. (2022, May). *Annual financial report 2021*. Retrieved from Global Fund website: www.theglobalfund.org/media/12003/corporate_2021annualfinancial_report_en.pdf

Government of Saudi Arabia. (2017, February 28). *Saudi Arabia's aid to world reaches nearly $33 billion in 10 years*. Retrieved from Reliefweb: https://reliefweb.int/report/world/saudi-arabia-s-aid-world-reaches-nearly-33-billion-10-years

Green Climate Fund. (2021). Retrieved from Green Climate Fund: www.greenclimate.fund/

Green Climate Fund. (2022). *2021 annual results report*. Retrieved from Green Climate Fund website: www.greenclimate.fund/sites/default/files/document/20220412-arr2021.pdf

Hernandez, D. (2017). Are "new" donors challenging world bank conditionality? *World Development*, 529–549.

Humanitarian Quality Assurance Initiative. (2020). *CARE international initial audit – Summary report IA- 2020/05/27*. Chatelaine, Switzerland: HQAI.

Humanitarian Quality Assurance Initiative. (2022a, August 4). *Save the children international renewal audit – summary report 2022/08/04*. Retrieved from HQAI website: https://hqai.contentfiles.net/media/documents/1_SCI_REV_Summary_2022-08-04.pdf

Humanitarian Quality Assurance Initiative. (2022b). *Plan international mid-term audit*. Chatelaine, Switzerland: HQAI.

Humanitarian Quality Assurance Initiative. (2022c). *Plan international mid-term audit*. Chatelaine, Switzerland: HQAI.

Inter-American Development Bank. (2022, March). *Annual report 2021 financial statements*. Retrieved from Interamerican Development Bank website: https://publications.iadb.org/publications/english/document/Inter-American-Development-Bank-Annual-Report-2021-Financial-Statements.pdf

International Monetary Fund. (2022a, April). *What is the IMF*. Retrieved from IMF website: www.imf.org/en/About/Factsheets/IMF-at-a-Glance

International Monetary Fund. (2022b). *Crisis upon crisis IMF annual report 2022*. Retrieved from IMF website: www.imf.org/external/pubs/ft/ar/2022/what-we-do/lending/

International Rescue Committee. (2022, September 30). *Consolidated financial statements.* Retrieved from International Rescue Committee website: www.rescue.org/sites/default/files/2022-07/internationalrescuecommittee incfy21fs.pdf

Islamic Development Bank. (2022). *2021 annual report.* Retrieved from IsDB website: www.isdb.org/publications/2021-annual-report

Kelly, G., Brazys, S., & Elkink, J. A. (2016). *The dragon's curse? China, the World Bank, and perceptions of corruption in Tanzania.* Williamsburg, VA: AidData.

Lancaster, C. (2007). *Foreign aid: Diplomacy, development, domestic politics.* Chicago: University of Chicago.

Larmer, B. (2017, May 2). Is China the world's new colonial power? *New York Times Magazine.*

Li, X. (2017). Does conditionality still work? Chinese development assistance and democracy in Africa. *Chinese Political Science Review, 2*(2), 201–220.

Linked In. (2022). *World vision.* Retrieved from Linked in website: www.linkedin.com/company/worldvision

Luijkx, W., & Benn, J. (2017). *Emerging providers' international co-operation for development.* Paris: OECD.

Mawdsley, E. (2012). *From recipients to donors: Emerging powers and the changing development landscape.* London: Zed Books.

Medicins San Frontieres. (2022a). *Our funding policy.* Retrieved from Medicins sans Frontieres website: www.msf.org/reports-and-finances

Medicins San Frontieres. (2022b). *International financial report 2021.* Geneva: Medicins Sans Frontieres.

Mercy Corps. (2021, June 30). *Mercy corps and affiliates consolidated financial statements and supplemental schedules.* Retrieved from Mercy Corps website: www.mercycorps.org/sites/default/files/2021-11/Final-MercyCorps_FS.pdf

Mercy Corps. (2022). *Who we are.* Retrieved from Mercy Corps website: www.mercycorps.org/who-we-are

Naim, M. (2007, February 15). Help not wanted. *New York Times,* pp. A–29.

New Development Bank. (2017–2021). *NDB's general strategy: 2017–2021.* NDB.

New Development Bank. (2022). *Annual report 2021.* Retrieved from NDB website: file:///Users/ppomeran/Downloads/NDB_AnnualReport2021_full_version-3.pdf

OECD. (1996). *The DAC list of aid recipients used for 1996 flows.* Paris: OECD.

OECD. (2015). *Multilateral aid 2015: Better partnerships for a post-2015 world – highlights.* Paris: OECD.

OECD. (2017). *Global private philanthropy for development: Preliminary results of the OECD data survey.* Retrieved from OECD website: www.oecd.org/dac/financing-sustainable-development/development-finance-data/Preliminary-results-philanthropy-survey.pdf

OECD. (2018a). *Development co-operation report.* Paris: OECD.

OECD. (2018b). *Private philanthropy for development.* Paris: OECD.

OECD. (2020). *Earmarked funding to multilateral organisations: How is it used and what constitutes good practice.* Paris: OECD.

OECD. (2021a). *Private philanthropy for development* (2nd ed.). Paris: OECD.

OECD. (2021b). *Big picture of total resource receipts, 2002–2017.* Retrieved from OECD: https://public.tableau.com/views/Bigpictureoftotalresourcereceipts

2002-2017/Receipts?:embed=y&:display_count=yes&publish=yes&:showViz Home=no#1

OECD. (2021c). *DAC list of ODA recipients effective for reporting on 2021 flows.* Retrieved from OECD: www.oecd.org/dac/financing-sustainable-development/development-finance-standards/DAC-List-ODA-Recipients-for-reporting-2021-flows.pdf

OECD. (2021d, May). *ODA to developing countries-summary.* Retrieved from ODA website: www.oecd.org/dac/financing-sustainable-development/development-finance-topics/Developing-World-Development-Aid-at-a-Glance-2021.pdf

OECD. (2022a). *ODA levels in 2021 – preliminary data.* Paris: OECD.

OECD. (2022b, July 1). *Development co-operation profiles.* Retrieved from OECD: www.oecd-ilibrary.org/sites/2dcf1367-en/index.html?itemId=/content/publication/2dcf1367-en

OECD. (2022c). *Aid for civil society organisations.* Paris: OECD.

OECD. (2022d). *DAC list of ODA recipients effective for reporting on 2022 and 2023 flows.* Retrieved from OECD website: www.oecd.org/dac/financing-sustainable-development/development-finance-standards/DAC-List-of-ODA-Recipients-for-reporting-2022-23-flows.pdf

OECD. (2022e). *Detailed aid statistics: Official and private flows.* Retrieved from OECD International Development Statistics (database): https://doi.org/10.1787/data-00072-en

OECD. (2022f, May 25). *ODA receipts and selected indicators for developing countries and territories – table 25.* Retrieved from DAC website: www.oecd.org/dac/financing-sustainable-development/development-finance-data/

OECD. (n.d.a). *Data – Net ODA.* Retrieved from OECD website: https://data.oecd.org/oda/net-oda.htm

OECD. (n.d.b). *Frequently asked questions.* Retrieved from OECD website: www.oecd.org/dac/financing-sustainable-development/development-finance-data/faq.htm

OECD. (n.d.c). *Country programmable aid.* Retrieved from OECD: www.oecd.org/dac/financing-sustainable-development/development-finance-data/cpa.htm

Oxfam International. (2018, February 19). *OXFAM releases report into allegations of sexual misconduct in Haiti.* Retrieved from OXFAM International website: www.oxfam.org/en/pressroom/pressreleases/2018-02-19/oxfam-releases-report-allegations-sexual-misconduct-haiti

Oxfam International. (2021). *Annual report 2020–2021.* Retrieved from Oxfam International website: https://oi-files-d8-prod.s3.eu-west-2.amazonaws.com/s3fs-public/2022-03/Oxfam%20International%20Annual%20Report%202020-21.pdf

Oxfam International. (2022). *Finances and accountability.* Retrieved from Oxfam website: www.oxfam.org/en/what-we-do/about/our-finances-and-accountability

Partners in Health. (2022). *Annual report 2021.* Retrieved from Partners in Health website: www.pih.org/annual-report-2021/

PATH. (2022). *Annual report 2021.* Retrieved from PATH website: https://media.path.org/documents/PATH-annual-report-2021.pdf

Petrikova, I. (2016). Promoting "good behavior" through aid: Do "new" donors differ from the "old" ones? *Journal of International Relations and Development, 19*(1), 153–192.

Plan International. (2022). *Directors report and financial statements for the year ending June 30, 2021*. Retrieved from Plan International website: https://plan-international.org/uploads/2022/02/plan_international_-_fy21_worldwide_financial_statements_-_fully_signed_-cover.pdf

Prizzon, A., Greenhill, R., & Mustapha, S. (2017). An age of choice for development finance: Evidence from country case studies. *Development Policy Review*, O29–035.

A question of definition. (2006, September 14). Retrieved from The Economist: www.economist.com/node/7878108

Radelet, S. (2006). *A primer on foreign aid*. Washington, DC: Center for Global Development.

Ratha, D., Kim, E., Plaza, S., Seshan, G., Riordan, E. J., & Chandra, V. (2021). *Migration and development brief 35: Recovery: COVID-19 crisis through a migration lens*. Washington, DC: KNOMAD-World Bank.

Reuters. (2018, February 14). *Doctors without borders fired 19 people for sexual abuse last year*. Retrieved from Reuters website: www.reuters.com/article/us-britain-oxfam-msf/doctors-without-borders-fired-19-people-for-sexual-abuse-last-year-idUSKCN1FY2QC

Save the Children International. (2022). *SCI trustees report and financial statements 2021*. Retrieved from Save the Children International website: https://resourcecentre.savethechildren.net/pdf/SCI-Trustees-report-and-financial-statements-2021.pdf/

Strand, J. R., Flores, E. M., & Trevathan, M. W. (2016). China's leadership in global economic governance and the creation of the Asian infrastructure investment bank. *Rising Powers Quarterly*, 55–69.

Swedlund, H. J. (2017). Is China eroding the bargaining power of traditional donors in Africa? *International Affairs*, *93*(2), 153–192.

TheDotGood. (n.d.). *Welcome to the world 200 top SGOs*. Retrieved from TheDotGood website: https://thedotgood.net/sgo/brac/

UNAIDs. (2022, June 2). *2021 financial report*. Retrieved from UNAIDs website: www.unaids.org/sites/default/files/media_asset/PCB50_Financial_Report_2021_EN.pdf

UNDP. (2022). *UNDP funding compendium 2021*. Retrieved from UNDP website: www.undp.org/sites/g/files/zskgke326/files/2022-08/Compendium_2021_Aug%2029.pdf

UNHCR. (2022, February 17). *Update on budgets and funding (2021 and 2022)*. Retrieved from UNHCR website: www.unhcr.org/6228afe24.pdf

UNICEF. (2022a, May). *Partnering to protect child rights in a time of crisis, supplement to annual report 2021*. Retrieved from UNICEF website: www.unicef.org/media/125196/file/UNICEF%20Annual%20Report%202021%20Partnerships%20Supplement.pdf

UNICEF. (2022b, August). *UNICEF funding compendium*. Retrieved from UNICEF website: www.unicef.org/media/124541/file/Funding%20compendium%202021.pdf

United Nations. (2013). *Technical note on definitions, sources and coverage*. Retrieved from United Nations website: www.un.org/en/ecosoc/qcpr/pdf/technical_note_on_funding.pdf

United Nations. (2021). *LDC identification criteria & indicators.* Retrieved from Development Policy and Analysis Division: www.un.org/development/desa/dpad/least-developed-country-category/ldc-criteria.html

UNSCEB (United Nations System Chief Executives Board. (2022). *Budget and financial situation of the organizations of the United Nations system.* Retrieved from UNSCEB: https://unsceb.org/sites/default/files/2022-12/A.77.507%20-%20Budgetary%20and%20financial%20situation%20of%20the%20organizations%20of%20the%20UN%20system_5%20Oct%202022.pdf

World Bank. (2020, April 22). *World Bank predicts sharpest decline of remittances in recent history.* Retrieved from World Bank: www.worldbank.org/en/news/press-release/2020/04/22/world-bank-predicts-sharpest-decline-of-remittances-in-recent-history

World Bank. (2022a). *FY 2022 data.* Retrieved from World Bank website: www.worldbank.org/en/about/annual-report/fiscal-year-data

World Bank. (2022b). *Annual report 2022.* Washington, DC: World Bank.

World Bank. (2022c, May 11). *Remittances to reach $630 billion in 2022 with record flows into Ukraine – Press Release.* Retrieved from World Bank website: www.worldbank.org/en/news/press-release/2022/05/11/remittances-to-reach-630-billion-in-2022-with-record-flows-into-ukraine

World Bank. (n.d.). *Russia and the World Bank: International development assistance.* Retrieved from World Bank website: www.worldbank.org/en/country/russia/brief/international-development#3

World Bank. (n.d.). *What we do.* Retrieved from World Bank website: www.worldbank.org/en/what-we-do

World Bank/IDA. (2022a). *Borrowing countries.* Retrieved from IDA: http://ida.worldbank.org/about/borrowing-countries

World Bank/IDA. (2022b, December). *IDA graduates.* Retrieved from IDA: http://ida.worldbank.org/about/ida-graduates

World Food Program. (2022, June 15). *Annual performance report for 2021.* Retrieved from WFP website: https://docs.wfp.org/api/documents/WFP-0000140791/download/?_ga=2.125176330.1464040828.1667167634-446459803.1667069408

World Health Organization. (2022). *Budget funding and implementation.* Retrieved from WHO website: www.who.int/about/accountability/results/who-results-report-2020-2021/budget-implementation#financing-programme

World Vision International. (2022a). *About US.* Retrieved from World Vision International website: www.wvi.org

World Vision International. (2022b). *Consolidated financial statements 2021.* Retrieved from World Vision website: https://wvusstatic.com/2022/financial-accountability/FY21-WVUS-Consolidated-Financial-Statements.pdf

Yanguas, P. (2018). *Why we lie about aid: Development and the messy politics of change.* London: Zed.

4   How Aid Works

Many discussions about foreign aid take place in the abstract without defining exactly what aid is and what it is not. It turns out that in many cases people are discussing "apples and oranges". Chapter 3 had a definition that served as a brief introduction to the concept of Overseas Development Assistance (ODA). The two previous chapters provided a brief look at the context for aid and the main actors. This chapter will provide more detailed aid definitions, outline how aid is packaged and delivered, and offer some snapshots on how much aid is provided to whom.

Definitions of "Aid" and "aid"

There are many definitions of aid. In the public discourse, frequently what is being talked about is what can be called Aid with a capital "A": that is, any assistance provided from a donor to a recipient (Williamson, 2018). There is no restriction on the type of recipient (public or private; nations, companies, or individuals), the financial status of the recipient (rich or poor), the kind of aid (grants; loans; in-kind donations), or its purpose. For example, one can read about US military Aid to Israel or Aid given by a private charity to private individuals following a natural disaster.

These examples are not what the development community views as aid (with a small "a" because the total amount is much smaller). Development aid is a subset of what the public refers to as Aid. Development aid has a variety of sub-definitions. The most important and well-known of these is Official Development Assistance (ODA). Up until 2017, the definition of ODA was:

> those flows to countries and territories on the DAC List of ODA
> · Recipients and to multilateral development institutions that are:
>
>   i   Provided by official agencies, including state and local governments, or by their executive agencies; and

DOI: 10.4324/9781003265320-5

ii Each transaction of which:

a) is administered with the promotion of the economic development and welfare of developing countries as its main objective; and

b) is concessional in character and conveys a grant element of at least 25 percent (calculated at a rate of discount of 10 percent).
(OECD, 2008, p. 1)

Starting in 2018, a new definition was adopted to reflect changes in concessionality. While the rest remained the same, point ii b) in the previous list was replaced with the following:

b) is concessional in character. In DAC statistics, this implies a grant element of at least

- **45 percent** in the case of bilateral loans to the official sector of LDCs and other LICs (calculated at a rate of discount of 9 percent).
- **15 percent** in the case of bilateral loans to the official sector of LMICs (calculated at a rate of discount of 7 percent).
- **10 percent** in the case of bilateral loans to the official sector of UMICs (calculated at a rate of discount of 6 percent).
- **10 percent** in the case of loans to multilateral institutions (calculated at a rate of discount of 5 percent for global institutions and multilateral development banks, and 6 percent for other organizations, including sub-regional organizations).

(OECD, 2021)

There are several important elements to both the old and revised definition of ODA. First is that countries must be low-income or middle-income countries with a per capita income below US$12,236 in 2020 (OECD, 2022d). So the first element is an *income test*. Second, the provider must be an official public agency. Foundations and NGOs provide Aid (with a capital "A"), but this is not counted as Official Development Assistance. So the second element is a *provider test*. Third, the objective is limited to the "promotion of the economic development and welfare of developing countries", so there is an *objectives test*. Finally, the aid must have a grant element, so there is a *cost to recipient test*.

What Counts as ODA?

The definition of ODA leaves a broad range of activities that can be financed by aid – virtually anything one can think of from small village schools to international airports. Aid can finance all of those, and not only infrastructure, but also all the goods, services, and people associated with those investments. Aid can also finance policy reforms to ensure that public and private investments and services yield the maximum benefits possible for the country and its citizens. There will be more on what aid finances in coming sections.

There are two broad kinds of aid within ODA: humanitarian aid and developmental aid. Humanitarian aid is given in emergency and crisis situations to mitigate further suffering and loss of life. It also is given in conflict and post-conflict situations where there are immediate needs and there is not yet a stable situation for longer-term investments or a government willing and able to guide development efforts. Developmental aid, in contrast, ideally takes a medium to longer-term perspective, hoping to promote investments and reforms that will lead to sustainable, equitable economic growth far into the future. Traditionally, the organizations and staff who provide each type of aid are separate, with little coordination and knowledge-sharing. This is known as the "humanitarian-development divide", which appears to be narrowing in this century. Increasingly, the definitions and activities between the two types of aid are becoming blurred. For example, when refugees flee to a neighboring country with little prospects for returning home, are their living and livelihood conditions a humanitarian issue or a development one? When a pandemic spreads to low and middle-income countries, as happened with COVID-19, is that a humanitarian or an economic development issue? Clearly, in those examples, the humanitarian and economic development issues and needed assistance are intertwined. Also, the time frames for both humanitarian and development assistance have begun to merge: development agencies tend to get involved earlier in conflict and disaster situations, while humanitarian agencies tend to stay longer than had been the case. Despite the shrinking divide, it still exists, and OECD continues to track humanitarian assistance separately even while it is part of ODA (Keller, 2017). Since the 2000s, the annual amount of humanitarian aid from OECD-DAC members has grown both in absolute terms and as a share of ODA, from US$2.1 billion in 2000 (4.6 percent of ODA) to US$18.8 billion in 2021 (an estimated 10.5 percent of ODA) (OECD, 2022e, 2022f, 2022h).

There are some things that are excluded from the definition of ODA. Loans at market rates do not count as ODA. For example, loans provided by IBRD, the International Bank for Reconstruction and Development – the World Bank – are not ODA. They are a form of Development Assistance (DA in OECD's terminology), and they are part of Aid with a capital "A". Export credits or trade financing also do not count as ODA. Grants by foundations, such as the considerable amount of funds provided globally each year by the Gates Foundation, do not count as ODA. NGO development programs are not considered ODA; when the source of funds is from an official donor, those funds are captured in bilateral aid totals.

What else is included or excluded from the definition? Funds to support a colony or overseas territory cannot be counted as ODA or aid. This topic came up in late 2017 when countries like Britain and France could not count disaster relief to their islands hard hit by hurricanes as ODA. One-off cultural events, such as a concert, cannot be counted as ODA, but the financing of museums, libraries, art spaces, and music schools can be considered aid. COVID-19 vaccine donations, as well as measures for prevention, treatment, and care have been included in ODA. Importantly, all costs to a donor for administering aid are included in aid totals.

ODA Modernization

Since 2012, the Development Assistance Committee (DAC) of OECD has launched a process of modernization of ODA, which involves a number of changes that have been agreed and are being implemented over time. These ongoing changes have involved expenditures for peace and security, how loans are counted, refugee costs, how private sector investment activities are counted, and how debt relief will be counted.

Peace and Security

Generally, military and security expenditures, as well as combatting anti-terrorism, are excluded from ODA. However, during the process of modernizing ODA, important exceptions have been agreed. Financing for police training and routine civil policing functions can now be reported as ODA, as well as training of recipient country military personnel in areas such as human rights, rule of law, protection of women, humanitarian law, disaster relief preparedness, prevention and treatment of communicable diseases, anti-corruption, and transparency. These trainings on prominent governance and development issues need to be conducted under civilian oversight. A second change is that, in some circumstances, where the military is used as a last resort to deliver humanitarian aid or development services, additional costs (excluding salaries and normal operating expenses) can be reported as ODA. Also, limited activities, such as community-based efforts or education aimed specifically at preventing violent extremism, are now eligible to be counted as ODA (OECD-DAC, 2016c). In addition, expenditures related to reforming and managing security systems, including enhancing civil society's role, can now be considered as ODA.

Another set of changes relates to post-war activities. Demobilization, weapons disposal, and reintegration of ex-combatants into the economy, as well as development of related laws, regulations, and procedures, are all now eligible to be categorized as ODA. So is the removal of land mines and explosives and associated awareness-raising and victim assistance. A variety of efforts aimed at preventing child soldiers and rehabilitating them are now considered ODA-eligible expenditures as well. Finally, donor engagement in civilian peace-building activities (e.g., conflict resolution training; international civilian peace missions) can be reported as ODA, as can participation in UN-sponsored peacekeeping activities (e.g., training missions; election monitoring). This does not include the costs of actual peace-keeping military forces or any costs borne by the United Nations. The underlying thrust of all these reforms is to recognize the military's involvement or impact in some aspects of development and the growing relationship between peace and security and development. The "fine line" for policymakers was making changes that did not have the effect of strengthening military capabilities to wage war or diluting the primary developmental purpose of ODA (OECD-DAC, 2016b, 2016c).

How Loans Are Counted

As mentioned at the start of this chapter, the definition of the degree of concessionality of loans counted as ODA has changed. In the past when ODA-eligible loans had a grant element of at least 25 percent, calculated at a discount rate of 10 percent, the entire loan amount could be counted as ODA. When aggregated, there was a concept of gross ODA (all funds provided in a given year) and net ODA (gross ODA minus loan principal repayments for previous loans). Beginning in 2018, the rule changed. With the change in the definition of ODA, only the grant equivalent part of a loan can now be counted as ODA, so eventually there will be no difference between gross and net ODA. The rationale behind this change is to simplify reporting and show more transparency and comparability of donor effort. The change was also meant to provide incentives for donors to offer more grants and highly concessional loans especially to low-income countries, attempting to avoid future debt crises.

Refugees

Basic assistance for 12 months for refugees and asylum-seekers from countries eligible to receive ODA has been counted as ODA for some time. Because of the surge in refugees arriving to donor countries in the 2010s, these costs became a significant part of ODA, reaching 11 percent of total ODA in 2016 (Harcourt, 2017). However, different donors were interpreting the rules differently. In 2017 and again in 2022, DAC clarified what could be included in counting a donor's ODA contribution as a result of hosting refugees. The list includes basics like food, shelter, subsistence allowance, and health care. It also includes schooling and language training, assistance in the asylum process, the costs to rescue refugees at sea, transport within the host country, and voluntary repatriation to a developing country, all in the first 12 months. The clarification also provided some general guidelines allowing for reasonable estimates as well as actual costs (OECD-DAC, 2017b; OECD, 2022h).

The clarifications had the general objective of making data related to refugee costs more consistent and transparent. During the period of mounting refugee expenses within donor countries, there was some concern that refugee expenses could dilute the availability of ODA within recipient countries and distort the purpose of ODA, which has *both* welfare and economic development objectives for developing countries. Many donors see temporary refugee expenditures as a form of humanitarian aid, while others see the costs more as a form of global welfare rather than aimed specifically at development. There are several members of DAC who decided not to report in-donor refugee costs as part of their ODA (OECD-DAC, 2017b).

In-donor refugee costs reached a peak in 2016; since then, they have leveled off to a certain extent, but with the advent of the war in Ukraine, in-donor refugee costs will rise sharply starting with 2022 aid reporting.

Promoting the Private Sector

For the last several years, DAC members, along with many others, have emphasized the importance of the private sector in development and have undertaken significant efforts to increase private sector engagement. Many donors, in addition to aid agencies or departments, have development finance institutions and other agencies or funds that provide resources to private enterprises in developing countries. DAC members have agreed that the efforts of official agencies in providing private sector finance to developing countries can be counted as ODA, provided that the main purpose is development-oriented rather than strictly commercial. According to DAC,

> The effort may be measured *either* at the point of transfer of funds to a vehicle providing PSI [Private Sector Instrument] to developing countries *or* for each PSI transaction between the vehicle and the private enterprise or institution in the partner country.
>
> (OECD-DAC, 2016b, p. 6)

While the final implementation rules are being worked out over a number of years, amidst technical and financial disagreements, donors are being allowed to report related efforts as ODA. Specifically, government contributions to Development Finance Institutions (DFIs) and other financing vehicles providing loans and equities to developing countries can be counted as ODA at face value (the so-called institutional approach). Alternatively, under the instrument approach, each private sector loan or equity transaction between a DFI and a private enterprise or institution in a developing country can be counted as ODA on a grant-equivalent basis (provided there is an adequate grant element) (OECDa, n.d.).

The inclusion of private sector financing in ODA is happening as part of DAC's adoption of blended finance aimed at increasing commercial finance in support of the Sustainable Development Goals (SDGs). The intent is to leverage large amounts of private finance with lesser amounts of aid (with varying degrees of concessionality depending on the circumstances). The idea is to "crowd in" commercial finance while using concessional funds to address market failures (OECD-DAC, 2017b, pp. 6–10).

Debt Relief

In 2020, DAC members agreed to new rules for treating debt relief as part of ODA. The rules were altered in the expectation that donors would be more generous in their debt relief if more debt from restructuring and forgiveness could be counted as ODA. Basically, any part of an official loan (principal and interest) that was not counted previously as ODA and is now subject to concessional debt relief can be counted as ODA, up to a ceiling of the original amount of the loan. If a non-ODA official loan is rescheduled and the new loan meets the ODA criteria for a concessional loan, then the grant element of the rescheduled loan can be counted as ODA. For loans previously counted as ODA and rescheduled, any resulting debt relief above the amounts previously counted as ODA can be counted up to the ceiling of the nominal amount of the loan. It was hoped that the agreement would make it easier for DAC members to implement debt relief (OECD, 2020a; OECD, 2020b). Nonetheless, a new round of debt relief for low-income countries has been slow to materialize, in part because reaching agreement is more difficult than in the past because there are more parties: more debt is now held by non-DAC official donors, especially China, and the private sector.

Going Beyond ODA – The Realm of Development Finance

The DAC's interest in modernizing ODA clearly shows its interest in moving beyond aid to the more general realm of development finance.

This is in tune with the Sustainable Development Goals that outlined an ambitious agenda in which aid can play only a small role. At the same time as the panorama becomes wider, there is also interest in drilling down on aid and trying to clearly identify those parts of aid that are actually spent within the borders of developing countries. The DAC has already adopted a measure for the latter: CPA, or Country Programmable Aid. To remind you of the definition of CPA from the last chapter, CPA measures:

> the portion of aid that providers can programme for individual countries or regions, and over which partner countries could have a significant say. . . . CPA is a closer proxy of aid that goes to partner [recipient] countries than the concept of official development assistance (ODA).
> (OECD-DAC, 2018)

As can be seen from Figure 4.1, CPA is significantly lower than ODA for DAC Donors. From 2011 to 2020, CPA for DAC country donors ranged from 44 percent to 39 percent, declining in the more recent period. As Table 3.3 showed, when the EU Institutions are included in DAC CPA, the percentage rises to about 50 percent. Although figures are not available for non-DAC donors, some have higher percentages of CPA, and if total "ODA-like" aid from all donors were considered, CPA would likely be higher, but below 60 percent. What this means is that the amount of aid actually available to low and middle-income countries, and over which

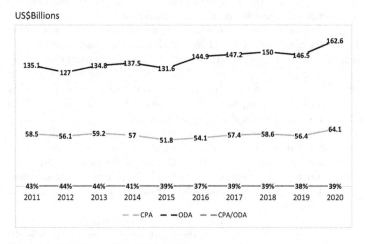

US$Billions

Figure 4.1 ODA Versus CPA 2011–2020

Source: OECD 2022g

Notes: DAC countries only

Current Prices

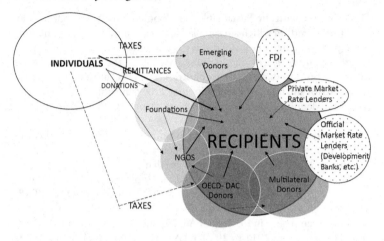

Figure 4.2 Development Finance From the Recipient Country's Viewpoint

Source: Author, adapted from OECD/DAC 2014

they can have some say, is much lower than the aggregate aid figures would indicate.

Even with increases in ODA, as has been the case for most of the past decade, it is clear that ODA alone will be insufficient to fund developing countries' burgeoning needs. From a developing country perspective, ODA is but one source of development finance. Figure 4.2 starts from the aid ecosystem in the last chapter and adds other sources of external finance. In addition to aid plus remittances and funds from foundations and NGOs, the figure now includes other sources of finance, such as official lenders who provide market-rate loans and/or export financing (e.g., multilateral banks, national development banks) and private sector finance through foreign direct investment and lending. Not all private finance has development objectives, and the size of those circles is very different depending on the country. If a country is low-income and not rich in natural resources (OECDb, n.d.), the circles on the right of the figure tend to be very small. In upper middle-income countries, those circles can be so large as to dwarf the rest of the picture, with official aid being very small.

Figure 4.2 also provides another view of how funds associated within a country are not necessarily in the hands of the country. It tells the same story as Figure 4.1, as most of the circles have areas outside of the recipient circle. Significant amounts of aid never actually reach developing countries. So ODA is a poor measure of actual external financing from both a developing country's perspective as well as from the perspective of providers such as multilateral banks who work with both concessional and non-concessional resource flows to developing countries.

TOSSD

It is for that reason, as well as to better support monitoring of the SDGs, that OECD/DAC began developing a new statistical measure of external assistance, referred to as TOSSD (Total Official Support for Sustainable Development). It is meant to monitor all "official resources and private finance mobilized by official interventions in support of their [developing countries] sustainable development" (OECDb, n.d.).

In 2017, an international working group with both donors and recipients began working on the TOSSD methodology. TOSSD has two pillars: one measures all cross-border official resources flowing into developing countries, and the other captures resources spent at regional and global levels to support international public goods and meet global challenges (OECD/DAC, 2016a; OECDb, n.d.). TOSSD would cover many of the items in Figure 4.2 that are considered "official", including private finance mobilized by official interventions. All TOSSD data is to be furnished by providers, with no new data reporting requirements for recipient countries. The idea of TOSSD is not to replace ODA, but to provide a complementary measure that more fully captures today's complicated external financing scenario for developing countries and the provision of global public goods. In today's world there is "aid", "Aid", and "Aid Plus". The first TOSSD data sets are available but are still a work in progress (OECD, 2022b). Pilot studies indicate that TOSSD is succeeding in capturing varying amounts of official funding that have not been previously reported to OECD or available at the country level (Gualbert et al., 2022). In some cases, the existing OECD systems may still be providing a more complete picture including private investment.

Does the advent of TOSSD mean that it is time to forget about aid and ODA as outdated concepts? The answer to that is a resounding no. A World Bank study reported that from 2000 to 2019, LDCs and other low-income countries received 94 percent of their official external financing as ODA (World Bank, 2021, p. v). Using 2015 data, OECD found that for upper middle-income countries (UMIC) ODA constituted less than 10 percent of their external resource flows, while for LDCs and other low-income countries, ODA was approximately 75 to 80 percent of those flows (OECD, 2018a). Figure 4.3 reinforces that message with more recent data. Using six countries with the most external flows in each income group according to 2020 TOSSD data, and using other OECD data on financial flows to developing countries, the figure shows that as per capita income increases, the percentage of ODA in total flows declines

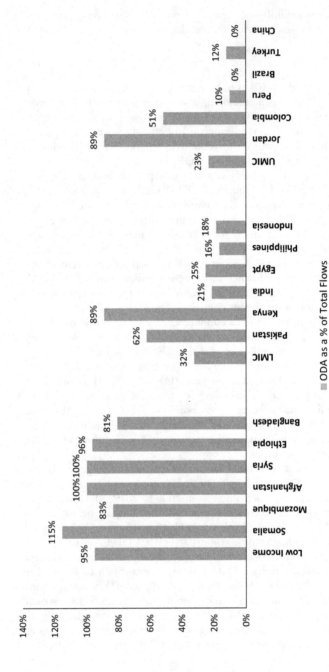

Figure 4.3 ODA as a Percentage of Total External Flows by Income Group – Selected Countries

Source: (OECD 2022b, 2022c)

Note: In the case of Somalia, ODA net flows were recorded as larger than total flows

on average from 95 percent on average to less than 32 percent (OECD, 2022c).

Consequently, aid is still extremely important to low-income countries. These are precisely the countries where growth has been elusive or, at least, not sustained over a long period of time. Moreover, the figure shows that for some middle-income countries (in this example, Kenya, Pakistan, Jordan, and Colombia) ODA continues to be an important source of external income due to circumstances related to conflict, security, and refugees.

A very real question is the role that aid has played in both low and middle-income countries. Is it helping to bring about positive change, or is it actually impeding progress? In many ways, that goes to the heart of the aid-effectiveness debate in subsequent chapters. To begin to answer that question, a more intensive exploration of aid is needed. The following sections discuss how aid is packaged and delivered and provide a deeper look at where the money goes.

The "Packaging" of Aid: Types, Modalities, and Channels

Forms of Aid

Recipient-focused aid for development can take a number of different forms. There are *grants* and *concessional loans* with a wide variety of terms (see the definitions in Chapter 3). These grants and loans can be disbursed in a number of different ways that will be discussed later in this section. There is *food aid*, where aid is in the form of physical food commodities. Food aid is just one form of *"in-kind" aid* where aid is provided in the form of physical inputs such as automobiles or virtually any imported commodity.

Technical assistance or technical cooperation is another form aid can take. A donor country makes short-term and/or long-term specialists available to a recipient. While generally technical assistance specialists are advisers, at times when there are serious capacity gaps, they are asked to fill line positions. Technical assistance in the past has frequently been in the form of tied aid and has had generally disappointing results (Berg, 1993) (Box 4.1). Another common form of aid, particularly in the early 2000s, is *debt relief.* When an official donor grants debt forgiveness to a country, it counts as foreign aid. A final form of aid is a non-market rate *guarantee.* With a guarantee, a donor agrees to back up a commitment made by the recipient government to a third party. That means the donor will make available an associated amount of funds in the event of a recipient government failure (for specific reasons like changes in government policy or political strife) to honor the terms of the contract. That amount would be used to compensate the third party.

Box 4.1   More on Tied Aid

Independent of the form that aid takes – grants, loans, in-kind aid, or technical assistance – aid can be *tied* or *untied*. *Tied aid* is when goods and/or services *must* be supplied from the donor country instead of purchased locally or by international competitive procurement. Studies have shown that tied aid is less efficient, with benefits from the aid declining by as much as 30 percent. For that reason, OECD-DAC has long advocated for the elimination of tied aid, especially for LDCs, countries that have been provided with HIPC debt relief, and more recently, other low-income countries and IDA-eligible countries (OECD, 2022k). As a consequence, many important donors, including the UK, Norway, and the Netherlands have virtually eliminated this practice. While tied aid has diminished in importance since the 1990s, it still exists and is important for some traditional and emerging donors. For example, the United States and EU Institutions still tie at least 28 percent of their aid, and a number of smaller donors, such as the Czech Republic and Poland, tie even greater percentages (OECD, 2022a, p. 34).

In some cases, tied aid and the benefits it brings to the donor country provide an important rationale for continuing or increasing aid. However, food aid is a particular form of tied aid that can have long-lasting negative effects on recipient countries. Except in emergency situations, food aid is problematic since it can depress local agricultural production and distort prices. In addition, there is evidence that food aid provided by its largest donor, the United States, is not necessarily provided to those countries most in need of food assistance (Qian, 2015).

Despite the OECD-DAC recommendation to end the practice of tied aid, developing countries generally accept tied aid as a "fact of life". As of 2020, about 18 percent overall of DAC members' bilateral ODA – as well as close to 10 percent of DAC bilateral aid to LDCs, other low-income countries, IDA-eligible and HIPC countries – remained tied (OECD, 2022h, pp. 23, 34). Non-traditional donors also use tied aid, and the overall percentage of tied aid may be significantly higher.

Modalities of Development Aid

Usually, aid is not just about writing checks to recipient governments. Development aid has a number of modalities that have different characteristics and disbursement channels. By far the most important forms of aid are loans and grants. Most loans and grants are directed towards *investment projects*.

Investment projects generally have fairly concrete and detailed plans specified in advance. Objectives, inputs, expected outputs, cost estimates, management, procurement (purchase of goods and services) arrangements, and monitoring and evaluation processes are usually spelled out in a document approved by both the donor government and the recipient government. Aid in investment projects is used to fund inputs. Consequently, maintenance of records and receipts is important, along with sound financial management and auditing. Donors may provide advances into a project account with accounting and reporting at specified intervals, or they may disburse into a project account against confirmed purchase receipts and signed contracts. Investment projects can be managed by a wide variety of actors: the donor itself; an individual or firm contracted by the donor; the recipient government, using either line agencies or a special project unit; or an NGO subcontracted by either the donor or the recipient (Box 4.2).

In contrast, *Programme* or *Program Aid* (which can also be called General Budget Support; Balance of Payments Support; Poverty Reduction Support; Structural Adjustment; or Development Policy Grants, Credits, and Loans) is aid granted usually to support policy and institutional change. The funds can be provided in one or more tranches

---

Box 4.2   Fishery Promotion in Sekondi: An Investment Project Example

The Japan International Cooperation Agency (JICA) provided a grant for a fishery promotion project in Ghana. The project, implemented between 2014 and 2018, aimed at providing a more stable supply of fresh fish in Sekondi. It financed infrastructure works and equipment to extend the mooring quay to alleviate congestion and improve related facilities. The implementing agencies were the Ghana Ports and Harbor Authority and the Sekondi Fishing Harbor. As a result, fresher fish is available, and some fishermen have increased their incomes. Project implementation was delayed by over a year because of an outbreak of Ebola fever. The grant amount was 2,102 million yen (US$18.71 million using average exchange rates 2015–2018). An external evaluation gave the project an overall rating of highly satisfactory.

Source: Keiko (2022)

(installments). Any associated policy conditions can be fulfilled in advance or with a series of actions with agreed deadlines, possibly tied to disbursements. The policy conditions can be economy-wide or focused on one or two sectors; they can be many or few. The funds are disbursed by the donor directly to the recipient government. This type of lending, which became popular in the 1980s and 1990s, became controversial under the umbrella of "structural adjustment" where recipient governments and others argued that donors were forcing the governments to undertake policy changes against their will. Because of this and the fact that recipient governments today have better articulated poverty action plans or national plans, there is now more agreement about most conditions. Although most people claim that conditionality has been streamlined and made more flexible, there are still multiple conditions attached to this type of lending (Cormier & Manger, 2022; Shah, 2017; Welham & Miller, 2022) (Box 4.3).

Other modalities lie on the spectrum between aid for discrete investment projects and program aid. *Sectorwide Approaches* or *SWAPs*, while still a specialized type of investment aid, are quite different from individual

---

Box 4.3   COVID-19 Crisis Response: A Policy-Based Operation Example

The African Development Fund, part of the African Development Bank, provided a UA 36 million credit (about US$ 51.7 million as of December 9, 2020, the effectiveness date of the credit) to Tanzania for the COVID-19 Crisis Response Budget Support Program (TCRBSP) during a one-year period covering 2021. The objective, through budget support, was to bolster the government's economic resiliency while mitigating the impact of the pandemic. It was aligned with existing strategies and programs, including other financing. The responsible agency was the Ministry of Planning, Economics, and Empowerment. Expected actions and outcomes were strengthening the Government's response to the pandemic, including testing and isolation, encouraging commercial banks to lend to the private sector, and providing more protection to highly vulnerable populations. There was a series of outcome and output indicators with 21 targets and an actual achievement rate of 68 percent. The project completion report rated the operation as satisfactory.

Source: African Development Fund (2022)

investment projects. As aid expanded in the new millennium, concerns about the lack of donor coordination and aid fragmentation became more evident. In contrast to investment projects, SWAPs are meant to cover most, if not all, investment and operating costs in a particular sector or subsector. Rather than having one or two donors, the SWAP is meant to encompass most, if not all, donors within the sector. Ideally, the recipient government and the donors, under the leadership of the recipient, sit down and agree on major objectives, sectoral strategy, priorities, and key activities within a medium-term investment plan, as well as common procurement, auditing, and reporting arrangements for the sector. Most SWAPs to date fall short of this ideal picture, but do try to reach agreement on objectives, strategy, and at least a good portion of a medium-term plan. Common financial and procurement arrangements have been more difficult to achieve, ostensibly because of weak recipient systems, but also because of entrenched practices and legal requirements of donors. Consequently, funds for SWAPs have generally been disbursed as in investment projects – against purchase of inputs – although there has been "basket funding" in a number of cases where donors establish a joint account to fund some of the activities in the SWAP. SWAPs are notable for their intent to tackle the problems associated with donor coordination. There is a clear understanding that SWAPS are managed and implemented by the recipient government using line management and agencies.

A more recent development has been a variety of aid operations known as Program for Results, Results-Based Aid or Lending, or Cash on Delivery (World Bank, 2022c; Birdsall & Savedoff, 2011). While each of these differs slightly, they are projects or programs where aid monies are disbursed upon achievement of results, as opposed to inputs. A donor and a recipient country agree on a program of investments and specify exactly how funds will be disbursed using a series of disbursement-linked indicators. Whenever specified achievements are reached, associated funding is released. The idea behind results-based aid is to remove donors from the day-to-day management of how development results are achieved. Before providing such aid, recipients are supposed to carry out institutional, environmental, and social assessments, with assistance as needed by the donor, in order to ensure that the recipient is prepared to be successful in achieving results. Not surprisingly, since its start in the early 2010s, it has become an increasingly popular aid modality (Box 4.4).

All of the previous modalities are country-based in the sense that they originate from either donor or recipient country strategies and plans specific to that recipient country. In contrast, there are also *Global Programs*, where objectives, targets, and administrative and funding procedures are determined at the global level. Although the mechanisms for global programs vary widely, generally countries can apply for and/or be granted funding

---

Box 4.4   Climate Action Through Landscape Management: A Program for Results Example

IDA approved an SDR360.9 million (US$500 million) grant for Ethiopia to finance a US$ 1.7 billion program to increase sustainable land management and expand access to secure land tenure in rural areas that are not range lands. The program started in 2019 and is programmed to finish in mid-2024. Disbursement is linked to a series of indicators, including the amount of land being managed under approved watershed management plans; an increase in securely registered lands in targeted areas; and actions to improve environmental and social management systems. The Ministry of Agriculture is the implementing agency though its Natural Resource Management Directorate and Rural Land Administration and Use Directorate (RLAUD). As of July 2022, implementation progress was rated moderately satisfactory, with more than US$125 million disbursed or about one-third of the funds programed under disbursement linked indicators. Both at the start and currently, the program has been rated as having substantial risks.

Source: World Bank (2019, 2022c)

---

for specific purposes. Once a grant has been approved, funding is available for an initial period. After performance and/or results are certified through financial and physical reporting on a semi-annual or annual period (usually), there are more disbursements. Additional grants or grant renewal is possible for countries with satisfactory track records. The Global Fund for Aids, Malaria, and Tuberculosis (The Global Fund) and the Global Alliance for Vaccines (Gavi) are examples of global programs. Although virtually all global programs originated with donors, most today have significant representation from developing countries on their boards and among their staff. Global programs have some attractive features. They are usually specific in purpose and clear about what they will fund, making them easier to monitor and to show results at the national and global levels. At the same time, because they have predetermined objectives and mechanisms, they can be difficult to coordinate with the recipient's national programming and budgeting and other country-based activities like SWAPs.

Aid Channels

All official aid ultimately comes from governments. In addition to types of aid and modalities, donor governments have a variety of choices on how to channel their aid to the ultimate beneficiaries. Some of the choices made by large DAC donors were shown in the last chapter in Table 3.3. The first choice that official donors have is whether they are going to keep control of their aid directly or whether they are going to give some of their aid to an international organization that will either be a financing or implementing agency and ultimately become responsible for what happens to those funds. If the donor keeps control, it is *bilateral aid*. If it goes to an international organization such as the United Nations, the Global Fund or IDA, and the original donor relinquishes control over how those funds are spent to the organization's governing body, it is *multilateral aid*.

With bilateral aid, there are further choices. Bilateral donors can provide some aid directly to NGOs for projects the NGOs undertake on behalf of recipients and beneficiaries. This is a common procedure when it comes to humanitarian aid and relief efforts. Some donors implement aid projects and programs themselves, or they sub-contract implementation to private companies, consultants, or NGOs. In all those cases, aid funds do not enter the recipient's national treasury and rarely are in their national budget.

Many donors provide aid directly to recipient governments through either a project account or a deposit into the recipient's national treasury. At that point, recipient governments also have choices. They can delegate responsibility either formally or informally to other parts of the government, NGOs, consultants, and private firms. Increasingly, aid channeled to recipient governments has been included in national budgets. This is important because having a line budget item can "nudge" thinking about what complementary national resources may be needed and how operational costs will be financed once the project is concluded.

A final choice for channeling aid funds has the confusing name of *multi-bilateral funding (multi-bi)*. OECD defines multi-bilateral funding as:

> These are resources to ODA-eligible multilateral agencies over which the donor retains some degree of control on decisions regarding disposal of the funds. Such flows may be earmarked for a specific country, project, region, sector or theme. They are bilateral resources channeled through a multilateral agency, and therefore technically qualify as part of bilateral ODA.
>
> (OECD, 2015, p. 4)

Multi-bi funds, depending on the agency, are also referred to as non-core contributions or trust funds. The essential point here is that donor governments retain some control over the use of the funds, and the funds are earmarked. Many times, these funds join together two or more donors who have a special interest in a specific area, but they also can be limited to a single donor.

The Basis for "Packaging" Decisions

Generally, it is the donor government that makes the decision on the forms and channels of aid that it prefers, especially when considering its overall program. Once those are made, modalities or the kinds of projects and programs it will fund in each individual country are generally undertaken with input from the recipient or based on the recipient's plans. Some recipients will also express views on their preferred forms of aid and even channels.

The preferences of donors regarding forms of aid tend to vary. While most donors provide both bilateral and multilateral aid, there is still a strong preference for bilateral aid. Some donors only provide aid in the form of grants (e.g., Sweden and the United States), while others prefer concessional loans. After the debt crisis and debt relief of the 1990s and 2000s, some major donors and policy analysts were urging the use of grants wherever possible to avoid the buildup of new debt (Klein & Harford, 2005; Clements, Gupta, Pivovarsky, & Tiongson, 2004). However, donors such as the Japanese and the World Bank's International Development Association (IDA) prefer concessional loans because they believe that form of aid can induce a greater sense of ownership among recipients, as well as ensuring some resources for aid through repayments over the longer term. Currently, some donors use a mixture of both grants and loans; concessional lending rose from 2018 to 2020 before falling slightly in 2021 (OECD, 2022f, p. 2). The revised ODA rule of counting only the grant equivalent part of a concessional loan may have implications for the mix of grants and loans in the future.

Many donors also use a mixture in terms of modalities and channels. Investment projects are the principal modality for almost all donors. Some donors steer completely clear of program aid popular in the early 2000s; the World Bank, European Institutions, and other multilateral banks still use this modality. Today, this type of aid is not popular among bilateral donors who are concerned about how their funds are being spent. In theory, the funds should be spent according to medium-term growth and poverty plans. In reality, yearly budget proposals, actual budgets, and budget outturns (expenditures) tend to vary among themselves and substantially from medium-term plans. Donors want to ensure that the funds that enter the recipient government's treasury are not being used for activities they disagree with or to fuel corruption. Most recipient governments, however, tend to prefer budget support that comes with more spending flexibility and fewer detailed accounting and reporting requirements. This preference holds true only if the aid is not heavily conditioned on difficult policy reforms.

While SWAPs were also widely used in the 2000s and continue in some countries, in most cases complementary individual projects have sprung up around them, thereby lessening the potential benefits of SWAPs to save transaction costs. An issue for donors with SWAPs is the resources required to prepare and negotiate a multi-partner SWAP.

Governments are also wary of the time commitment, but they very much appreciate the objectives of a SWAP. One concern, also a concern with multi-donor general budget support, is that it can increase the leverage of the donors against the recipient government when there is a disagreement.

A number of donors are experimenting with results-based aid, which has also found support among recipients. Recipient ministry of finance officials like those modalities that offer the country the greatest flexibility and can be included in their annual budgets. Sectoral ministries tend to favor earmarked sectoral aid for investment projects, SWAPS, or results-based aid since that will help ensure that their ministries will receive adequate funding.

A number of larger donors also like using Global Programs as delivery modalities for their aid. Through their participation on the board of a program, they can make their influence felt while avoiding the direct transaction costs involved in bilateral aid. Even some smaller donors are enthusiastic in their support for Global Programs because it may give them more influence – "a seat at the table" – than is the case with individual country-based bilateral funding. Some low-income recipients have issues with Global Programs because they may not dovetail with their national plans and country-based budgeting efforts, complicating an already cluttered aid scenario. They also may not feel they are adequately represented in overall policies and decision-making for the programs. Middle-income countries, especially higher middle-income countries, are enthusiastic about global programs because they are one of the only ways in which they are able to get grants and concessional loans.

Finally, as far as channels are concerned, the recipients' clear preference is to have all aid monies channeled to and through their national treasuries. Recipient governments are particularly wary of aid projects where the funds and control remain with the donor or its contractor. They are also wary of funds channeled directly to NGOs. Donors do this when they are leery of providing funds directly to the government and/or they wish to support and strengthen civil society. For some donors, maintaining control is important for accountability vis-a-vis their authorizing environments back home. Other donors insist that recipient government ownership and accountability for aid funds are essential to further long-term capacity and development goals.

Consequently, there is a great deal of heterogeneity in how aid is "packaged". Different donors have different preferences, and donor preferences do not perfectly match recipient preferences. While serious mismatches still occur, the evolving scenario is one that is much improved from earlier times when recipients had virtually no say in how "their" aid was delivered.

How Much Aid Is There?

Size of Aid

Figure 4.4 shows how ODA has evolved since 1990. As the figure shows, there has been a sharp and fairly steady increase in aid beginning in the early 2000s (World Bank, 2022b). This has resulted in a doubling of ODA in real terms over a 20-year period. Moreover, these figures do not include "ODA-like flows" from countries not reporting to OECD. Nonetheless, most aid is still coming from the traditional OECD-DAC donors as noted in the previous chapter.

Preliminary figures for 2021 showed a continuation of high levels of ODA, with a total of about US$178.9 billion from OECD/DAC donors alone (and an increase of over 4 percent in real terms from 2020). Most of the increase was due to the need for additional support for COVID-19 expenses in the form of vaccine donations. COVID-19-related expenses averaged about 10 percent of the aid from OECD/DAC donors in both 2020 and 2021 (OECD, 2022f, pp. 1, 13).

Sectoral Composition of Aid

According to OECD, of the total ODA of about US$196 billion in 2020, US$129 billion or about 66 percent was bilateral aid, and about US$67 billion or 34 percent was multilateral aid. In 1990, the share of multilateral aid was lower, around 20 percent (OECD, 2022i). Figure 4.5 breaks down bilateral aid by major purpose. As can be seen from the figure, social infrastructure and services are by far the largest category. While COVID-19 increased health and other social expenditures considerably, traditionally this category has always been the largest. Support for economic infrastructure and production (e.g., agriculture, industry, mining) had been increasing slowly before the COVID-19 pandemic and continues to do so.

In-donor refugee costs have seen a sharp increase in recent years, although there was a decrease from 2017 through 2021 as the flow of refugees to Europe slowed. However, these costs are expected to increase sharply because of refugees from Ukraine as well as a growing number of "climate refugees". The relatively low percentages for debt relief and program assistance (budget support) are evidence of how once important categories of aid at the turn of the century have declined. However, debt relief is likely to become important again given the growing number of developing countries in debt distress after the COVID-19 pandemic, the war in Ukraine, and accompanying worldwide financial and economic difficulties.

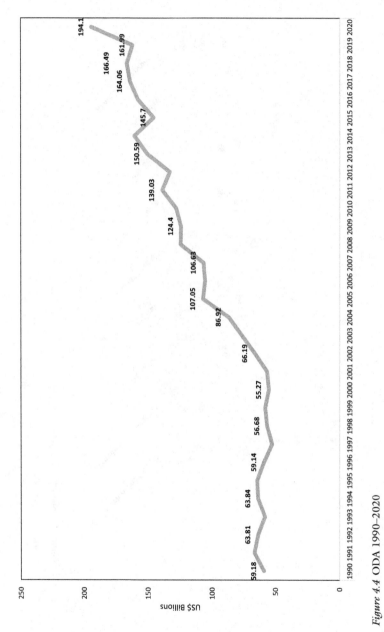

Figure 4.4 ODA 1990–2020
Source: World Bank 2022b

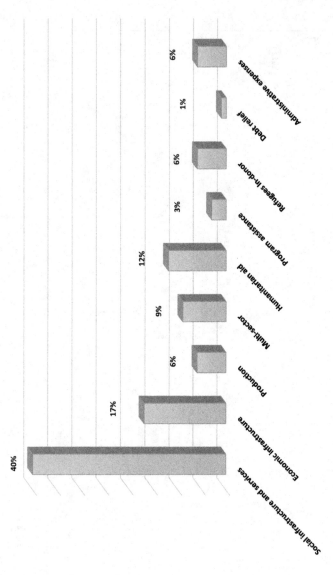

Figure 4.5 Bilateral Aid by Major Purpose

Source: OECD 2022i

Note: DAC country members only; 2020 data

Regional Distribution

Figure 4.6 shows the regional distribution of aid. Africa is the largest recipient with about 40 percent of aid, and Asia is close behind with 30 percent. It should be noted that Africa has only 20 percent of the population of aid recipient countries while Asia has 65 percent of that population. Oceania, comprised mainly of small, relatively sparsely populated Pacific Islands, has the highest aid per capita but accounts for only a small amount of total aid.

Aid by Income Grouping

Figure 4.7 shows the distribution of aid by income grouping. As noted in Chapter 3, somewhat surprisingly, LDCs and other low-income countries do not receive more aid than middle-income countries. The figure, which excludes the sizeable amount of unallocated aid, shows that low-income countries receive 48 percent of aid from DAC and multilateral donors, while middle-income countries receive 52 percent. An increased share of aid for low-income countries is unlikely in the near future given donors' pandemic-related aid in middle-income countries, the need to increase climate-related spending in some large middle-income countries (e.g., Brazil and Indonesia), and an increase in aid to Ukraine and other European aid recipients.

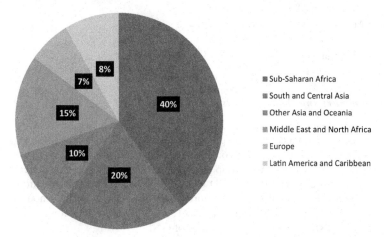

Figure 4.6 Aid by Region
Source: OECD 2022i
Notes: Includes multilateral and bilateral DAC aid
Excludes aid unspecified by region
Data is 2019–2020

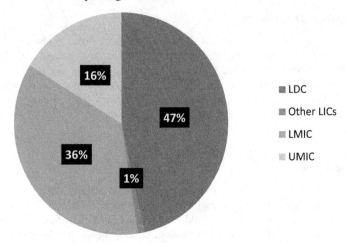

Figure 4.7 Aid by Income Grouping
Source: OECD, 2022i
Notes:
LDC = Least Developed Countries
LICs = Low-Income Countries
LMIC = Low Middle-Income Countries
UMIC = Upper Middle-Income Countries
Includes multilateral aid
Excludes unspecified aid
Data is 2019–2020

Summarizing Donors' Efforts

As mentioned earlier, since the mid-1960s, the recommendation has been for aid-providing countries to provide 0.7 percent of their Gross National Income (GNI) as aid. Most countries have fallen far short of that target, and the DAC donors as a group have never achieved close to that target. Figure 4.8 elaborated by OECD gives a good snapshot of the situation using 2021 preliminary data. Figure 4.8a shows the absolute amount provided by each DAC donor in 2021, while Figure 4.8b shows what that represents in terms of percentage of GNI.

There are several points to note in relation to Figure 4.8. First, as noted in an earlier chapter, the United States is by far the largest donor, followed by Germany and Japan. Germany has met the 0.7 percent of GNI target for ODA, while Great Britain, after meeting the target for several years, significantly reduced its assistance to half of one percent (0.5) in 2021. The United States is only at 18 percent of GNI, the lowest

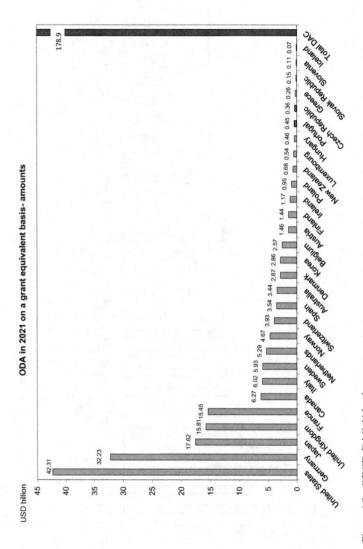

Figure 4.8a OECD-DAC Aid – Amounts

Source: OECD, 2022f, p.9

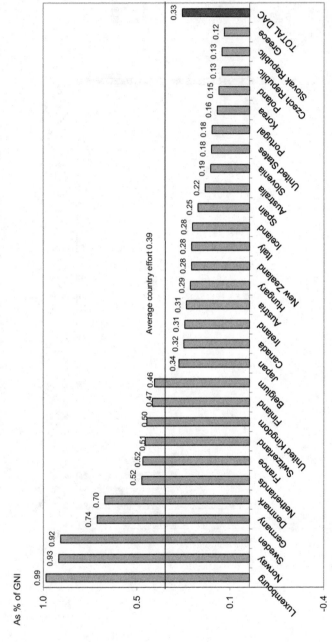

Figure 4.8b As a Percentage of Gross National Income
Source: OECD, 2022f, p.9

of any G7 country. Given the size of the US economy, that represents a sizable amount. While US aid contributions may wax and wane with different federal governments, the overall picture has remained remarkably stable, with US aid trending upward since 1998 (OECD, 2018b). In 2021, US ODA increased by more than 14 percent over 2020, largely due to vaccine purchases for developing countries and an increase in contributions to multilateral organizations (OECD, 2022f, p. 4).

A second thing to note is that Norway, Denmark, Sweden, and Luxembourg have consistently achieved or exceeded the recommended benchmark for aid. While OECD does not have verified figures for every major aid provider outside of the DAC, Turkey, an important non-DAC donor, also exceeded the 0.7 target in 2021 and has done so in prior years. Collectively in 2021, the DAC donors reached .33 percent of GNI, significantly less than the target but an increase over previous years.

As much as money is important, aid is not just about the amount of funds provided. Because the "how" is as important as the "how much", the next chapter focuses on donor quality and how it is measured. Each donor has its own priorities and decision-making mechanisms, and the differences among them matter to recipient countries and to the overall picture of aid effectiveness.

Bibliography

African Development Fund. (2022). *Tanzania, COVID-19 response budget support program (TCRBSP) project completion report.* AfDB.

Berg, E. (1993). *Rethinking technical cooperation: Reforms for capacity building.* New York: UNDP.

Birdsall, N., & Savedoff, W. D. (2011). *Cash on delivery: A new approach to foreign aid.* Washington, DC: Center for Global Development.

Clements, B., Gupta, S., Pivovarsky, A., & Tiongson, E. R. (2004, September). Foreign aid: Grants versus loans. *Finance and Development,* 46–49.

Cormier, B., & Manger, M. S. (2022). Power, ideas, and World Bank conditionality. *The Review of International Organizations, 17*(3), 397–425.

Gualbert, G., Xu, S., Lessard, M., Sangare, C., Dagtekin, A., Micek, C., & Benn, J. (2022). *Total official support for sustainable development – data comparison study for Bangladesh, Cameroon, and Colombia, OECD development co-operation working papers, no. 109.* Paris: OECD.

Harcourt, S. (2017, November 1). *Aid donors met to discuss how to change the rules; here is what happened.* Retrieved from ONE website: www.one.org/international/blog/aid-donors-met-to-discuss-how-to-change-the-rules-here-is-what-happened/

Keiko, A. (2022). *Republic of Ghana: FY2020 ex-post evaluation report of Japanese aid project "the project for fishery promotion in Sekondi".* Tokyo: JICA.

Keller, J. M. (2017, May 1). *Bridging the humanitarian-development divide: Three priorities from three global leaders.* Retrieved from Center for Global Development.

Klein, M., & Harford T. (2005, March). *Grants or loans? Public policy for the private sector.* Washington DC: World Bank.

Lancaster, C. (2007). *Foreign aid: Diplomacy, development, domestic politics*. Chicago: University of Chicago.

Luijkx, W., & Benn, J. (2017). *Emerging providers' international co-operation for development*. Paris: OECD.

OECD. (2008). *Is it ODA*. Paris: OECD.

OECD. (2012). *What do we know about multilateral aid? The 54 billion dollar question*. Paris: OECD.

OECD. (2015). *Multilateral aid 2015: Better partnerships for a post-2015 world – highlights*. Paris: OECD.

OECD. (2018a). *Resource flows beyond ODA in DAC statistics*. Retrieved from OECD website: www.oecd.org/dac/stats/beyond-oda.htm

OECD. (2018b, April 9). *Development aid stable in 2017 with more sent to poorest countries*. Paris.

OECD. (2020a, 30 July). *Donors agree on aid treatment of debt relief*. Retrieved from OECD website: www.oecd.org/newsroom/donors-agree-on-aid-treatment-of-debt-relief.htm

OECD. (2020b). *Reporting on debt relief in the grant equivalent system*. Paris: OECD.

OECD. (2021). *Official development assistance – definition and coverage*. Retrieved from OECD: www.oecd.org/development/financing-sustainable-development/development-finance-standards/officialdevelopmentassistancedefinitionandcoverage.htm

OECD. (2022a). *2022 report on the implementation of the DAC recommendation on untying official development assistance*. Paris: OECD.

OECD. (2022b). *Data visualization tool*. Retrieved from TOSSD website: https://tossd.online/

OECD. (2022c). *Geographical distribution of financial flows to developing countries 2022: Disbursements, commitments, country indicators*. Paris: OECD.

OECD. (2022d). *DAC list of ODA recipients effective for reporting on 2022 and 2023 flows*. Retrieved from OECD website: www.oecd.org/dac/financing-sustainable-development/development-finance-standards/DAC-List-of-ODA-Recipients-for-reporting-2022-23-flows.pdf

OECD. (2022e). *Humanitarian assistance*. Retrieved from OECD website: www.oecd.org/dac/financing-sustainable-development/development-finance-topics/humanitarian-assistance.htm

OECD. (2022f). *ODA levels in 2021 – Preliminary data: Detailed summary note*. Paris: OECD.

OECD. (2022g). *Query wizard for international development statistics*. Retrieved from OECD website: stats.oecd.org/qwids

OECD. (2022h). *Report on the implementation of the Clarifications on ODA reporting of in-donor refugee costs*. Paris: OECD.

OECD. (2022i, May 25). *Statistics on resource flows to developing countries – Various Tables*. Retrieved from OECD website: www.oecd.org/dac/financing-sustainable-development/development-finance-data/statisticsonresourceflowstodevelopingcountries.htm

OECD. (2022j, May). *Table 19*. Retrieved from www.oecd.org/dac/financing-sustainable-development/development-finance-data/statisticsonresourceflowstodevelopingcountries.htm

OECD. (2022k). *Tied aid*. Retrieved from OECD: www.oecd.org/dac/financing-sustainable-development/development-finance-standards/untied-aid.htm

OECD. (n.d.a). *Modernisation of the DAC statistical system.* Retrieved from OECD: www.oecd.org/dac/financing-sustainable-development/development-finance-standards/modernisation-dac-statistical-system.htm

OECD. (n.d.b). *Total official support for sustainable development (TOSSD).* Retrieved from OECD: www.oecd.org/dac/tossd/

OECD. (n.d.c). *Untied aid.* Retrieved from OECD: www.oecd.org/dac/financing-sustainable-development/development-finance-standards/untied-aid.htm

OECD/DAC. (2014). *The new development finance landscape: Developing countries' perspective (working draft).* Paris: OECD.

OECD/DAC. (2016a). *TOSSD: A new statistical measure for the SDG era.* Paris: OECD.

OECD-DAC. (2016b). *DAC high level meeting communique.* Paris: OECD.

OECD-DAC. (2016c). *The scope and nature of 2016 HLM decisions regarding the ODA-eligibility of peace and security-related expenditures.* Paris: OECD.

OECD-DAC. (2017a). *2017 report on the DAC untying recommendation.* Paris: OECD.

OECD-DAC. (2017b). *DAC high level communique.* Paris: OECD.

OECD-DAC. (2018). *Country programmable aid (CPA).* Retrieved February 2018, from OECD.org: www.oecd.org/dac/financing-sustainable-development/cpa.htm

Qian, N. (2015). Making progress on foreign aid. *Annual Review of Economics,* 277–308.

Radelet, S. (2006). *A primer on foreign aid.* Washington, DC: Center for Global Development.

Shah, A. (2017). *Development assistance and conditionality: Challenges in design and options for more effective assistance.* Paris: European Commission/OECD.

Welham, B., & Miller, M. (2022, October 4). *Managing a new era of IMF lending conditions.* Retrieved from ODI website: https://odi.org/en/insights/managing-a-new-era-of-imf-lending-conditions/

Williamson, V. (2018, March 19). *Americans overestimate foreign aid? Not so fast.* Retrieved from Brookings Institution: www.brookings.edu/blog/fixgov/2018/03/19/americans-overestimate-foreign-aid-not-so-fast/

World Bank. (2019). *Program appraisal document, Ethiopia climate action through landscape management program for results.* Washington, DC: World Bank.

World Bank. (2021). *A changing landscape: Trends in official financial flows and the aid architecture.* Washington, DC: World Bank.

World Bank. (2022a). *Implementation status and results report, Ethiopia climate action through landscape management program for results.* Washington, DC: World Bank.

World Bank. (2022b). *Net official development assistance received (CurrentUS$).* Retrieved from World Bank Data website: https://data.worldbank.org/indicator/DT.ODA.ALLD.CD

World Bank. (2022c, September 29). *Program-for-results finance(PforR).* Retrieved from World Bank: www.worldbank.org/en/programs/program-for-results-financing

Yanguas, P. (2018). *Why we lie about aid: Development and the messy politics of change.* London: Zed.

Part II

Effective Aid

Debates and Trends

5 Judging Donors' Performance

The preceding chapters have provided a glimpse of aid's operating environment, a summary of the key donors, and a basic understanding of the complexities of aid. This is background to gain an appreciation of how aid works. It also provides a foundation to begin thinking about aid effectiveness.

Aid effectiveness is a multi-faceted concept. There are at least three major – and complex – questions that need to be examined before venturing opinions on aid effectiveness. The first is: Are aid providers performing satisfactorily? What exactly makes a "good donor"? The second big question is: Is aid doing the "right" things? Defining what are the "right" things is the crux of the matter. And the third is: Is aid having a positive impact on poverty reduction, quality living standards, economic growth, and the resolution of global issues? Here too, issues related to attribution and measurement, among others, make clear answers difficult. To sum this up in more familiar language: With regard to aid, are donors doing things the right way, and are they doing the right things? Most importantly, is it making a positive difference in people's lives?

These questions will be explored in the next chapters. In this chapter, the emphasis is on judging donor performance. The topic is challenging: From whose perspective are donors being judged? Donors have their home country constituencies, who usually expect them to provide aid in an efficient way and to reap home-country benefits out of their largesse. Aid recipients have their own concerns related to how aid is given. Recipients want aid that matches their priorities and timeframes, whether those priorities are related to meeting citizens' expectations or achieving short-term personal and political gains. Finally, academics and development practitioners want donors to provide aid in ways that do not get in the way of achieving results on the ground.

So how does one go about evaluating donor performance? One way to do this is to review the theories and indices that have developed over the years to measure donor quality. While the relevant articles and indices have substantive and methodological issues, it is possible to glean from them indicators or criteria that can be useful (and used) for judging how a particular donor is doing in relation to others.

DOI: 10.4324/9781003265320-7

Samuel Huntington's four criteria for institutionalization – adaptability, complexity, autonomy, and coherence – can also be applied to donor agencies (Huntington, 2006, p. 12).

Autonomy, in the aid agency context, means the ability to make decisions based solely on developmental or humanitarian considerations, independent of political mandates or constraints. Lancaster (1999) used Huntington's theory as part of her hypotheses related to analyzing aid agencies in the 1990s, simplifying the organizational characteristics down to autonomy and capacity. In her conception, capacity was related to local field presence, the ability to be flexible, handle complexity, adapt to recipient circumstances, encourage recipient "ownership", and demonstrate general competence and coherence (Box 5.1).

Box 5.1   Classroom Exercise: Autonomy and Capacity as Key Components of Donor Performance

Make a list of some of the principal aid donors, and have the class decide how to judge them based on autonomy and capacity. Use Low (L), Medium (M), and High (H) to score, with L/M and M/H used sparingly.

The matrix would look something like this:

Donor	Autonomy	Capacity
France		
Germany		
Japan		
Sweden		
UK		
US		
China		
EU		
IDA/WB		
Gates Foundation		
Global Fund		

The exercise demonstrates useful lessons, including how subjective the ratings are and how they depend on the weight given to variables within each of the broad categories. It also shows some broad trends. To mention just two: multilateral and private institutions generally have a greater degree of autonomy than bilateral aid agencies. Capacity in aid agencies – defined beyond just technical expertise – is highly variable and cannot be taken for granted.

Source: Author, based on Lancaster (1999)

By the end of the 1990s, an international conversation on aid effectiveness was in full swing. As part of that, studying donors' performance and trying to perfect and measure the criteria on which that performance should be judged became part of the aid dialog. It quickly became apparent that knowledge about how aid agencies worked was surprisingly limited. Perhaps it should not have come as such a surprise since the emphasis in most of the previous discussions on aid effectiveness had centered on the recipients' performance.

The problem of judging donor performance became even more complex: not only was there debate over the significance of various indicators (e.g., Was increased field presence always positive?), but there were data limitations. Data limitations were twofold: some information about aid agencies had never been requested and, therefore, it had never been collected. In addition, there was reluctance on the part of many aid agencies to share data on their internal workings. Partly for this reason, the studies tended to emphasize aid practices (and of course, amounts) that could be observed by recipients and third parties.

The oldest effort examining donor aid practices is OECD's Peer Reviews, which have been ongoing since 1962 (OECD, 2006). Continuing until the present day, the Peer Reviews of individual DAC country members are conducted by two senior officials from other DAC countries and take place on average every five to six years. The reviews assess member countries on their aid practices and adoption of DAC guidelines along with a broader range of topics (e.g., aid amounts, strategy, major priorities) related to aid effectiveness (OECD/DAC, 2021). For some DAC members, the reviews have been valuable inputs into donor agency reforms and perceived improvements in aid delivery. While the usual practice in peer reviews has been to consult with selected recipient officials, recipients play a limited role in these reviews, especially in terms of agenda-setting.

The Paris Declaration on Aid Effectiveness in 2005 was the most notable attempt to bring donors and recipients into a dialog on what matters for aid effectiveness. As noted in Chapter 2, the five guiding principles were: recipient *ownership*, donor *alignment* with recipient strategies and systems, donor *harmonization* and improved coordination, *managing for results* with strengthened monitoring and performance indicators, and *mutual accountability* with broader consultations and more timely information. Along with the five principles, 15 indicators were established. While six of the indicators were primarily the recipient's responsibility or a joint responsibility, nine indicators were primarily the donors' responsibility and provide some clues as to which areas were considered important to improve donor performance. Table 5.1 provides a list of those indicators. The indicators showed the growing importance of the themes of country ownership, use of a recipient country's systems and institutions, better coordination among donors, and more predictability in aid flows.

Except for coordinated technical assistance, by the target date (2010) none of the Paris Declaration indicators had been met, although substantial

Table 5.1 Paris Declaration Indicators

Donors Primarily Responsible

- **Aid flows align on national priorities**
  % of aid for the government sector reported on the government's budget
- **Strengthen capacity by coordinated support**
  % of technical co-operation implemented through coordinated programs consistent with national development strategies
- **Use of country public financial management (PFM) systems**
  % of aid for the government sector using partner countries' PFM systems
- **Use of country procurement systems**
  % of aid for the government sector using partner countries' procurement systems
- **Strengthen capacity by avoiding parallel Project Implementation Units (PIUs)**
  Total number of parallel PIUs
- **Aid more predicable**
  % of aid for the government sector disbursed within the fiscal year for which it was scheduled and recorded in government accounting systems
- **Aid untied**
  % of aid that is fully untied
- **Use of common arrangements or procedures**
  % of aid provided in the context of program-based approaches
- **Joint missions**
  % of donor missions in the field undertaken jointly

Recipients Primarily Responsible
- **Operational development strategies**
  % of countries having a national development strategy rated "A" or "B" on a five-point scale
- **Reliable public financial management (PFM) systems**
  % of countries moving up at least one measure on the PFM/CPIA[1] scale since 2005
- **Reliable procurement systems**
  % of countries moving up at least one measure on the four-point scale since 2005
- **Results-oriented frameworks**
  % of countries with transparent and monitorable performance assessment frameworks

Joint Responsibility
- **Joint country analytic work**
  % of countries analytic work undertaken jointly
- **Mutual Accountability**
  % of countries with mutual assessment reviews in place

Source: (OECD, 2011, p. 19)

progress had been made on some of them. Specifically, two of the indicators within the recipients' scope of responsibility – the development of sound national development strategies and results-oriented monitoring frameworks – had been developed in several countries (OECD, 2011).

More progress on some of these indicators has been made in the last decade (although few of the indicators are being tracked in their original form). There has been notable progress in recipients' development planning and improved public financial management (PFM) systems. While donors have increased their alignment with country priorities and objectives, less progress has been made in donor use of country monitoring systems and results frameworks, and there is some indication that alignment is now declining. Recipient PFM systems have continued to improve, but this has not been accompanied by significantly greater use by donors. According to the Global Partnership for Effective Development Co-operation (GPEDC), use of those systems is determined more by length of country engagement and the relative size of a donor's aid within the recipient's public sector budget (GPEDC, 2020a). The overall picture from these global assessments connected with the Paris Declaration is one where recipient performance has improved more rapidly than donor performance.

At the Busan High Level meeting in 2011, the emphasis was changed from aid effectiveness to development effectiveness in recognition of the broad-based partnerships necessary for successful development. Four principles of development effectiveness were agreed: *country owner-ship, focus on results, partnerships for development,* and *transparency and shared responsibility,* and these have subsequently been used by GPEDC to monitor progress. GPEDC's monitoring efforts and indicators will be discussed later in this chapter.

Ranking Donors – Donor Perspectives

The Easterly-Williamson Series

The conversations both prior to and after the Paris High-Level Meeting on Aid Effectiveness spawned a "cottage industry" of focusing on donor practices and trying to rank donors' performance. William Easterly, a noted development economist, collaborated with Tobias Pfutze on an academic article in 2008 called "Where Does the Money Go? Best and Worse Practices of Foreign Aid". The article said explicitly that the ranking of aid agencies was based on aid practices and not on impact. The categories used were *transparency, overhead costs, degree of specialization/fragmentation, selectivity,* and *ineffective aid channels.* Data availability was an issue for some categories, especially transparency and overhead costs. As with all performance rankings, how each of the categories is measured is critical to the final ranking. For example, a selectivity score for each donor is a composite score of aid going to democratic and less-corrupt governments as well as aid giving to low-income countries. Box 5.2 shows an example of the relationship between performance criteria and indicators. Table 5.4 later in this chapter shows the top ten ranking using the Easterly and Pfutze methodology (Easterly & Pfutze, 2008).

Box 5.2   Inside Performance Ranking: Performance Criteria, Rationales, and Proxy Indicators: An Example From the Ranking Series Starting With Easterly and Pfutze

Performance Criteria	Rationale	Proxy Indicators
Transparency	Information to hold agencies accountable to recipients and taxpayers in donor countries in lieu of feedback directly from beneficiaries Improving donor coordination	• Data reporting to OECD • Data on employment, administrative expenses, salary and benefits, and aid disbursed – website, direct inquiry
Low Overhead Costs	Measure of efficiency Ensuring aid goes to beneficiaries and not agency bureaucracy	• Ratio of administrative expenses to aid • Ratio of salary and benefits to aid • Aid disbursed per employee
Less Fragmentation (specialization)	Less duplication of efforts and confusion among agencies Efficiency and more individual accountability Lower transaction costs for recipient	• Specialization by country • Specialization by sector (Herfindahl Indices)
Selectivity	Aid not sustaining authoritarian governments Aid not supporting corrupt governments Aid given to those who need it most	• % of aid going to "free" countries • % of aid going to less-corrupt countries • % of aid going to low-income countries
Effective Aid Delivery Channels	Efficiency Aid supporting recipient interests rather than donor interests	• % of aid that is tied • % of aid as food aid • % of aid as technical assistance

• Are these criteria and indicators the most important ones for donor performance?
• Are the indicators good proxies for the criteria? Are the indicators sufficient proxies for the criteria?
• Are the criteria and indicators focused mainly on the donor's perspective or on the recipient's perspective?
• Which of these would be most important from the recipient's perspective?

Source: Easterly and Pfutze (2008), Easterly and Williamson (2011), Palagashvili and Williamson (2021)

Easterly, this time collaborating with Claudia Williamson, updated the findings in 2011. They found that transparency and data availability were slowly improving, and there was a noted decline in the use of ineffective aid channels, especially tied aid and food aid. Selectivity and fragmentation continued to demonstrate poor performance. Multilateral agencies ranked better than bilateral agencies, except for UN agencies, which were generally among the worst performers (Table 5.4). As the article notes:

> This study attempts to measure if donors follow best practices, as outlined in the Paris Declaration, aid agency documents, and the academic literature, and if agency behavior is improving. The general answer is no and no, with the exceptions noted.
>
> (Easterly & Williamson, 2011, p. 1946)

Liya Palagashvila, along with Claudia Williamson, again updated the findings, this time including both OECD-DAC bilateral donors and non-DAC bilateral donors, as well as multilateral and UN agencies. The focus of their article was to assess how non-DAC donors were performing according to the same criteria used previously to judge more traditional aid donors. Those performance criteria had mainly been derived from traditional aid donor and Western academic sources. What they found was broadly consistent with previous findings: multilateral donors consistently performed better than bilateral donors. Non-DAC donors and DAC donors performed poorly, with little distinction between them. While DAC donors provided more transparency in reporting, non-DAC donors engaged in less aid fragmentation across countries and made less use of ineffective aid channels (tied aid, food aid, technical assistance). They also found that larger donors tended to perform better than smaller ones, chiefly because of greater transparency and lower overhead costs[2] (Palagashvili & Williamson, 2021).

QuODA

One of the best-known exercises to rank aid donors' performance is the Quality of Official Development Assistance (QuODA). It began in 2010 as a joint project between the Brookings Institution and the Center for Global Development (CGD). It was spearheaded by noted development economists Homi Kharas and Nancy Birdsall. QuODA uses data from other sources, while it provides inputs to at least one other index. As is the case with the Easterly-Williamson series, there is no attempt to judge aid's impact. Its objective is to assess the performance of official donors with respect to the commitments they have made and best practices in the evolving aid literature.

QuODA was originally planned to come out annually, but so far it has been repeated five times: 2010, 2011, 2014, 2018, and 2021.[3] Its coverage is limited to OECD-DAC bilateral donors and the most important multilateral donors. Over the years, it has undergone a series of changes in methodology, data sources, multilateral coverage, and indicators. Some changes in indicators may reflect changes in data availability. However, the evolution of indicators also reflects changing views about what matters in donor performance.

From 2010 through 2018, the four dimensions tracked by QuODA were *maximizing efficiency, fostering institutions, reducing the burden on recipients,* and *transparency and learning.* From 2011 through 2018, the four dimensions were represented by 31 indicators, reduced to 24 indicators in 2018. Table 5.2 lists the 2018 indicators and those that were dropped. Some indicators – coordinated technical assistance, missions, and analytical work – that had been part of the Paris Agreement

Table 5.2 QuODA 2018 – A Pared Down Index

Maximizing Efficiency	Fostering Institutions	Reducing Burden	Transparency and Learning
	QuODA Indicators 2018		
Share of allocation to poor countries	Share of aid to recipients' top development priorities	Significance of aid relationships	Membership in IATI*
Share of allocation to well-governed countries	Share of aid recorded in recipient budgets	Fragmentation across donor agencies	Making information on development funding publicly available
High country programable aid share	Share of development interventions using objectives from recipient frameworks	Median project size	Recording of project title and descriptions
Focus/ specialization by recipient country	Use of recipient country systems	Contribution to multilaterals	Detail of project description
Focus/ specialization by sector	Share of scheduled aid recorded as received by recipients		Reporting of aid delivery channel
Support of select global public good facilities	Coverage of forward spending plans/ Aid predictability		Completeness of project-level commitment data

Maximizing Efficiency	Fostering Institutions	Reducing Burden	Transparency and Learning
Share of untied aid			Share of evaluations planned with recipient
Dropped Indicators			
Low administrative unit costs	Avoidance of Project Implementation Units Coordination of technical cooperation	Coordinated missions Coordinated analytical work Use of pro-grammatic aid	Quality of evaluation policy

Source: (Center for Global Development, 2018, pp. 6, 29)

*International Aid Transparency Initiative

monitoring were dropped because they were now considered too specific for a broad index. The dropping of those indicators surely also reflects the more limited attention being given to donor coordination after 2011. Adding to the perennial reluctance of sovereign actors to voluntarily constrain their scope of action, the growing importance of non-OECD/DAC donors, many of whom want to distinguish themselves from the traditional aid donors, thwarted coordination efforts. Similarly, the avoidance of project implementation units (PIUs) and the use of programmatic aid were dropped because of changing views over the decade. While aid recipients tend to support those indicators and view related progress as part of increased ownership, donors have continued to require PIUs in many instances, largely on efficiency and fiduciary grounds. Similarly, most donors have sharply curtailed their use of programmatic aid, which earlier had been seen as a sign of increased trust in recipients and their systems. Instead, more attention is being paid to aligning aid projects with the objectives of recipient development strategies.

The shift in thinking about which indicators matter for donor performance continued with QuODA 2021. Both the dimensions and indicators were revised for the fifth edition of QuODA. The four dimensions were changed to *prioritization, ownership, transparency and untying,* and *evaluation*. These dimensions are supported by 17 indicators, of which 9 are new. Of the remaining 8, several are composites of previously separate indicators. Table 5.3 lists the 2021 indicators, showing which are new and which have been dropped entirely.

Table 5.3 QuODA 2021 – A Changing Index

Prioritization	Ownership	Transparency and Untying	Evaluation
QuODA Indicators 2021			
ODA spent in partner countries	Alignment at objectives level*	Aid reported to IATI [i]	Evaluation systems (quality)
Poverty focus	Use of country financial systems **	CRS coverage and comprehensiveness [ii]	Learning systems (quality)
Contributions to under-aided countries – "orphans"	Reliability and predictability ***	Timeliness of reporting to CRS and IATI	Results-based management systems (quality)
Core support to multilaterals	Partner feedback	Untied aid (official)	
Support to fragile states and global public goods		Untied aid (contracts) ****	
Dropped Indicators			
Significance of aid [iii] relationships	Aid share to recipients' top development priorities	Membership in IATI	
Fragmentation across donor agencies [iii]		Making information on development funding publicly available	
Median project size [iii]			
Aid share to well-governed countries			
Focus/specialization by country			
Focus/specialization by sector			

Source: (Mitchell, Calleja, & Hughes, 2021b, pp. 2, 21–23, 2021a)

Note: Shaded boxes are new indicators in QuODA 2021 not in previous QuODA versions. Lighter grey box reflects that half of the composite indicator is new (i.e., support to fragile states).

*   share of interventions from recipient country objectives and share of evaluations planned with recipient countries
**   share of ODA recorded in recipient country budget and use of country's public financial management systems
***   share of ODA received as scheduled and donor-forward spending plans
****   share of development contracts awarded to donor country companies adjusted for market share
i   International Aid Transparency Initiative
ii   OECD's Creditor Reporting System
iii   Formerly part of Reducing the Burden on Recipients

The large shifts in the QuODA 2021 dimensions and indicators again reflect changing views in the foreign aid community. While fostering institutions and ownership are similar in concept and remain an important ranking dimension, reducing the burden on recipients is no longer a dimension. Transparency and evaluation have been elevated in importance, now accounting for two dimensions.

These shifts are even more apparent when looking at individual indicators. Looking at the dropped indicators in Table 5.3, five of the nine dropped indicators relate to aid fragmentation, the need for improved donor coordination, and improved country/sector specialization among donors. This continues the trend already evident in 2018 to downplay donor coordination as an important aspect of donor performance. Fragmentation is a complex issue because there are different definitions and ways to measure it. While aid fragmentation poses difficulties, there are also potentially negative aspects of aid coordination. Among others, increased coordination can carry with it substantial transaction costs and a possibility of cartel formation among donors (McKee, Blampied, Mitchell, & Rogerson, 2020). Whatever the intrinsic value of aid coordination, the increase in the number and diversity of aid donors has made coordination more difficult. At the same time, it is debatable whether the implicit (and sometimes explicit) competition among donors or a "go it alone" strategy has resulted in improved donor performance, either individually or overall. For those recipients who are "aid darlings" rather than "aid orphans", greater aid fragmentation with less coordination has brought with it increased transaction costs and most likely efficiency losses (Klingebiel, Negre, & Morazan, 2017).

Some other changes are also noteworthy. The one governance indicator in QuODA – share of aid going to well-governed countries – has also been dropped. The rationale for this change focuses on the inherent tension between this indicator and those related to aid to fragile states and underfunded aid "orphans". This change also reflects trends within the aid community. Specifically, dropping the governance indicator highlights the move away from the official view widely held since the late 1990s that "aid works best in a good policy environment" (World Bank, 1998). It also points to the difficulties in agreeing on what good governance means in different country contexts (McKee et al., 2020, pp. 2, 48). Finally, the move is one more sign of the diminishing importance given to "good governance" in aid allocation. This importance has always been more rhetorical than real since there is little evidence that it has ever been rigorously applied in practice (Clist, 2011; Easterly & Williamson, 2011; Palagashvili & Williamson, 2021).

In contrast, two new indicators reflect a renewed focus on support to under-aided countries and fragile states, particularly in the last decade. This focus is undoubtedly based on the increasing concentration of extreme poverty in fragile states and the United Nations' "leave no one behind" as a key tenet of achieving the Sustainable Development Goals. Projections indicate that by 2030 most of the extreme poor will live in fragile states. Moreover, people living in extreme poverty will constitute more than a third of the total population in those nations (Baier, Kristensen, & Davidson, 2021). Nonetheless, apart from humanitarian aid, providing additional support to fragile states does not garner much support from the population in many donor countries who do not want to see their tax dollars going to waste, even if somehow linked to security and anti-terrorism concerns. The reduction in aid to Afghanistan, along with the US and its allies' military withdrawal from Afghanistan in 2021, are but one recent demonstration of this.

Two final changes worthy of note in QuODA 2021 are two new indicators related to reporting to the International Aid Transparency Initiative (IATI) and three new indicators related to evaluation, learning, and management (Table 5.3). These five indicators plus one on reporting to OECD constitute more than one-third of the 17 QuODA indicators. This clearly shows how transparency, data, and evidence have gained importance in both evaluating donors' performance, as well as in the thinking about what constitutes a good donor.

International Aid Transparency Initiative

The International Aid Transparency Initiative (IATI) is both the result of and part of the impetus for increased attention to transparency and the availability of data from aid providers.

The first Aid Transparency Index came out in 2011. Since then, it has undergone a series of changes in methodology and coverage. Through the changes, the index's objectives have remained constant: to improve the provision of timely, comprehensive, forward-looking data on aid and development finance that meets the needs of developing countries and other stakeholders. Since 2014, it has been published every two years. It assesses major bilateral, multi-lateral, and private aid donors' transparency using 35 detailed indicators grouped under five components: organizational commitments and planning, finance and budgets, project attributes, "joining-up development data" (linking data for a user-friendly complete picture), and performance (Publish What You Fund, 2022a). To be included in the index, an organization must meet three of four criteria: majority public ownership; aid or development finance as its primary purpose; spending of at least US$1 billion annually; and a leading role in setting policy in its home country, region, or specialization. In 2020, the index covered 47 organizations; in 2022, five organizations were dropped while eight were added, for a total of 50.

Table 5.4 provides the list of ten donors who were ranked in the "very good" category in the 2022 Index (Publish What You Fund, 2022b). IATI found no general decline in transparency due to the COVID-19 pandemic, but the UK, Canada, and the Global Fund dropped in ranking from the "very good" category. As has generally been the case, multilateral donors represent the majority of the best performers; the US (MCC – Millennium Challenge Corporation) is also represented in the top tier. In the last decade, IATI maintains that transparency has improved markedly among most donors, and well over half of all donors covered in the index were rated "very good" or "good" in 2022. It also believes that "[t]he Index continues to drive behaviour towards greater transparency and openness among aid donors" (Publish What You Fund, 2020a, p. 4).

There have been several other recent ranking exercises, among them, the Principled Aid Index (2018 and 2020), the Real Aid Index (2020), and Donor Scorecards by the ONE campaign (2019). These ranking exercises have either limited coverage, focus on donor motivation rather than performance per se, or so far have been limited efforts, published once or twice. What these indices have in common, along with the ones discussed in this chapter, is that they were produced by academics, think tanks, or NGOs mainly from donor countries. While some try to incorporate recipient views to a certain extent (e.g., highlighting the importance of ownership), they tend to use indicators that are important from the traditional donors' point of view and reflect those changing views.

Table 5.4 shows the "top ten" donors from the Easterly-Williamson ranking series, from QuODA 2018 and 2021, and from Aid Transparency 2022. Multilateral organizations dominate throughout. Other than that, there is little consistency among the "top ten" in terms of bilateral donors. While there is a constant presence of multilateral organizations, different criteria and indicators lead to different results for bilateral aid providers.

Ranking Donors – Recipient Perspectives

Listening to Leaders

AidData, a research initiative housed at the College of William and Mary, did its first report on Listening to Leaders in 2015, using data from 2014. Its second report was based on 2017 data and released in 2018. Its third report was issued in 2021, with data from 2020, and a complementary report was issued in 2022. This initiative is based on survey data from recipients and other stakeholders at the country level, as opposed to expert analysis and data largely from a donor's point of view. There are

Table 5.4 Donor Performance: Different Indices, Different Years, Different Results?

Index	Easterly and Phutze (2008)	Easterly and Williamson (2011)	Palagashvili and Williamson (2021)	QuODA (2018)	QuODA (2021)	Aid Transparency Index (2022)
Top Ten	IDA	Nordic Devt. Fund	AfDB	New Zealand	IFAD	AfDB – Sovereign^
	UK	Global Fund	Global Fund	AsDB	AfDB	IDA
	AfDB	AsDB	UNECE***	AfDB	IDA	IDB
	AsDB	AfDB	GAVI	IDB Special	Global Fund	AsDB – Sovereign^
	IDB	UK	IMF	IDA	GAVI	US MCC***
	Norway	Japan	AsDB	Denmark	Sweden	UNICEF
	Sweden	UNRWA**	GEF	Global Fund	UNDP	UNDP
	Japan	New Zealand	Nordic Devt. Fund	Ireland	Finland	UN-OCHA***
	Switzerland*	Germany	Arab Funds	GAVI	Denmark	AsDB – Non-Sovereign^
	Portugal*	IDA	UNPBF***	Australia	Canada	Canada, Global Affairs
	France*					GAVI

Source: Easterly and Pfutze (2008), Easterly and Williamson (2011), Palagashvili and Williamson (2021), Mitchell and McKee (2018), Mitchell et al. (2021a), Publish What You Fund (2022)

^ AfDB and AsDB – Sovereign includes projects that are approved with the guarantee of an official entity; AsDB – Non-Sovereign Includes private sector projects approved without an official guarantee from a national or sub-national entity.

* all ranked 9

** United Nations Relief and Works Agency for Palestine Refugees in the Near East

*** UNECE – United Nations Economic Commission for Europe; UNPBF – United Nations Peace Building Fund: US MCC – Millennium Challenge Corporation; UN-OCHA – United Nations Office for the Coordination of Humanitarian Affairs

somewhat different themes in each of the reports, but the overarching objective, as stated in the first report, remains the same:

> This first-of-its-kind survey was explicitly designed to provide timely, detailed, and accurate data on the trustworthiness, influence, and performance of 100+ Western and non-Western development partners, as observed and experienced by the in-country counterparts of development partners.
>
> (Custer, Masaki, Latourell, & Parks, 2015, p. 12)

The 2015 report focused on reform efforts and explored four variables: frequency of communication, usefulness of advice, agenda-setting influence, and helpfulness in reform implementation. In 2018, the focus was on whether priorities were aligned, with a ranking of donors on two aspects: influence and helpfulness. In 2021, the report focused again on the congruence of priorities, the characteristics that recipient country leaders value most in a development partner (donor), the "footprint" of donors, influence, and helpfulness (Custer et al., 2015; Custer et al., 2018, 2021).

In terms of priorities, the 2018 and 2021 reports concluded that donors and recipient country leaders share a commitment to strong institutions and health. Leaders in developing countries place a greater priority on education and employment than do donors (as measured by their spending). Both the 2018 and 2021 reports show a continuing misalignment of priorities among citizens, government leaders, and donors in several areas. It is, therefore, not surprising that leaders valued donors' ability to adapt their strategies to country needs as the characteristic they valued most. When asked what makes a donor "adaptable", the top answers were adapting projects to the local context, aligning projects with national strategies, and consulting local stakeholders (Custer et al., 2021, pp. 11–12).

Other valued characteristics for donors were long-term planning, useful advice or support, adherence to international standards, and providing substantial resources. Leaders said that building institutional capacity, prioritizing long-term impacts, and planning for project continuity were the most important when it came to long-term planning (p. 12). From the responses they received, the AidData team also concluded that "leaders prefer development projects that are transparent and generous, focused on infrastructure, and provide political cover to lock in desirable reforms" (p. 13).

In terms of "footprint" or how many recipients interacted with a particular donor, three multilateral agencies – the World Bank, the United Nations Development Program, and the European Union – were the largest, working with at least 40 percent of the survey respondents from

137 countries. Other UN system agencies, such as UNICEF, WHO, and FAO, as well as large OECD aid providers, such as the US, Germany, Japan, and the UK also had large "footprints". China was the leader among non-OECD bilateral donors, ranking 18th among all aid providers and 9th among bilateral donors. There are, of course, many donors who specialize in a particular region (e.g., the Asian Development Bank) or topic (the Food and Agriculture Organization) whose "footprint" is important in those areas (pp. 16–18).

The question is whether having a broad presence translates into a donor having more influence and influence that is perceived as positive by the recipient. In terms of influence, defined as helping to shape domestic policy priorities, the answer is mostly yes. The World Bank, the IMF, the EU, the US, Germany, UNICEF, UNDP, WHO, and the UK are ranked in the "top ten" for "footprint" and in the top quintile for influence (p. 29). Regional and sectoral aid providers (the European Bank for Reconstruction and Development [EBRD], IDB, AfDB, ADB, and the Global Fund) show up as strong influencers as well. Perhaps the most interesting finding is that China occupies the 8th place in terms of influence.

Influence does not always translate into positive influence. According to the report, regional or sector-focused multilaterals (e.g., ADB, the Development Bank of Latin America – CAF and small bilaterals [e.g., Ireland, New Zealand]) were viewed most positively. Japan was the only G-7 DAC donor in the "top ten" donors viewed most positively. China and the IMF were "top ten" in influence, but their influence was viewed less positively. In terms of helpfulness in implementing reforms, the story is much the same, except that both the US and IMF reappear in the top grouping for helpfulness.

Table 5.5 recaps the top donors in terms of influence, positive influence, and helpfulness. Multilateral and international organizations comprise most of the list. WHO appears in all three categories for the first time, no doubt because of the global pandemic. In some cases, donors are viewed among the most helpful, but they have less overall influence (e.g., New Zealand, GAVI). There are also a few cases where influence does not translate into positive influence and/or helpfulness. China is in the top ten for influence but moves down to 17 when adjusted for positive influence and moves to 32nd place for helpfulness. Portugal is 16th in influence and moves up two places when adjusted for positivity. It moves down to 36th place for helpfulness. The IMF, while in the top spot for influence and 3rd for positivity-adjusted influence, is ranked 14th for helpfulness. The report's authors have some reasonable conjectures regarding the mixed ratings for China (economic clout) and the IMF (more involved in the policy formulation phase than in implementation), but these explanations do not come directly from the recipients (Custer

Table 5.5 Listening to Leaders 2021: The Top Donors in Influence, Positivity-Adjusted Influence, and Helpfulness

Donor Rank	Influence	Adjusted for Positive Influence	Helpfulness
1	IMF	World Bank	Global Fund
2	World Bank	EU	WHO
3	US	IMF	UNICEF
4	EU	WHO	EU
5	WHO	US	World Bank
6	EBRD	IDB	UNDP
7	IDB	EBRD	US
8	China	UNDP	EBRD
9	UNDP	Global Fund	ADB
10	UK	UK	IDB
11	AfDB	AfDB	New Zealand
12	Global Fund	UNICEF	WFP
13	UNICEF	ADB	GAVI
14	ADB	Portugal	IMF
15	Germany	WFP	UK

Source: Custer et al. (2021)

Note: Shaded donors appear in top 15 on all three criteria.

et al., 2021). A follow-up report emphasized that leaders, in addition to financial resources, were interested in capacity building and advice and helping to mobilize external and domestic support for improving government accountability (Custer, Horigoshi, Hutchinson, Choo, & Marshall, 2022).

The *Listening to Leaders* series is valuable because it focuses on recipient views. Nonetheless, it is important to note that the topics themselves, the questions, the ranking indicators, and the interpretation of results are not formulated by the recipients, but by the US-based AidData research team.

Davies and Pickering

Another survey of aid recipient views on development cooperation and aid partners was commissioned by OECD's Development Assistance

Committee and carried out by the Australian National University's Development Policy Center. The survey, carried out in 2014 and published in 2015 and 2017, included 40 countries that were recipients of ODA (Davies & Pickering, 2015; Davies & Pickering, 2017). The survey's objective was to capture how aid recipients from the public sector see aid evolving over the next five to ten years. Much smaller in scope (61 respondents) than AidData's *Listening to Leaders*, the online survey was complemented by follow-up interviews with just under half of the recipients. Consequently, many of the findings are accompanied by explanations directly from recipients.

This survey is different from the others in that it only ranked broad categories of donors (i.e., OECD-DAC bilateral, non-DAC bilateral, and multilateral). Instead, it ranks recipient responses on topics including current and future development challenges, the changing demand for development assistance, the quality of aid, transitioning away from aid, and the performance of aid providers. Recipients saw aid providers' role changing over five to ten years from one of mostly filling funding gaps and supporting basic service delivery to a more enabling role, providing high-level technical and policy advice, and helping to mobilize private funding (Davies & Pickering, 2015, p. 19). In terms of aid modalities, the respondents expressed a clear preference in the future for general and sector budget support, while recognizing that projects would persist. This is in stark contrast to the continuing predominance today of project interventions by both OECD-DAC and non-DAC aid providers. The report concludes that "**countries favour modalities that provide alignment and flexibility**. . . . Typical reasons for preferring general budget support were that it strengthened alignment, country ownership and country systems . . . as well as reducing fiscal and balance-of-payments deficits" [emphasis in the original] (Davies & Pickering, 2015, p. 26).

The need for aid providers to practice alignment and flexibility was reinforced when the survey asked directly about the most important qualities that donors would need in the future. Alignment with country priorities, using country systems, aid on budget, predictability, and flexibility were the top five answers. These were followed by harmonization, clear policy conditions, advisory support, and untied aid. Transparency, monitoring and evaluation/learning, and efficiency were at the bottom of the list. These categories were provided by the survey designers, and the answers are indicative of relative, rather than absolute, importance (p. 27). In terms of their satisfaction with types of providers, the respondents were most satisfied with multilaterals, followed by OECD-DAC donors and non-DAC bilateral donors (p. 29). Respondents noted in the interviews that these categories were broad, and there was considerable variation within each grouping (p. 29). Although each category had its strengths and weaknesses, alignment, use of country systems, predictability, transparency, and accountability were most frequently mentioned as the areas for improvement across the board (p. 34). Unpredictability was viewed as the biggest risk to high-quality aid in the future (p. 35).

Interestingly, more than half of the recipients saw benefits in increased competition among aid providers, although officials from low aid-dependent countries, middle-income countries, and East Asia and the Pacific had the most doubts about this. As the report points out, these categories of countries are able to lead aid coordination efforts and can see benefits from increased coordination. Officials in favor of increased competition thought that it could help their government achieve more control over its aid relationships and improve the donors' collective performance (pp. 35–36).

The insights contained in the Davis and Pickering work support some of the themes related to donor performance that were also prominent in AidData's work and the expert-driven indices. Despite the use of different indicators in each, multilateral and international organizations figure prominently at the top of nearly all the indices. Ownership and alignment are prominent themes in nearly all the indices. Use of country systems, predictability, and aid on budget are also prominent, especially on the recipient side. Nonetheless, AidData's reports pointed out that alignment is far from complete and that forward planning and use of country systems are "works in progress".

In addition to areas of congruence, at least in principle, there are areas where tensions between donor and recipient views can be noted, or where views are contested within the international aid community. While prioritization and selectivity by donors are emphasized in the expert-led indices, this is much less evident in recipient views. Most recipients want to maximize the amount of aid received and are reluctant to turn down offers of aid. Consequently, most do not seem troubled by fragmentation among countries or even within countries. Recipients react favorably to what they see as a scenario for more choice, more control, and healthy competition among donors. Because of the increase in the number of donors and their diversity, as well as recipient views welcoming competition, harmonization has virtually dropped off the table as a performance indicator for donors. At the same time, fragmentation within countries, leading to increased transaction costs and less coherent programming, was flagged by some recipients. The issue of coordination/harmonization versus competition/fragmentation is still an unresolved one in the aid community.

Another area of seemingly different emphasis captured by the indices is the relative importance of transparency and evaluation. While changes in QuODA over the years imply an increased emphasis on these topics as indicators of good donor performance, this is less evident in the views of recipients. As the Davies/Pickering report noted, these topics, although not unimportant, were of relatively less priority for recipients when asked about desirable donor characteristics. A final area of difference in emphasis is aid modalities. While tied aid is still an issue for all, recipients seem less concerned about it overall. The reverse is true for budget support. Recipients want donors to provide general and sector budget support. Donors are reluctant, and budget support from bilateral donors has decreased markedly since the early 2000s.

GPEDC Monitoring and the Commitment to Development Index

The Global Partnership for Effective Development Co-operation (GPEDC) monitoring exercises and the Commitment to Development Index (CDI) will be the final efforts outlined in this brief examination of indices and ranking exercises on donor performance. As is the case with the rest of the indices and studies in this chapter, it is the characteristics or indicators that are of most interest, rather than the ranking of who is the best. These two efforts are different from most of the other indices under review because they are more comprehensive, albeit in different ways. GPEDC's monitoring looks at progress and indicators for both donors and recipients. This harks back to the Paris Declaration monitoring; GPEDC's monitoring, jointly sponsored by OECD and UNDP, is the successor effort. The CDI initiative by the Center for Global Development is one of the oldest ranking efforts. It reviews aid but also analyzes other policies and actions of aid-providing countries that could hamper global development efforts.

GPEDC Progress Reports

GPEDC was established at the Busan High-Level Meeting on aid in 2011. It was meant to provide a platform for learning and monitoring progress on development effectiveness from the viewpoint of multiple stakeholders: donors, recipients, NGOs, and the private sector. The Global Partnership tracks progress in monitoring the four agreed development effectiveness principles agreed at Busan: country ownership, a focus on results, inclusive partnerships, and transparency and mutual accountability. Those four effectiveness principles were to be tracked using ten indicators, with survey data primarily from recipient countries but also from donors. Progress reports have been published in 2014, 2016, and 2019 (OECD/UNDP, 2014, 2016, 2019). Table 5.6 shows the GPEDC monitoring framework through 2019. Some 86 aid recipient countries (including nearly all LDCs) and some 117 aid providers provided information for the 2019 report.

Of the 13 indicators (3 of the original ten indicators now have two parts), 5 were donors' primary responsibility with 2 more shared with recipient countries (OECD/UNDP, 2016, p. 5). Of course, donors also are involved in many of the other indicators (e.g., civil society

Table 5.6 GPEDC Monitoring Framework (through 2019)

Principle	Indicator No.	Indicator	Primary Responsibility
A focus on results	1a	Development partners use national development strategies and results frameworks	Donors
	1b	Countries have quality strategies and results frameworks in place	Recipient governments
Country ownership	5a	Annual predictability of development cooperation	Donors
	5b	Medium-term predictability of development cooperation	Donors
	9a	Quality of developing countries' public financial management systems	Recipient governments
	9b	Development partners use public financial management systems	Donors
	10	Aid is untied	Donors
Inclusive partnerships	2	Civil society operates within an environment that maximizes engagement and contribution to development	Recipient governments
	3	Public-private dialog promotes private sector engagement and contribution to development	Recipient governments
Transparency and mutual accountability	4	Transparent information on development cooperation is publicly available	Recipient governments/Donors
	6	Development cooperation is included in budgets subject to parliamentary oversight	Recipient governments/Donors
	7	Mutual accountability is strengthened through inclusive reviews	Recipient governments
	8	Public allocations for gender equality and women's empowerment are tracked	Recipient governments

Source: OECD/UNDP (2014, 2016, 2019)

engagement, mutual accountability). Most of the indicators for which donors had primary responsibility are familiar from other donor ranking exercises, most notably QuODA, which used GPEDC monitoring data for several of its indicators. The GPEDC monitoring does not rank individual donors but gives data for six different types of donors: vertical funds, UN agencies, multilateral development banks, other international organizations, OECD-DAC members, and non-DAC bilateral donors.

Increasingly, GPEDC monitoring has also tried to align itself with the Sustainable Development Goals and the 2030 Agenda for Sustainable Development, which came after GPEDC established its monitoring framework. Because of this and other feedback from its stakeholders, GPEDC has undergone a two-year exercise of reviewing and revising its monitoring framework. At the High-Level Summit in December 2022, the new framework was launched, which will include changes on what is measured and how it is measured. More emphasis is expected on adapting monitoring to fragile states, south-south cooperation, global challenges, and private sector activities. The framework and processes will substantially change starting in 2023 (GPEDC, 2022).

The structure of the GPEDC monitoring framework up until 2023 confirms the changes in the last 20 years in the development community's views on donors' and recipients' performance. Comparing the Paris Declaration and GPEDC monitoring frameworks shows *continuing emphasis on alignment with recipient country priorities, use of countries' own systems, predictability of aid flows, untied aid,* and *mutual accountability* in some form. Transparency, tracking gender-related public expenditures, and involvement of civil society and the private sector are prominent elements in the GPEDC monitoring framework that were absent in the Paris Declaration framework. Elements in the Paris Declaration monitoring that are no longer present include all forms of harmonization among donors, avoiding parallel Project Implementation Units, program-based approaches, and strengthening capacity through coordinated technical assistance. QuODA also dropped all these indicators in either 2018 or 2021 (Tables 5.2 and 5.3).

While GPEDC does no explicit ranking, it tracks trends over time for the six different types of donors for most indicators. Box 5.3 summarizes some highlights from GPEDC's 2019 report.

Future GPEDC monitoring will surely align more closely with the SDGs and the 2030 Agenda for Action. Monitoring of the SDGs is a work in progress, given the large number of indicators reflecting the 17 main goals. Its information on development partnerships to achieve the goals (Goal 17) is taken from other sources (e.g., GPEDC, OECD) already mentioned. Because the SDGs are so broad, their monitoring framework and indicators are not particularly useful in discerning aid priorities or judging the quality of donors.

Box 5.3 Highlights From GPEDC's 2019 Monitoring Report (*2018 Monitoring Round*)

- Recipient countries have strengthened national development plans and strategies (just under two-thirds have them), and most donors align project objectives to those plans. However, the overall share of project objectives drawn from national plans decreased from 2016 to 2018 (from 85 percent to 83 percent) (p. 100).
- Donors' use of recipient country results, statistics, and monitoring systems decreased from 2016 to 2018, with the noted exception of multilateral development banks (MDBs). Use ranged from 40 percent for non-DAC donors to 70 percent for MDBs to 86 percent for vertical funds. The overall average for indicator use was 59 percent, while the average for data use was 50 percent (p. 102).
- The annual predictability of donor aid disbursements improved from 2016–2018, with the share disbursed in the planned year rising from 83 percent to 87 percent. Progress since 2011 has been marginal when the figure was 85 percent (p. 108), and multi-year planning has weakened.
- Use of recipient public financial management (PFM) systems has improved since 2011; donors' use of those systems has not kept up with the pace of improvement. In 2011, 49 percent of funds were disbursed using those systems (budget execution, financial reporting, auditing, and procurement); in 2018, the figure was 53 percent. The MDBs and OECD-DAC members lead in using country systems, 57 percent and 55 percent, respectively (p. 115).
- Formal progress has been made in untying aid, with the share of untied aid rising to 82 percent in 2017. However, the share of untied aid received by 17 of the least-developed countries *decreased* from 2015 to 2017. Even without formal tying, many contracts are awarded to a donor country's firms. In 2015–2016, for nine OECD-DAC donors, 70 percent of contract amounts went to suppliers based in their own country (pp. 120).
- The environment for CSOs (Civil Society Organizations) in developing countries is deteriorating, with fewer protections. As for donors, "CSOs do not consider development partners' funding mechanisms to be predictable, transparent, or accessible to a diversity of CSOs and report that funding received is primarily driven by the providers' own interests and priorities"

(p. 15). Some 15 percent of the largest development projects approved in 2017 were implemented by CSOs (the third largest implementer, following the government (35 percent) and donors themselves (19 percent) (p. 131).

- Some 61 percent of aid was included in recipient country budgets subject to legislative oversight. This is a decline from 2016, when the corresponding figure was 66 percent. The decline may reflect continuing issues with reporting and direct disbursements to implementing entities outside of the public sector (pp. 50, 110).
- Transparency continues to improve at the global level with more comprehensive data from more donors. Most recipient countries have aid management systems in place, and 83 percent of donors report to these systems. Nonetheless, improvements in consistency and the quality of reporting are needed at the country level (p. 15).

Source: OECD/UNDP (2019)

Commitment to Development Index

The Commitment to Development Index (CDI) is one of the oldest and best-known efforts at ranking nations who assist developing countries. The CDI not only ranks nations on the quality and quantity of development finance (ODA, ODA-like grants, and concessional lending) but also on seven other areas of global exchange and public goods: investment, migration, trade, environment, health, security, and technology. Policies in these areas are important to developing countries. CDI shows that donors may adopt policies that thwart objectives of economic growth, environmental sustainability, and poverty reduction in the countries where they provide aid and other forms of development finance. Conversely, less-than-generous donors may adopt policies in other areas that help developing countries achieve sustainable growth.

Started in 2003, the CDI ranks donors in each of the categories and overall. Initially, the CDI only covered OECD-DAC donor countries and had only "aid" and six other categories. It added other countries as they became aid donors and joined the DAC (27 countries from 2012–2018). Starting in 2020, the index went through a significant overhaul. "Aid" was broadened to "development finance", and the structure changed into three broad themes (development finance, policies on exchange, and global public goods). Indicators, data sources, and methodologies changed in several categories. In 2021, no doubt in part as a response to the COVID-19 pandemic, "health" was added to the global public goods theme. Most importantly, in 2020, the coverage broadened significantly to include 13 new countries (mostly non-DAC G-20 members) for a total of 40 (Robinson, Cichocka, Ritchie, & Mitchell, 2020). Box 5.4 shows the evolution of CDI coverage, a concrete reflection of the growing diversity of countries providing aid (whether classified as ODA or not).

Looking specifically at development finance, the CDI gives equal weight to both quantity and quality of finance to get an overall ranking. The quantity measure differs from ODA. It only includes cross-border grants and the grant equivalent of concessional lending. It also includes contributions to multi-laterals. It excludes in-donor refugee costs, scholarships, and other items spent within the donor country. It is expressed as a percentage of GNI (Robinson et al., 2020, pp. 16–17).

Box 5.4 Evolution of CDI Coverage

Original	*Added 2008–2012*	*New in 2020*
Austria	South Korea	Argentina
Belgium	Czech Republic	Brazil
Canada	Hungary	Chile
Denmark	Luxembourg	China
Finland	Poland	India
France	Slovakia	Indonesia
Germany		Israel
Greece		Mexico
Ireland		Russia
Italy		Saudi Arabia
Japan		South Africa
Netherlands		Turkey
New Zealand		United Arab Emirates
Norway		
Portugal		
Spain		
Sweden		
Switzerland		
United Kingdom		
United States		

Source: Adapted from Robinson et al. (2020, Table 5.1, p. 5)

Obviously, donor performance is more than just the amount of finance provided, but it is a good reminder that money does matter. As for determining quality, the CDI gathers data on five indicators of bilateral finance quality, calculates a measure of multilateral quality, and weighs each according to their relative share in total finance for that donor. The five bilateral indicators (and their respective weights) of development finance quality are:

- Focus on poorer countries (40 percent)
- Share to fragile states (10 percent)
- Transparency of development finance data (20 percent)
- Share of untied finance (20 percent)
- Ownership – projects aligning with recipient objectives (10 percent)

These indicators should be relatively familiar by now; they also appear in CGD's other aid ranking exercise, QuODA. There are differences in the scoring and weighting between the two, and QuODA has more variables and covers multilateral institutions. CDI attributes multilateral aid back to bilateral donors and sets the quality measure for multilateral aid at the 67th percentile of the overall bilateral quality, weighted in accordance with its share in that bilateral donor's total. Table 5.7 compares results between CDI's and QuODA's bilateral 2021 rankings. It also compares CDI's development finance rankings with its overall rankings for the same year.

The CDI-QuODA comparisons shown in Table 5.7 make the by-now obvious point that different indicators and weights can produce quite different rankings. The CDI rankings are particularly influenced by the quantity of aid provided as a percentage of GNI, as well as the structure of the quality component. In comparing the CDI development finance rankings with the CDI overall rankings, a few things stand out. First, two non-traditional donors, Turkey and UAE, were ranked in the top ten for development finance, while in the overall ranking the newly included donors clustered at the bottom. Second, five countries figure in the top ten of both rankings: Sweden, Norway, Denmark, the UK, and the Netherlands, all OECD-DAC traditional donors. Clustering is even more pronounced where seven countries appear at the bottom in both rankings; all are countries added in 2020 (Center for Global Development, 2021; Mitchell et al., 2021a).

The Grand Finale

Taken all together, what do these studies and ranking exercises say about being a "good donor"? In recent years, there appears to be a consensus among donors, recipient governments, other stakeholders, and observers

Table 5.7 CDI and QuODA 2021 Country Rankings

QuODA Bilateral	CDI – Development Finance	CDI – Overall
Sweden	Luxembourg	Sweden
Finland	Norway	France
Denmark	Sweden	Norway
Canada	Turkey	Australia
Belgium	Denmark	UK
UK	UK	Netherlands
Ireland	Netherlands	Germany
South Korea	Ireland	Finland
Netherlands	Belgium	Canada
Iceland	UAE	Denmark
Australia	Finland	Australia
Luxembourg	Germany	Portugal
New Zealand	Switzerland	Switzerland
Norway	Saudi Arabia	Luxembourg
Switzerland	Canada	New Zealand
Germany	France	Belgium
Japan	Italy	Japan
Italy	Portugal	Ireland
Spain	South Africa	Italy
France	US	Spain
US	Austria	Czechia
Portugal	Greece	US
Austria	Spain	Slovak Republic
Czech Republic	Japan	South Korea
Poland	Slovak Republic	Hungary
Hungary	Czechia	Chile
Slovenia	Australia	Greece
Slovak Republic	Poland	South Africa
Greece	Indonesia	Turkey
	South Korea	Poland
	Brazil	Brazil
	Hungary	Saudi Arabia
	Russia	Indonesia
	Argentina	Mexico
	Chile	Israel
	New Zealand	China
	Mexico	Russia
	China	Argentina
	India	UAE
	Israel	India

Source: Center for Global Development, 2021; Mitchell et al. (2021a)

Turkey = shading represents countries added in 2020

that aligning with recipient objectives and priorities is important for donor performance, although country ownership has become somewhat muted, at least among donors. Donor flexibility and adaptability are seen as key, especially since many countries are experiencing rapid transitions and unforeseen challenges.

Recipients would like to see more predictability in aid flows and an expanded use of country systems (budgeting, procurement, monitoring, and auditing) by donors, especially where those systems have improved substantially. Donor transparency and information at the country level and processes for mutual accountability between donors and recipients are also important for recipients. As countries transition to higher income status, recipients want continued development finance, but also more advice (not conditionality) and dialog with donors they view as helpful. For recipients, the expansion of choice and the possibility of more control outweigh the transaction costs of dealing with more aid providers.

On the donors' side, the situation is a bit less clear. Donors see an increased need to provide evidence of their efforts and to demonstrate concrete results. Transparency, results monitoring, and evaluation have all gained prominence over the last two decades. Related to the need to show results, most donors are not ready to let go of project management units and have pulled back on general budget support and program-based aid. Coordination among donors has lessened in importance. Most donors practice selectivity of some kind in distributing their aid. However, there is little agreement on what selectivity means or what it should mean. Should aid go to states who are the poorest or the most fragile? Should aid go to neighbors, historical connections, or to lagging regions? Should aid go to recipient nations with weak governments or to those who are able to fully benefit from the resources? There is also little agreement on the desirability of specialization. Are donors who provide broad programming, with possibilities for synergies and cross-sector lessons, better than those that have specializations with clearer mandates and easier monitoring? Are donors that prioritize global public goods better than donors who prioritize national or sub-national public goods?

Given the differing views between donor and recipient countries and the diversity among donors, the various rating exercises and studies are not able to come up with a snapshot of the perfect donor. Multilateral agencies (a few UN agencies, multilateral banks, and vertical funds) tend to score better than bilateral donors across the board. There is only one bilateral, the UK, that appeared in the "top ten" of most indices reviewed in this chapter. Since DFID was abolished and aid moved to the newly merged Development, Commonwealth, and Foreign Office in 2020, along with serious aid budget cuts, it is unlikely that the UK will figure in the "top ten" of many indices going forward. As mentioned in an earlier chapter, DFID was the rare bilateral aid agency responsible for both policy and implementation. It was influential in many developing countries and multilateral venues, and it had a poverty focus, a competent staff, a good degree of autonomy, and positive influence. It may be that Huntington's characteristics of adaptability, complexity, autonomy, and coherence turn out to be the most helpful among all the various analyses in guiding the aid community on the necessary criteria for a well-performing aid agency.

As this chapter has attempted to show, the indices provide helpful clues and a good starting point to discern what matters to various stakeholders when they look at donor performance. Different criteria and weighting in the various indices also demonstrate the lack of consensus about what matters. It is a mistake to look to these studies and indices to reveal a definitive model of donor performance leading to increased aid effectiveness. Without going deeply into each study's methodology, what can be said is there are missing and imperfect data, assumptions (some reasonable, some not), less-than-perfect proxy indicators for some criteria, a bias towards issues that matter more to donors than recipients, and not infrequent changes in methodology, data sources, coverage, criteria, and indicators. While most attempt to use data as much as possible to establish the rankings, there are unavoidable instances of subjectivity or judgement calls. In the end, rankings are an attempt to provide a quantitative answer to a subject – performance – that has many qualitative aspects (Box 5.5).

Box 5.5 Student Views on "What Makes a Good Donor"

After reviewing much of the same content as this chapter, graduate students were put in small groups and asked to agree on the top five characteristics for a well-performing donor. The students were a mixture of US nationals and international students. This exercise was repeated 13 different times from 2007 to 2019 with a total of 49 small groups.

There was no list to choose from, so all responses were in students' own words and then grouped into categories. The most frequently cited and the number of times each was cited are given in the following list. Throughout the years, transparency and accountability, alignment, and reliability were strong themes.

- Transparency and accountability (42)
- Local ownership and alignment (24)
- Long-term commitment and reliability (24)

- Coordination and harmonization (22)
- Efficiency/Donor capacity (22)
- Specialization and selectivity (21)
- Autonomy (16)
- Capacity-building (15)
- Flexibility/Adaptability/Less conditionality (14)
- Untied aid (13)
- Local engagement and knowledge (13)
- Amount (8)

Source: Compiled from Pomerantz, 2007–2019

Policymakers and the public at large like rankings. They are easy to understand and foster competition to promote specific and, hopefully, beneficial policy or implementation changes. They are meant to recognize and encourage good performers and to "name and shame" those that are lagging. Those that are lagging receive specific "tips" on how they can advance. However, for all the reasons cited earlier, the rankings do not provide a particularly astute tool for determining donor performance or the quality of aid. At best, they are a helpful start. The next chapters go on to look beyond donor performance to the yet more difficult topic related to aid effectiveness: Are donors doing the right things?

Notes

1 CPIA is the Country Performance and Institutional Assessment tool used by the World Bank to judge IDA-eligible recipient performance. More information on the CPIA can be found on the World Bank's website (World Bank, n.d.).
2 The purpose of this chapter is to look at the performance criteria included in ranking studies and not methodological issues, but a couple of points need mentioning. The list of UN agencies varied substantially among the three studies; improved average results for UN agencies in the P&W study is partly the result of the inclusion of new UN agencies, such as UNECE (United Nations Economic Commission for Europe) and UNPBF (United Nations Peace Building Fund). Also, the P&W study does not include China, an important non-DAC donor (understandably, for lack of data), and there is a nine-year lag between the data and its publication.
3 It now is managed solely by CGD.

Bibliography

Baier, J., Kristensen, M. B., & Davidson, S. (2021, April 19). *Poverty and fragility: Where will the poor live in 2030?* Retrieved from Brookings – Future Development Blog: www.brookings.edu/blog/future-development/2021/04/19/poverty-and-fragility-where-will-the-poor-live-in-2030/

Center for Global Development. (2018). *Quality of official development assistance: QuODA 2018 methodology.* Washington, DC: Center for Global Development.

Center for Global Development. (2021). *Commitment to development index 2021 brief.* Washington, DC: Center for Global Development.

Clist, P. (2011). "25 years of aid allocation practice: Whither selectivity?" *World Development, 39*(10), 1724–1734.

Custer, S., DiLorenzo, M., Masaki, T., Sethi, T., Harutyunyan, A., & Custer, S. (2018). *Listening to leaders 2018: Are donors tuned-in or tone-deaf?* Williamsburg, VA: AidData.

Custer, S., Horigoshi, A., Hutchinson, A., Choo, V., & Marshall, K. (2022). *Aid reimagined: How can foreign assistance support locally-led development?* Williamsburg, VA: AidData at William & Mary.

Custer, S., Masaki, T., Latourell, R., & Parks, B. (2015). *Listening to leaders: Which development partners do they prefer and why?* Williamsburg, VA: AidData.

Custer, S., Sethi, T., Knight, R., Hutchinson, A., Choo, V., & Cheng, M. (2021). *Listening to leader 2021: A report card for development partners in an era of contested cooperation.* Williamsburg, VA: AidData.

Davies, R., & Pickering, J. (2015). *Making development co-operation fit for the future: A survey of partner countries.* Paris: OECD-DAC Working Paper.

Davies, R., & Pickering, J. (2017). How should development co-operation evolve? Views from developing countries. *Development Policy Review, 35*(S1), 010–028.

Easterly, W., & Pfutze, T. (2008). Where does the money go? Best and worst practices in foreign aid. *Journal of Economic Perspectives, 22*(2), 29–52.

Easterly, W., & Williamson, C. R. (2011). Rhetoric versus reality: The best and worst of aid agency practices. *World Development, 39*(11), 29–52.

GPEDC. (2020a). *Making development co-operation more effective: Headlines of Parts I and II of the global partnership 2019 progress report.* OECD/UNDP.

GPEDC. (2020b). *How we partner together: Work program 2020–2022.* Retrieved from GPEDC website: www.effectivecooperation.org/system/files/2020-11/GPEDC_2020-2022_Work_Programme_FINAL_15May%20%281%29.pdf

GPEDC. (2022). *Rebuilding trust through effective development co-operation – special report.* GPEDC.

Huntington, S. W. (2006). *Political order in changing societies.* New Haven: Yale University Press.

Klingebiel, S., Negre, M., & Morazan, P. (2017). Costs, benefits and the political economy of aid coordination: The case of the European Union. *European Journal of Development Research, 29*, 144–159.

Lancaster, C. (1999). *Aid to Africa: So much to do so little done.* Chicago: University of Chicago Press.

McKee, C., Blampied, C., Mitchell, I., & Rogerson, A. (2020). *Revisiting aid effectiveness: A new framework and set of measures for assessing aid "quality".* Washington, DC: Center for Global Development.

Mitchell, I., Calleja, R., & Hughes, S. (2021a). *The quality of office development assistance (results brief).* Washington, DC: Center for Global Development.

Mitchell, I., Calleja, R., & Hughes, S. (2021b). *The quality of official development assistance: QuODA 2021 methodology.* Washington, DC: Center for Global Development.

Mitchell, I., & McKee, C. (2018, November 15). *How do you measure aid quality and who ranks highest?* Retrieved from Center for Global Development.

OECD. (2006). *DAC in dates: The history of OECD's development assistance committee.* Paris: OECD.

OECD. (2011). *Aid effectiveness 2005–10: Progress in implementing the Paris declaration.* Paris: OECD.

OECD/DAC. (2021). *Peer reviews of DAC members.* Retrieved from OECD.org: www.oecd.org/dac/peer-reviews/

OECD/UNDP. (2014). *Making development co-operation more effective: 2014 progress report.* Paris: OECD Publishing.

OECD/UNDP. (2016). *Making development co-operation more effective: 2016 summary report.* Paris: OECD Publishing.

OECD/UNDP. (2019). *Making development co-operation more effective: 2019 progress report.* Paris: OECD Publishing .

Palagashvili, L., & Williamson, C. R. (2021). Grading foreign aid agencies: Best practices across traditional and emerging donors. *Review of Development Economics,* 654–676.

Pomerantz, P. (2007–2019). *What makes a good donor.* Duke University: Durham, NC

Publish What You Fund. (2020a). *Aid transparency index 2020.* Retrieved from Publish What You Fund: https://www.publishwhatyoufund.org/the-index/2020/

Publish What You Fund. (2022a). *2022 transparency index technical paper.* International Aid Transparency Initiative.

Publish What You Fund. (2022b). *Aid transparency index 2022.* Retrieved from Publish What You Fund: https://www.publishwhatyoufund.org/the-index/2022/

Robinson, L., Cichocka, B., Ritchie, E., & Mitchell, I. (2020). *The commitment to development index: 2020 edition, methodological overview paper.* London: Center for Global Development Europe.

World Bank. (1998). *Assessing aid: What works, what doesn't and why.* New York: Oxford University Press.

World Bank. (n.d.). *IDA resource allocation index (IRAI).* Retrieved from World Bank: https://ida.worldbank.org/financing/resource-management/ida-resource-allocation-index

6 The Great Aid Effectiveness Debate

In the previous chapter, the discussion focused on donor performance and how it should be measured from both the donor and recipient point of view. There are many other aspects to aid effectiveness, including open questions about how aid monies are best spent and how to maximize aid's impact on growth and poverty reduction. The great aid effectiveness debate goes one step further and questions whether developmental aid should exist at all. Even before the end of the 20th century when the debate heated up, there were earlier concerns about aid from critics such as Milton Friedman, a Nobel laureate and one of the leaders of the neo-classical Chicago school of economics at the University of Chicago, and P.T. Bauer, a Hungarian economist who taught at the London School of Economics (Friedman, 1995; Bauer, 1984). There were also highly sophisticated champions of aid, including President Harry S. Truman of the United States and Robert McNamara, a US Secretary of Defense who went on to become the president of the World Bank.

The debates on aid effectiveness have been extensive, boisterous, and occasionally, enlightening. After nearly three decades of intense debate, there are few definitive conclusions. This chapter will recap the debates among several well-known academics and public intellectuals that focus on some of the "big questions" surrounding aid. It will end by highlighting some of the problems involved in evaluating aid that partially explain why the debates have been, in the end, inconclusive.

The Public Debate Heats Up

The public debate on aid effectiveness stems from the events in the 1980s and 1990s – the structural adjustment, "Washington Consensus" era. Despite extensive reforms in the neo-classical tradition, growth stagnated in many of the reform countries in Latin America and Africa. The reforms, supported with aid, brought social and political unrest to many countries. Not all of the unrest was negative: political unrest in Africa led to a "third wave" of democratization. Generally, however, there was

DOI: 10.4324/9781003265320-8

a widespread feeling of disappointment. Similarly, after the break-up of the Soviet Union and the adoption of market economies in many of the "new" countries, results were highly variable. Steep declines in GDP and economic depression lasting ten years, despite aid, were the norm for many, including Russia, with sharply deteriorating standards of living. At the same time, there was rapid growth in Asia, especially in India, China, and Vietnam. Those countries had also reformed, but not by following the prescriptions of donor countries. By the mid-1990s, the donors themselves were experiencing "aid skepticism" and "donor fatigue"; ODA amounts started dropping.

Against this backdrop, it is not surprising that a public debate surrounding aid roared to life. Among many participants, a few voices stand out: Professors Jeffrey Sachs and Joseph Stiglitz, along with Bono, as proponents of aid and Professors William Easterly and Angus Deaton, along with Dambisa Moyo, as opponents of aid. This public debate questioned the fundamental reasons for aid and its impact. Most critics did not question the need for humanitarian or emergency aid, but they were focused on longer-term developmental aid.

The Sachs-Easterly debate began publicly in 2005, when Sachs published *The End of Poverty*. The book portrayed global poverty and tried to explain why it persisted. It was an eloquent entreaty to the industrialized nations to end the "poverty trap" that imprisons people and nations. Sachs' conclusion essentially was that aid needs to increase to end extreme poverty. In addition to laying out a rational argument, the book was an emotional plea: "The effort required of the rich is indeed so slight that to do less is to announce brazenly to a large part of the world, 'You count for nothing'" (Sachs, 2005, p. 288). Easterly, in both a *Washington Post* review and a subsequent academic article, likened Sachs' approach to the "Big Push" popular in the 1950s and 1960s, when many economists thought that development was largely a problem of filling financial gaps. "The danger is when the utopian dreams fail (as they will again) the rich-country public will get even more disillusioned about aid" (Easterly, 2005, p. BW03).

Over the next few years, Easterly became even more critical of aid, arguing a few salient points in books and articles. The key point was that large amounts of aid had been given with much less than expected returns. The reasons for this included where the aid was given (to corrupt and incompetent governments), who gave the aid and to whom (bureaucrats with perverse incentives and little or no accountability), and how the aid was given (with no involvement of the intended *beneficiaries* who know more than the bureaucrats and "experts" about what they need) (Easterly, 2006, 2013b).

Sachs argued that what needs to be done is "not rocket science", and the knowledge to improve people's lives exists and is readily accessible (for example, Sachs, 2014). On the other hand, Easterly pointed to all the policies that have not worked and emphasized that there are no silver bullets that produce growth and end poverty (Easterly, 2002). Furthermore, rapid growth incidences, such as those experienced by India, China, and Vietnam, happened with relatively little aid as a percentage of GDP (Easterly, 2007, p. 329). While Sachs touted all the knowledge that development experts have in areas like education, health, and agriculture, Easterly was highly skeptical that "experts" could design the type of localized, bottom-up interventions that poor people need.

Sachs decided that a "proof of concept" would help convince policymakers and the public of the feasibility of ending poverty with relatively modest amounts of aid per capita and technical expertise. In 2005 he started the Millennium Villages Project with the first village, Sauri, in western Kenya. The idea was that a set of integrated investments and actions, costing US$110 per capita over a period of five years and guided by some dedicated technical specialists, would allow chosen villages to reach the Millennium Development Goals (MDGs), including ending extreme poverty. The project was later extended to 2015, and costs per capita rose. At its height, the MVP had 14 sites encompassing 80 villages with half a million people in ten countries. The project was controversial from the onset. There was enthusiasm in some quarters. For example, US university students started raising money for the project and hoped to do internships in the villages. In other instances, it was met with skepticism about its paternalism and doubts about its replicability and sustainability (Rich, 2007). The villages demonstrated some successes in the provision of health and education infrastructure and immunizations, but they were unable to show sustainable income increases. The MVP final evaluation pointed to some asset accumulation and other accomplishments but admitted that only one-third of the goals were met (Mitchell et al., 2018). An independent evaluation of the MVP in northern Ghana documented similar accomplishments and shortfalls. It also pointed to the need to ensure there was local testing and adaptation for project activities, even for interventions with successful track records elsewhere (e.g., bed nets, vaccinations). It concluded that sustainability remained a key challenge (ITAD, 2018).

This was not a surprise. Earlier, in 2013, Nina Munk, who had followed Sach's "experiment" for years, came out with an influential and moving book that documented Sach's determination and ultimately his failure. Time after time, things did not go as planned. In one instance, controlling malaria was one of Sach's priorities, and distributing treated bed nets, especially for use by children, was one of the project's interventions. However, things did not go as planned in one of the villages. As she relates:

> Traditionally, nomadic pastoralists rely on smoke to keep mosquitoes from attacking their livestock. . . . "It is easier to simply use the nets to protect the animals," said Ahmed, explaining why in Dertu some nets were being diverted from a child's bed to a herd of kid goats. "And in a pastoral community, the livestock have more value than humans."
>
> (Munk, 2013, p. 55)

Easterly, in his review of Munk's book, *The Arrogance of Good Intentions*, sums up the MVP:

> Sachs offered a seductive message to Westerners: that they could be the saviors who could end poverty in Africa with a modest amount of effort. After reading Munk's superb book, nobody will ever again think ending poverty is really that easy.
>
> (Easterly, 2013a, p. 32)

For all the publicity that Easterly garnered for his verbal jousts with Sachs and for his books with expressive titles – *The Elusive Quest for Growth: Economists' Adventures and Misadventures in the Tropics, The White Man's Burden: Why the West's Efforts to Aid the Rest Have Done So Much Ill and So Little Good*, and *The Tyranny of Experts: Economists, Dictators, and the Forgotten Rights of the Poor* – it was Dambisa Moyo's first book that kicked the public debate on aid into high gear. Moyo, a Zambian economist who spent her adult life living outside of Africa, published *Dead Aid* in 2009. In *Dead Aid* and elsewhere, she takes a more extreme view than Easterly, arguing that aid has, in fact, been harmful to Africa and is responsible for millions of people remaining in abject poverty (Moyo, 2009).

> The problem is that aid is not benign – it's malignant. No longer part of the potential solution, it's part of the problem – in fact aid *is* the problem.
>
> (p. 47)

She likened Africa to a drug addict.

> Africa is addicted to aid. For the past sixty years it has been fed aid. Like any addict it needs and depends on its regular fix, finding it hard, if not impossible, to contemplate existence in an aid-less world. In Africa, the West has found its perfect client to deal to.
>
> (p. 75)

The arguments against aid that Moyo used were, for the most part, already prevalent in some parts of the aid community. According to Moyo, aid creates a vicious cycle, propping up corrupt governments that then interfere with the rule of law, institutions, and civil liberties. The unfavorable conditions created then make domestic and foreign private investment unattractive. This leads to fewer employment opportunities and increasing poverty, resulting in more aid. In addition, aid makes corruption worse: the additional money in the public sector attracts the unprincipled and creates a situation of rent-seeking and endemic corruption. Some of the stolen funds find their way back into the economy, but large sums leave the country. When donors place conditions on their aid to regulate its use, conditions are seldom enforced. Moreover, the traditional donors frequently equate a good policy environment with democracy out of a belief that democracy helps to sustain economic growth. However, Moyo argues that democracy can be harmful in the early stages of development and gives examples of high-growth scenarios under autocracies such as Pinochet's Chile and Fujimori's Peru.

Somewhat contradictory to her argument of corruption siphoning off much of the funds, she also argues that aid serves to reduce savings and investment, including directly crowding out high-quality foreign investment. She also makes the case that aid can be inflationary, further choking off investments and making exports more expensive. All in all, aid diverts people's attention from productive activities to politics, weakens accountability, and diminishes overall social capital and trust in the society. Aid is also, therefore, a culprit in fomenting social unrest and conflict, one of the most serious obstacles to economic growth in Africa.

Moyo found a ready audience among Africa's youth and in some of the academic communities in the United States and Europe. Part of *Dead Aid*'s allure was that it was written by an African woman. She was largely dismissed in the aid practitioner community because she had never worked on the ground in development or with aid and because many of her claims remained unsubstantiated. Unlike Easterly and Sachs, who published academic papers with (albeit contested) technical evidence to underlie their claims, Moyo's book was based largely on anecdotal evidence and was an emotional plea to wean Africa off aid. Ironically, by making aid and external actors the central cause of the continent's problems, Moyo joins Western donors in placing too much emphasis on donor influence and the centrality of aid in African development.

Nonetheless, *Dead Aid* energized public and academic debates about aid effectiveness around the world. Furthermore, Moyo was joined by some critics who could not be dismissed so easily. One of the most prominent was Angus Deaton, a Nobel Laureate, professor at Princeton

University, and noted scholar on poverty. Like Moyo, he argues that aid is an obstacle to poverty reduction (Deaton, 2013).

> This is one central dilemma of foreign aid. When the "conditions for development" are present, aid is not required. When local conditions are hostile to development, aid is not useful, and it will do harm if it perpetuates those conditions.
>
> (p. 273)

Specifically, giving aid to governments with poor institutions and "toxic politics" is harmful. He also returns to the question of motivations for bilateral aid, which is mostly guided by the donor's domestic and global interests, rather than the needs of the poor in the recipient country. He notes, as shown in Chapter 4, that much ODA does not go to low-income countries and that aid may be less important for poor countries than other resources such as trade, innovative technologies, and remittances. In addition, for a variety of reasons, aid does not work like investment as a source of capital that can help foster growth. For Deaton, aid is more like a commodity boom that can come and go divorced from domestic needs and local politics, increasing government expenditure in a way that may not be sustainable (Deaton, 2013).

Moreover, Deaton argues that aid causes harm by diverting the recipient government's attention from more important tasks. Beyond that, the most serious harm comes in countries where aid forms a large part of government spending and breaks the feedback and accountability link between the government and the governed. The recipient government, if accountable to anyone, is accountable to the donors and not to its citizens. Consequently, aid has a dampening effect on civil society and democracy and undercuts the institutions needed to foster long-term growth. Moreover, accountability to the donors does not work well. He asks, together with Easterly, "Who put *us* in charge?" (Deaton, 2013, pp. 312, 349); why should donor views preempt local ones? In addition, donors do not have the same direct experience and are not as informed as the local population. Even when donors know what is going on, they are reluctant to exercise sanctions, enforce conditions, and stop aid because of a complex set of professional incentives along with the knowledge that an abrupt halt to aid could make the situation even worse. So threats and face-saving compromises take the place of real consequences in most cases.

Despite these sharp criticisms, there is a powerful case for aid with important advocates. In addition to Sachs, the foreign aid establishments in many countries are in favor of aid as part of their diplomatic toolbox. The merging of aid agencies into foreign policy ministries is one concrete signal of this. As many have noted, during the Cold War, aid was given not necessarily for developmental purposes, but to gain alliances and stave off gains by the other side. So, as noted earlier when discussing the motivations for aid, aid has an instrumentality that goes far beyond its developmental role. As for its developmental role, aid is seen as increasing savings and financing investment in poor countries to generate growth. It can also help provide needed foreign exchange in poor countries to finance growth-inducing imports. Further, aid can fund investments in health and education, valuable in themselves, but also able to increase labor productivity and directly contribute to economic growth. Aid is also seen as valuable as a conduit for the transfer of technology and knowledge from rich countries to poor countries (Radelet, 2006).

In the public debate on aid effectiveness, by far the most prominent argument in favor of aid is its role in helping the poor escape from misery. As early as 1973, Robert McNamara, then president of the World Bank, in a well-known speech in Nairobi, Kenya, made a powerful case for aid:

> And are not we who tolerate such poverty, when it is within our power to reduce the number afflicted by it, failing to fulfill the fundamental obligations accepted by civilized men since the beginning of time? . . .
>
> There are of course, many grounds for development assistance: among others, the expansion of trade, the strengthening of international stability, and the reduction in social tension.
>
> But in my view the fundamental case for development assistance is the moral one. The whole of human history has recognized the principle – at least in the abstract – that the rich and the powerful have a moral obligation to assist the poor and weak.
>
> (McNamara, 1973, pp. 7–8)

Since that time, his sentiments have been echoed by many. For example, Nicholas Kristof, noted *New York Times* columnist, after touting some of aid's successes, strikes an even more emotional note:

> Smallpox was a great success but not a fluke. Among other historical foreign aid successes are immunizations, oral rehydration therapy and the green revolution.
>
> More broadly, when we pay a few hundred dollars for fistula surgery so that a teenage girl no longer will leak urine or feces for the rest of her life, that operation may not stimulate economic growth. But no one who sees such a girl's happiness after surgery can doubt that such aid is effective, for it truly saves a human being.
>
> (Kristof, 2007, p. A19)

Others have also touted aid's positive accomplishments. Steve Radelet, arguing against cuts in US foreign aid, noted that aid programs have played a significant role in health improvement, including lives saved among those suffering from HIV-AIDS, tuberculosis, polio, and malaria. He also cited the important role aid played in the gains in girls' education in Afghanistan, an accomplishment today sadly in jeopardy (Radelet, 2017). Bill and Melinda Gates, in their Annual Letters from the Gates Foundation, have defended aid and touted its accomplishments. And in the *Wall Street Journal* Bill Gates has called his funding of health delivery through the Global Fund, GAVI, and the Global Polio Eradication Initiative (GPEI) "the best investment I've ever made" (Gates, 2019).

One more set of Nobel Laureates has weighed in on the aid effectiveness debate, perhaps somewhat unintentionally. Abjihit Banerjee and Esther Duflo were awarded the Nobel Prize for their espousal and practice of randomized controlled trials (RCTs) to evaluate development interventions. They have consistently argued that there is plenty of room for improving specific policies and actions leading to better results. While no single RCT can bring about improvements in overall aid and development effectiveness, over time, a set of RCTs together can yield findings that can result in improved effectiveness on a wider scale. They took this route intentionally, having been convinced that the big questions regarding whether and under what circumstances aid or development "works" are unanswerable. In direct contradiction of Moyo's and Deaton's views, Duflo had this to say in 2011:

> The primacy of politics over policy that is at the heart of the institutionalist view is perhaps overemphasized. What we term the political-economy view is that without good politics, there won't be good policies, and conversely, that good policies will follow from politics. I want to argue that neither is true. It might even be possible to reverse the argument: perhaps good politics will follow good policies.
>
> (Duflo, 2011, p. 2)

More recently, Banerjee and Duflo have been even more direct in their skepticism of those seeking answers to big questions:

> Economists, ourselves included, have spent entire careers studying development and poverty, and the uncomfortable truth is that the field still doesn't have a good sense of why some economies expand and others don't. There is no clear formula for growth. . . .
>
> At a more fundamental level, these efforts to discover what causes growth make little sense. Almost every variable in a given country is partly a product of something else. . . . Trying to tease out single factors that lead to growth is a fool's errand.
>
> (Banerjee & Duflo, 2020, pp. 22, 24)

That article, published in *Foreign Affairs*, elicited a written response from Jeffrey Sachs:

> They understand poverty as a big puzzle to be solved mainly through experiments, notably randomized controlled trials. . . . There are not huge mysteries about what is needed to end extreme poverty. Practical solutions are largely known and within reach; what poor countries need is not more economists performing randomized trials to confirm what experts already know but good governance and development assistance to cover financing gaps. . . .
>
> The rejection of development aid, combined with a disdain for existing development knowledge, is the real cause of the continuing crisis of extreme poverty in the midst of great global wealth.
>
> (Sachs, 2020, pp. 186, 189)

The one thing that seemingly unites Sachs, Easterly, Moyo, and Deaton – and differentiates them from a major part of the academic development community today – is their skepticism that the answer to aid and development effectiveness follows the route of numerous RCTs conducted by trained economists focusing on specific, micro-level issues within projects. There will be more on RCTs and their findings in the next chapter.

What to make of these starkly differing views on aid in the public domain? In this age of data and evidence, why is it so hard to evaluate aid effectiveness? Before reviewing the evidence on aid effectiveness at the macro and micro level in the next chapter, it is timely to reflect on exactly why it is so hard to have a clear picture of aid's impacts.

Issues With Evaluating Aid Effectiveness

There are serious issues that stand in the way of evaluating aid effectiveness at both the macro level (overall effectiveness) and the micro level (individual interventions or projects). Some of these issues can be overcome with good analysis, while others are more difficult to resolve.

Unclear or Multiple Objectives

The type of aid discussed in this book is presumed to be given for developmental or humanitarian purposes. Harking back to the aid motivations discussed in Chapter 3, the reality is far more complex. While interventions can be evaluated based on stated intentions, this may not yield valid results in the case of aid. In fact, aid with stated developmental objectives may be given for other reasons, such as security concerns, fear of contagious disease spread, global warming, alliance-building, and vote-buying in the United Nations (see, for example, Dreher, Nunnenkamp, & Thiele, 2008). Some academics argue that aid allocation may increasingly be a product of "targeted development" – both developmental and in the donor's self-interest (Bermeo, 2017). Others argue that at least some aid of that type should not be considered developmental at all: the financing of global public goods benefits the world as a whole and can be viewed as a type of compensatory finance to recipient countries for their outsized contribution to fighting global bads that others created (Kaul, Isabelle, & Stern, 1999; Kaul, Blondin, & Nahtigal, 2016). While there has been some debate about this, including at COP-27, the 2022 environmental conference in Egypt, the concessional financing of global public goods in developing countries is today an integral and growing part of aid. On the topic of aid with multiple objectives, Lancaster concluded, "It is, therefore, irrational and potentially highly misleading to evaluate *all aid* according to only one of its purposes" (Lancaster, 2007, p. 222). Evaluating aid effectiveness correctly under these circumstances is more complex and costly.

Apart from aid with purposes that are not strictly developmental, many aid projects suffer from multiple objectives. It is not unusual, especially in large projects, to have project descriptions that point to increasing incomes for a specific group, capacity building for one or more levels of government and/or communities, providing sustainable infrastructure, training technicians, and so on. These objectives are not necessarily at odds with each other, but implementation will almost certainly be uneven. The amount of funds designated for each objective is generally not a sound basis on which to prioritize objectives. Moreover, the objectives and related project components were put together for a reason (in theory, if not always in practice), so treating each one as separate has its perils. How then to judge the overall effectiveness of a project with uneven implementation? As many project evaluators will say, this is a matter of judgment. Unclear or multiple objectives "muddy the waters" when it comes to judging aid effectiveness.

Attribution

A single donor is seldom the only player in a developmental initiative. For most development interventions, whether policy or investment-based, there are several sources of finance – from the government, other donors, beneficiaries, and so on. In addition, there is a long results chain. Donors put funds in, and after that, many things happen. Even with good monitoring, it is hard to attribute success or failure to any one player or link in the chain. While RCTs can perhaps establish attribution for the success or failure of a specific type of intervention under controlled circumstances, most projects and programs are far more opaque. Confusion on this point is understandable because both donors and recipients are quick to claim responsibility for successes and to attribute failures to other parties.

The structural adjustment loans and grants of the 1990s and 2000s mentioned in Chapter 2 are a good example of attribution difficulties related to aid effectiveness. Donors, especially multilateral donors such as the IMF and the World Bank, played key roles. They recommended policy changes and provided funds to help with the transition period. Even today, many years later, there are still questions and disagreements as to why the programs, also dubbed the Washington Consensus, did not result in an immediate resumption of growth in many countries and made the situation worse in others, causing social unrest and increased misery. For the last 20 years or so, it has become fashionable to attribute failure to flawed policies designed by the donors. Most mainstream economists would rebut this and insist that the failure was due to implementation flaws directly attributable to the governments: lack of high-level commitment and integrity, lack of technical expertise, and lack of knowledge of the political economy within their own societies. In reality, the mix of these design and implementation issues differed from country to country, with the likelihood that both donor and recipients shared responsibility. Consequently, attribution for aid effectiveness, or the lack thereof, is difficult and time-consuming in each country. This matters because if you don't know definitively what went wrong, it is impossible to improve.

Time Consistency

To make judgements about aid effectiveness even more complicated, there are issues with time. The time needed to judge whether a policy or an investment intervention has been effective varies. Furthermore, with many interventions, benefits only come to complete fruition years later. One of the biggest issues is when to evaluate a project and program. Most project evaluations have traditionally been done when the investment period has been completed. This is a reasonable checkpoint to ensure that project inputs, financed by aid, have been provided. However, it is far too early to make judgements about positive impact, and importantly, the sustainability of that impact. Most development professionals have had the disappointment of going to visit what was deemed a successful project intervention in the past, only to discover that little or nothing is left of the project. Even in those instances, it may be overstated to conclude that the project was a complete failure, since project activities may have been useful during a critical period or beneficial as a transition.

With a renewed emphasis on results-based or performance-based aid, more attention is being paid to monitoring and evaluation. This has also meant a push for doing evaluation as early as possible, in some cases, even before inputs have been fully delivered. This can result in aid volatility as donors conclude prematurely that a project will not be effective (Bour-guignon & Sundberg, 2007, p. 319). On the other hand, evaluating a project intervention after a long period of time has elapsed also has issues. The more time that has passed between the intervention and the evaluation of the benefits, the more difficult it is to discern the exact role of aid. If there are no long-term benefits, it perhaps is clear that aid has not been effective, but again, there is little way of knowing precisely what went wrong in the results chain without intensive investigation. If there are long-term benefits, it becomes quite difficult to discern whether these were directly caused by the aid provided, or if, in the meantime, other things happened to bring about the results. If the project was planned to have an experimental or quasi-experimental evaluation design, things may be somewhat clearer, but those types of evaluation are still relatively rare and have their own set of issues, as will be discussed in the next chapter.

To continue with the example of structural adjustment, early evaluation showed highly disappointing results in many countries (e.g., Zambia), while a handful of countries showed some immediate response (e.g., Tanzania, Uganda). However, from today's vantage point, there is accumulating evidence that countries that underwent some type of structural adjustment have done relatively better over time than countries that did not undergo structural adjustment (Easterly, 2019). Easterly, using this case, also emphasizes the perils of early evaluation:

> The results are an interesting case study in the use of evidence in the political economy of reform. When new reforms are announced with as much fanfare as the Washington Consensus, there is pressure to evaluate the reforms as soon as possible. This can lead to what this paper documents, to premature pessimism about reform before the reform process is even complete and before enough post-reform growth is available. Later results may show this pessimism to be mistaken, but there is much less interest in evaluating reforms by that point.
>
> (p. 34)

Exogenous Variables – "Stuff happens"

Another difficulty is that aid interventions do not take place in a laboratory setting. In the real world, things happen that can easily derail development efforts. Droughts, floods, epidemics, and coups are just a few of the many things that can delay or wipe out project activities and benefits. This seems to make for an easy evaluation: aid was not effective because something exogenous (an event outside of the project) happened.

If only it were that easy! In countless examples, excessive optimism keeps projects open – and funds disbursing – long after it becomes clear that the environment is not conducive to success. Where aid administration by the government and/or the donor is nimble and flexible, it may be possible to redirect the funds relatively quickly to humanitarian relief or other more suitable uses given the changed circumstances. In many of these cases, however, donors are not quick to recognize the threat to project viability or cannot easily amend agreements to change the use of aid monies. Excessive optimism, a donor's limited knowledge of the context or extent of the issue, poorly motivated donor and recipient staff, and rigid rules and processes can each conspire to keep aid flowing when there is little hope of it being used productively. When it comes time to evaluate the aid, the story becomes that the project or program did not work because of the floods, the coup, or other event. That, of course, is not the whole story. The decisions and actions (or the lack thereof) by the involved recipients and donors most certainly played a role. Even apparently simple evaluations of aid effectiveness have their own complexities.

Aid Based on Need and Fragile States

The poorest and most fragile states rely on aid. These are precisely the types of places where governments are generally weak or not committed to the needs of the poor or to development in general. Aid granted to those governments is unlikely to be effective. Some donors attempt to get around this problem by providing aid directly or through local organizations and NGOs, bypassing the government in hopes that the funds will reach the ground and do some good. Other donors risk providing aid to the government in hopes of building capacity and having at least some funds reach the beneficiaries.

With humanitarian aid, especially one-time efforts, it may be either necessary or desirable to bypass the government and work with other organizations when states are truly fragile and the needs are critical. There is less of a case to be made for developmental aid extending over a period of years. Bypassing the government is not a recipe for more effective public goods and service delivery over the long term. This brings the discussion right back to where it started, with the varying objectives of aid and what is meant by aid effectiveness. It is attractive to believe that there is room for multiple objectives (and there *is* some room) in aid interventions, but the trade-offs also need to be acknowledged. Rapid delivery may mean slower capacity-building. Relying on NGOs to deliver development assistance may have the effect of sustaining a weak or uncaring government in power. On the other hand, aid in the hands of a weak or corrupt government may never reach the intended beneficiaries at all or may serve to prop up the regime. Without incentives and commitment, building longer-term capacity is an illusion.

Evaluating aid granted to fragile states is extremely difficult. How much "leakage" through corruption or mismanagement is acceptable? Should the focus be entirely short-term? How does one contribute to a lessening of fragility over time? In other words, how do you measure success in those circumstances? One measure may be lives saved, but not all aid to fragile states is emergency aid. Once again, there may be different meanings as to what is a good outcome and what constitutes effective aid.

With so many issues involved in evaluating aid, it is no wonder that the "Great Aid Effectiveness Debate" took place and continues until today. Yet, despite the issues and the many gaps, progress has been made in evaluating the impact of aid. The next chapter relies on an existing framework for thinking about aid effectiveness and uses the framework to review the evidence and current practice.

Bibliography

Banerjee, A. V., & Duflo, E. (2020, January–February). How poverty ends: The many paths to progress – and why they might not continue. *Foreign Affairs*, *99*(1), 22–29.

Bauer, P. (1984). *Reality and rhetoric: Studies in the economics of development.* Cambridge, MA: Harvard University.

Bermeo, S. B. (2017). Aid allocation and targeted development in an increasingly connected world. *International Organization*, *71*(Fall), 735–766.

Bourguignon, F., & Sundberg, M. (2007). Aid effectiveness: Opening the black box. *American Economics Review*, *97*(2), 316–321.

Deaton, A. (2013). *The great escape: Health, wealth, and the origins of inequality.* Princeton, NJ: Princeton University Press.

Dreher, A., Nunnenkamp, P., & Thiele, R. (2008). Does US aid buy UN general assembly votes? A disaggregated analysis. *Public Choice, 136*, 139–164.

Duflo, E. (2011). Policies, politics: Can evidence plan a role in the fight against poverty? In *Sixth annual Richard H. Sabot lecture.* Washington, DC: Center for Global Development.

Easterly, W. (2002). *The elusive quest for growth.* Boston, MA: MIT Press.

Easterly, W. (2005, March 13). A modest proposal. *The Washington Post*, p. BW03. Retrieved from www.washingtonpost.com/wp-dyn/articles/A25562-2005Mar10.html.

Easterly, W. (2006). *The White man's burden.* New York: Penguin Press.

Easterly, W. (2007). Was development assistance a mistake. *American Economic Review*, *97*(2), 328–332.

Easterly, W. (2013a, October 7). The arrogance of good intentions. *Barron's*, p. 32.

Easterly, W. (2013b). *The tyranny of experts.* New York: Basic Books.

Easterly, W. (2019). *In search of reforms for growth: New stylized facts on policy and growth outcomes.* Cambridge, MA: National Bureau of Economic Research .

Friedman, M. (1995). *Foreign economic aid: Means and objectives.* Palo Alto, CA: Hoover Institute.

Gates, B. (2019, January 16). *Bill Gates: The best investment Ive ever made.* Retrieved from Wall Street Journal online: www.wsj.com/articles/bill-gates-the-best-investment-ive-ever-made-11547683309

ITAD. (2018). *Impact evaluation of the SADA millennium villages project in Northern Ghana: Endline summary report.* Retrieved from ITAD: https://www.itad.com/wp-content/uploads/2020/02/MV-Eval-FINAL-report-for-website_8.10.18-ID-181622-2-1.pdf

Kaul, I., Blondin, D., & Nahtigal, N. (2016). Understanding global public goods: Where we stand and where to next. In I. E. Kaul (Ed.), *Global public goods* (pp. xiii–xcii). Cheltenham: Edward Elgar.

Kaul, I., Isabelle, G., & Stern, M. A. (1999). *Global public goods: International cooperation in the 21st century.* New York: Oxford University Press for UNDP.

Kristof, N. D. (2007, August 9). Bono, foreign aid, and skeptics. *The New York Times*, p. A19.

Lancaster, C. (2007). *Foreign aid: Diplomacy, development, domestic politics.* Chicago: University of Chicago Press.

McNamara, R. S. (1973). Address to the board of governors. *World Bank/IMF annual meetings.* Nairobi, Kenya: IBRD.

Mitchell, S., Gelman, A., Ross, R., Chen, J., Bari, S., Huynh, U. K., . . . & Namakula, P. (2018). The millennium villages projects: A retrospective, observational, endline evaluation. *The Lancet, 6*(5), e500–e514.

Moyo, D. (2009). *Dead aid: Why aid is not working and how there is a better way for Africa.* New York: Farrar, Straus and Giroux.

Munk, N. (2013). *The idealist: Jeffrey Sachs and the quest to end poverty.* New York: Doubleday.

Radelet, S. (2006). *A primer on foreign aid.* Washington, DC: Center for Global Development.

Radelet, S. (2017, May 8). *Once more into the breach: Does foreign aid work?* Retrieved from Brookings Institution Future Development website: www.brookings.edu/blog/future-development/2017/05/08/once-more-into-the-breach-does-foreign-aid-work/

Rich, S. (2007). Africa's village of dreams. *The Wilson Quarterly, 31*(2), 14–23.

Sachs, J. D. (2005). *The end of poverty: Economic possibilities for our time.* New York: Penguin Press.

Sachs, J. D. (2014, June 23). *The global goal everyone forgot.* Retrieved from jeffsachs.org: www.jeffsachs.org/newspaper-articles/6nhpa463b88ar2dr27ctygxcjj8ykf

Sachs, J. D. (2020, May–June). Trials and tribulations: A response to "how poverty ends". *Foreign Affairs, 99*(3), 186–189.

7 Opening the "Black Box" of Aid Effectiveness

With multiple objectives, a long results chain, varying times from inputs to impact, and a host of other issues, aid is an elusive subject for evaluation. It is no wonder that determining aid effectiveness is frequently difficult, not only in the aggregate but even at the project level.

Francois Bourguignon and Mark Sundberg, in a well-known article, had this to say: "Trying to relate donor inputs and development outcomes directly, as through some kind of black box,[1] will most often lead nowhere" (Bourguignon & Sundberg, 2007, p. 317). Instead, they argue for disaggregating the results chain (or the causality chain, as they call it) into three separate linkages or relationships:

- Policies to outcomes (Knowledge)
- Policymakers to policy (Governance)
- External donors to policymakers (Aid relationships)

After briefly examining the meaning of these linkages, this chapter will use the framework to examine the evidence and some recent trends in thinking about aid effectiveness.

Opening the "Black Box"

Policies to Outcomes

Much of the aid effectiveness literature has focused on the first relationship of policies to outcomes. Of the three relationships, this is the most technical and the priority for development economists. Some may argue that not much is known (given that there are multiple studies about "big picture" questions with greatly varying results). Others may add that results are country-specific and difficult to generalize. Even so, as many economists have pointed out, there are some things that have been learned over the last 60 or so years, even with the understanding that caveats and exceptions will always exist. For example, there is a consensus

DOI: 10.4324/9781003265320-9

that macroeconomic stability is critical for investment and that economic growth has been the best route to poverty reduction in many countries. Knowledge at the micro and project level has also expanded, thanks to RCTs and other forms of experimental or quasi-experimental research designs. However, just because knowledge has been generated does not mean it will be used by either aid recipients or donors in their decisions on aid. That is why the other two relationships are so critical.

Policymakers to Policy

The second relationship – policymakers to policy – is fundamentally about governance and how decisions are made within a nation. There is a long-standing argument about what good governance means and how important it is. There was a period during the structural adjustment era when it was thought that improving governance was the missing link to economic growth and aid effectiveness (Rodrik, Subramanian, & Trebbi, 2004). More recently, Acemoglu and Robinson have argued that inclusive societies produce better policies and better outcomes (Acemoglu & Robinson, 2012, 2019). However, there is no consensus on this. As seen in the previous chapter, Banerjee and Duflo are skeptical about the role of institutions, arguing that perhaps good policies lead to better institutions and not necessarily vice versa. Others, including Jeffrey Sachs, have pointed out that while institutions are important, they are just one of a number of variables involved in economic development (Sachs, 2003). Dani Rodrik, one of the early enthusiasts, issued a *mea culpa* for placing too much emphasis on institutions' role in economic development and issued a sharp critique of what he termed "institutional fundamentalism" (Rodrik, 2006, p. 979).

The contested role of governance in economic development means that there is less certainty around the relationship of policymakers to policy, other than the basic fact that it matters. The question in practical terms boils down to how decisions are made. The *Growth Report* of some years ago clearly stated that the type of regime – democratic or otherwise – did not seem to make much difference. What the commission who produced the report deemed important was "an increasingly capable, credible, and committed government" (Commision on Growth and Development, 2008, p. 3).

There is a good deal of wisdom packed into that short phrase. A capable government has the ability to gather and digest relevant information and can take sound decisions within an appropriate timeframe. A credible government is one that both citizens and partners recognize as a sovereign authority that does what it says it will do. A committed government is one whose values and actions are aligned with those of poverty reduction and economic development. And finally, it is a government that does not stagnate, but adapts to changes and gets better over time.

That still leaves much to be discovered about how policymakers make policy in a particular moment in a particular country. The extent of consultation and debate, the degree of decentralization and participation, the formation and "mental models" of key policymakers, as well as the overall internal and external environment, all contribute to the process. In many developing countries, aid is an important part of the external environment, which leads to the last relationship.

Donors to Policymakers

Aid relationships are particularly difficult to categorize because the rhetoric does not always match the reality. It has been fashionable for some years now to talk about partnership and government ownership of aid efforts. However, the reality is much more complex and contested. There are at least three basic ways to characterize the relationship of donors to recipient country policymakers:

- Principal-agent relationship
- Contractual relationship
- Partnership

Note that these are not conceptually similar in their formation nor mutually exclusive: they are characterizations or models and not categorizations.

Aid as a Principal-Agent Relationship

In this characterization of aid, the donor is considered the principal and the recipient is the agent. Donors provide aid because they want the recipient to do something, e.g., build a bridge or educate children. Donors cannot do this directly, so they must rely on governments as agents. If the donor and government interests are perfectly aligned, this is a smooth relationship. However, a perfect alignment between donors and recipients seldom exists, and recipients frequently will take the donors' money and use it differently or imperfectly. The donor does not necessarily have good information on what is happening because feedback from the ultimate recipients is missing or because the agent is also responsible for providing the information (Paul, 2006; Martens, Mummert, Murrell, & Seabright, 2002).

Looking at aid as a principal-agent relationship gives rise to some consequences. It acknowledges and cements an unequal relationship between donor and recipient, continuing the type of relationship that began with conquest and colonialism. It negates the principle of recipient ownership since the ultimate owner is the aid provider. It creates resentment and secrecy on the part of the recipient government while nurturing arrogance and mistrust on the donor side. It makes recipient governments primarily accountable to donors, as opposed to local citizens, and the relationship is perceived as a threat to national sovereignty. Consequently, recipients look for ways to diminish their aid dependency over time while recognizing they have limited leeway in the short-term. Donors often look for ways to mitigate the risk in the situation. At times, this means looking for another agent, bypassing the government, and providing aid through alternative agents such as consulting firms, NGOs, or grassroots organizations. At other times, this means insisting on conditionality to bind the recipient agent to do the principal's bidding exactly as the principal wishes. It can also involve trying to educate the recipients so that they will ultimately understand that the donor's views are the "correct" ones.

The characterization of aid as a principal-agent relationship is intellectually attractive because it is clear-cut and corresponds to the way that aid was practiced, particularly in those countries where the former colonial power became a chief aid donor or where one donor, through the sheer size of its aid budget, was able to become the dominating force. It is precisely this formulation of aid that has drawn so much criticism, first on moral and political grounds, but also because of a noted lack of aid effectiveness. How much donor-recipient relations still adhere to this model is an open question, but it is safe to say that principal-agent dynamics are still widespread in aid relationships, especially in low-income countries.

Aid as a Contractual Relationship

Aid as a contractual relationship stands in contrast to the paternalism of the principal-agent characterization of aid relationships. Here there is a presumption of two independent entities agreeing on the boundaries and details of their relationship. In return for funds provided, recipients have obligations (for example, specified reporting requirements). Some of the newer models of aid delivery, Cash on Delivery and Program for Results, are based on this, with funds only released after agreed targets are met. In this model, there is no need for discussion of overarching common objectives or approval of a government's overall budget and priorities. It requires a relationship, but one that does not go beyond that forged in a contractual "deal". If the contract is not honored on either side, the relationship breaks. In the 1990s and 2000s, several donors, including some multilateral institutions, began referring to recipients as "clients" to further the idea of a service industry bound by contract to a client. While this has receded in favor of partnerships, today some non-traditional donors, such as China, tend to follow this model, emphasizing mutual benefit and non-interference in sovereign affairs.

Advanced middle-income countries, who can lead the aid dialog and negotiate with donors, tend to fit this characterization better. Lower-income countries, particularly those who have an arrangement with the IMF and/or are aid-dependent, have difficulties in negotiating on a contract-by-contract basis. It's also difficult for low-income countries to have limited, contractual relationships with former colonial powers. There is too much shared history and continuing ties to treat a negotiation as a one-off deal executed by equal (at least in this context) parties. In addition, traditional donors are seldom satisfied by the limited extent of dialog implied in this model.

Aid as a Partnership

Since the early 2000s, it has become fashionable to refer to aid relationships as partnerships. Donors are referred to as development partners, while recipients are called country partners. The idea is that both parties are together in the development enterprise, with true "ownership" of policies and actions by the country and with development partners acting consistently with country objectives and strategies. Instead of the one-way accountability of the principal-agent model, there are clearly understood mutual obligations and accountability. Plans are discussed in advance and agreed by both partners, with comprehension of the limitations on each side. It is a relationship that goes beyond a single contract. For example, partner countries are expected to improve their financial management systems for projects and other sector operations. Development partners are committed to helping in this and, most importantly, to use those systems when they are deemed strong enough.

Whatever the rhetoric, the reality on the ground is far different. Frequently, there is disappointment on both sides, with both sides claiming that the other has not lived up to expectations. For true partnerships to exist, solid trust is needed on both sides. In turn, trust is built on a foundation of common objectives, commitment over the long haul, reliability, transparency, and open and honest communication (Pomerantz, 2004). While some of these conditions can exist for some period between a country and an individual development partner, it is rare for true partnerships to endure because of changes in senior officials and policies on either side. Oftentimes, policy changes come from above for reasons that are beyond the specific aid relationship. Successful partnerships do sometimes develop at the project level and last for several years, but those are also subject to personnel changes and are finite. Characterizing aid relationships as a partnership is aspirational. The problem is that it is confusing for newcomers and leads to disillusion and cynicism among experienced staff.

Conflict and Bargaining

Whatever form aid relationships take, they can be passive, peaceful, or conflictual. Pablo Yanguas, in his analysis of aid, remarks on the inevitability of conflict in a process that is fundamentally about change.

> The fiction of aid as a technical, accounting process crumbles upon contact with reality. Development is not a series of fixes to be measured but of battles to be fought. Transformational change is predicated on institutional change, which is bound to create winners and losers.
>
> (Yanguas, 2018, p. 204)

It is more likely that aid relationships will be conflictual than peaceful. However, passivity is also part of the overall picture. In a principal-agent relationship, the agent may choose to be passive, hoping that passivity will allow the game to continue. Pritchett, Woolcock, and Andrews have written extensively about how governments, encouraged by donors, go ahead with "best practice" reforms to obtain financing. Donors then see the reforms unravel for a variety of reasons, including lack of capacity, suitability, or commitment. They characterized this practice as isomorphic mimicry, and where relationships fit the principal-agent model, it is likely extensive (Andrews, Pritchett, & Woolcock, 2017).

Others see the relationship as a continual bargaining process independent of the characterization of aid relationships as principal-agent, contractual, or partnership. However, neither side can guarantee it will live up to its commitments, and enforcement is weak. Swedlund and Lierl used a bargaining framework to explain the rapid rise and decline of general budget support as an aid modality. Recipients wanted budget support because it was more reliable than aid for individual projects. Donors, in turn, wanted budget support because it bought them "a seat at the table": involvement in larger policy discussions, including how the government's budget was spent. Thus, the bargain was struck. However, when donors did not live up to their commitments and stopped budget support for reasons unrelated or only partially related to economic reform, the bargain unraveled (Swedlund & Lierl, 2019). Dijkstra countered that the recipients preferred budget support not because it was more predictable, but because it allowed recipient governments more leeway in their spending preferences. The decline in budget support was much more one-sided: the donors lost interest over the last decade in "ownership" and the aid effectiveness agenda, with aid policies dictated increasingly by foreign policy and business concerns (Dijkstra, 2021, p. 1034). Despite the debate on what happened to budget support, the bargaining framework is useful because it makes the point that not all the power and the leverage are on the donor's side in the relationship.

Disaggregating the "black box" into three distinct linkages involving knowledge, governance, and relationships helps to demystify the aid process. It provides a structure to begin to analyze aid effectiveness in any given situation. Yet, it does not necessarily make aid effectiveness easier to achieve or to evaluate, especially when most of the attention has been paid to the technical aspects of projects or reforms. It is of little wonder that the evidence on aid effectiveness is plentiful but frequently contradictory. Now that it is clear how complex it is to assess aid effectiveness, it is time to turn to that evidence.

The Evidence on Aid Effectiveness

In this section, some of the evidence on aid effectiveness is reviewed using the three linkages – policies to outcomes, policymakers to policies, and donors to policymakers – as the organizing principle. The first section on the technical knowledge base is divided in two: the evolving picture on macro effectiveness and the evolving picture on micro (project level) effectiveness.

Policies to Outcomes – the Knowledge Base

In many ways, this linkage should be the easiest to understand and to assess: Did *x* produce *y* result? However, the difficulties in assessing aid, including time consistency and attribution issues, come into play. Not surprisingly, the answers look quite different from the "big picture" macro perspective as compared to the micro perspective closer to the ground.

The Evolving Macro Picture

The economic literature on macro aid effectiveness seeks to answer two fundamental questions: Does aid increase economic growth and, if yes, under what conditions?

As the backdrop to these questions, it is worthwhile to recall that economic growth and poverty reduction in low and middle-income countries were relatively strong in recent times up until the outbreak of the coronavirus pandemic. That, of course, is not evidence of aid effectiveness, since aid is but one relatively small variable in the overall equation, and some of the fastest growing economies, such as China, had relatively small amounts of aid.

What does the economic literature say about aid effectiveness? To be direct, it says: "yes, no, maybe", using increasingly complex statistical techniques and cross-country regressions. Since the 1960s, there have been several waves of aid effectiveness studies. In the 1970s and 1980s, there were a series of academic articles that focused on aid's impact on domestic savings. More savings meant more investment and more growth according to the theory of that time. Aid champions thought that aid would lead to a dollar-for-dollar increase in savings. However, many of the results indicated that it increased domestic saving less than expected because of "leakages", including poor government expenditure choices and corruption. This was also the period when the concept of the "micro-macro paradox" emerged. While many aid projects were reported as successes, their collective impact did not show up at the macro-level (Mosley, 1996). Using more sophisticated econometric methods, Boone's work reinforced pessimism about aid's contribution to economic growth (Boone, 1994). The *Economist* article about his work on aid was titled "Down the Rathole" (Anonymous, 1994). In short, the 1990s constituted a period of aid pessimism, with a sizeable literature questioning aid effectiveness. This correlated with what was happening in reality: "aid fatigue" had set in, and aid budgets were cut.

The new millennium began on a different note. Craig Burnside and David Dollar published a World Bank working paper and an *American Economic Review* article, supported by a new data base and analysis, that argued that aid has a positive impact on growth, but only in developing countries that have good fiscal, monetary, and trade policies (Burnside & Dollar, 1997, 2000). This message was reinforced and brought into the aid practitioner community by a widely circulated World Bank report *Assessing Aid: What Works, What Doesn't, and Why* with the mantra that aid works best in a good policy environment. This message was intuitively attractive to aid officials involved every day in the reform process. It essentially argued for selectivity as opposed to conditionality that was increasingly difficult to enforce in countries that were reluctant reformers. It is hard to overestimate the influence that *Assessing Aid* had on the donor community, continuing until the present day. While donors may have chosen for many reasons not to follow its advice, there was little doubt in their minds that it was true.

"Aid works best in a good policy environment" was not without its critics. In addition to the sticky problems of precisely defining "good" and sustainable policies in a specific context, or what the implications were for countries with poor policies, Burnside and Dollar's work led to a new wave of studies that found the original analysis far from robust. Some of those studies argued that a positive aid-growth relationship occurred independent of specific policies, while others argued that there was little or no effect from aid on growth. Still others argued that the type of aid mattered, or the time period studied (see among others, Hansen & Tarp, 2000; Easterly, Levine, & Roodman, 2004; Rajan & Subramanian, 2005; Clemens, Radelet, Bhavnani, & Bazzi, 2012). There was also a renewed emphasis on the role of institutions and governance as part of the "good environment", another area with contested evidence.

By the second half of the 2000s, there had been so many studies on the overall impact of aid that new efforts began on meta-analysis or analyzing the studies together to see whether a robust conclusion was possible.

Doucouliagos and Paldam initiated the trend in 2008, with updates in 2011 and 2013 (Doucouliagos & Paldam, 2008, 2011, 2013). Their conclusion is that, in the aggregate, aid has had little economic importance in generating growth, although they note that aid has had a positive impact on growth in Asia and that some elements of aid, such as debt relief, could have a positive effect on growth. Their findings have been rigorously contested by Channing, Jones, and Tarp, who consistently find an overall positive relationship between aid and growth. Finally, Mekasha and Tarp updated their earlier meta-analysis to match the time period of Doucouliagos and Paldam's analysis and continued to find a positive and statistically significant relationship between aid and growth (Mekasha & Tarp, 2013, 2019). Macro aid effectiveness studies are ongoing for individual countries, time periods, or sectors.

The hopeful answer from all these studies and debates is that at least some aid is effective. Nonetheless, the statistical and econometric techniques presently available, coupled with continuing data difficulties, are perhaps not quite sharp enough to produce a clear-cut answer to the question as to whether aid, in the aggregate, helps to produce growth. Meanwhile, the studies of macro aid effectiveness continue.

The Evolving Micro Picture – Project-Level Evaluation

Up until the 1970s, evaluation of development projects was largely ad hoc. USAID created an Office of Evaluation in 1968, and in 1973, based on earlier efforts, Robert McNamara, the President of the World Bank, created OED, the Operations Evaluation Department. USAID's Office was largely project-based, using a log-frame approach, identifying project goals, objectives and strategy, activities, and results, with corresponding indicators derived from baseline data. OED had a somewhat broader mandate, and by the mid-1970s had a Director-General with the rank of Vice President who reported directly to the Board of Directors (as opposed to bank management). The basis of the World Bank evaluation system that evolved was the Project Completion Report (PCR), written by the responsible operations department, with the assistance of the borrowing country. OED was to review the PCR and issue a Project Performance Audit Report (PPAR). A yearly review of PPARs would provide an annual "scorecard of performance" (Willoughby, 2003, p. 9), as well as identify trends by country, issue, or sector that could be subject to additional evaluation. Other bilateral and multilateral donors followed suit in the 1970s and created their own evaluation units.

The project evaluations produced by the various donors are far from uniform or universal. Even today, many do not go beyond reporting on the inputs provided or are issued only in the donor's principal language and not translated into English or the recipient country's language. Other evaluations provide information on outputs and the fulfillment of project objectives, and some agencies perform comprehensive reviews for groups of projects like those done by the World Bank's OED (now called IEG – Independent Evaluation Group). To try and standardize norms for evaluation, OECD DAC adopted a set of principles for the evaluation of development assistance in 1991, aimed at future improvement of development efforts and to provide accountability along with public information on performance. After a series of reviews and subsequent revisions, DAC approved quality standards for development evaluation in 2010. The standards were comprehensive in scope, meant to apply to reviews of development agencies and broad themes, as well as individual projects. Among other factors, the standards stressed independence, ethical behavior, partnership, and quality in the evaluation process (OECD DAC Network on Development Evaluation, n.d.).

While OECD's initiative has been useful, in practice development agencies continue to "do their own thing", and evaluations continue to have variable quality and usefulness. Aid agencies, despite an avowed dedication to learning from the past to improve performance, are understandably reluctant to showcase failures given their dependence on government budgets. Consequently, many agency evaluations emphasize the positive and attempt to show satisfactory performance. As an example, the latest public balanced scorecard on performance produced by the World Bank showed that IEG considered over 82 percent of the completed operations reviewed during fiscal years 2019 to 2021 as having satisfactory outcomes (World Bank, 2022). It should be noted that the World Bank continues to be a positive exception since it reviews and issues project completion reports for every operation; many agencies do not have a comprehensive system, and evaluation is still sporadic or fairly rudimentary. However, even the World Bank cannot escape the subtle biases that argue in favor of declaring that a project has substantially met its objectives.

Aid pessimism and the falling aid totals of the 1990s led to a renaissance in project level evaluation in the early 2000s. The renewed interest in project evaluation was also a reaction to the contradictory and confusing macro aid effectiveness analyses and the feeling that standard prescriptions for growth, like the Washington Consensus, were not working. Donors and academics alike wanted more robust evidence on the conditions under which development interventions could work and how aid projects could be improved. The Abdul Latif Jameel Poverty Action Lab (J-PAL) was established in 2003 as a global research center associated with the Massachusetts Institute of Technology (MIT), "working to reduce poverty by ensuring that policy is informed by scientific evidence" (Abdul Latif Jameel Poverty Action Lab, 2022). Ester Duflo and Abjihit Banerjee were the driving force behind J-PAL and the rise of randomized impact evaluations (RCTs – randomized controlled trials, as they were called in medical research) in development work. Innovations for Poverty Action (IPA), with close ties to J-PAL, was created around the same time as a non-profit doing similar kinds of research, impact evaluations, and dissemination of results. Box 7.1 gives a brief description of the methodology and uses of RCTs. In 2008, the International Initiative for Impact Evaluation (3IE) was created. 3IE conducts RCTs, other types of formative and impact evaluations, systematic reviews, and evidence-gap analysis, combining a diverse set of quantitative and qualitative evaluation tools.

Box 7.1   What Exactly Is a Randomized Controlled Trial (RCT) in Development Work?

RCTs have been prominent in the scientific and medical community for some time. In medicine, their purpose is to measure the effectiveness of a new intervention. Researchers select the population, the type of intervention (treatment) to be compared, and the potential outcomes. The number of participants is calculated to ensure statistical reliability, and participants are recruited and randomly assigned to either a group receiving the intervention or to a comparator or control group. In medicine, RCTs are often blinded so that the involved parties (i.e., participants, doctors, nurses, researchers) do not know what treatment each participant is receiving. The fundamental objective of an RCT is to be able to determine cause and effect with as little bias as possible. In a methodological article, medical researchers called it "the gold standard for effectiveness research" (Hariton & Locascio, 2018).

Since the early 2000s, RCTs have been increasingly used in development to assess whether a particular intervention is having the forecast impact or to find out what kind of impact an intervention is having. In other words, this is experimentation in the "real world" on the ground. For both practical and ethical reasons, many development RCTs have a cluster design, where the intervention and the control groups are clusters of participants, e.g., villages or sub-districts, so that everyone in the group receives or does not receive the intervention. There is a statistical determination ("power calculation") of how many clusters and how many participants within each cluster need to be randomly sampled for the results to be considered valid (White, Sabanwal, & de Hoop, 2014). RCTs have been used in a wide variety of contexts: to evaluate the impact of different methods of cash transfers to the poor, specific health interventions, new curricula in schools, and job training programs, among many others. The use of RCTs has sparked controversy among practitioners and academics about its role in determining aid effectiveness (Boxes 7.2 and 7.3).

With the push of J-PAL and IPA especially, RCTs became the evaluation method of choice and have been embraced by many social science researchers engaged in development work. RCTs are considered by some to be the "gold standard" for project impact evaluation, while others consider that they are but one tool among many in the toolbox and not necessarily the best one. Boxes 7.2 and 7.3, respectively, list some strengths and limitations of RCTs.

Box 7.2 Strengths of Randomized Controlled Trials in Development Work

- RCTs have brought new vitality to development evaluation and primary data collection.
- RCTs can be used to test innovations and alternative delivery mechanisms and modes.
- RCTs eliminate many (but not all) sources of conscious and unconscious bias in evaluation.
- RCTs need to be planned well ahead of the intervention with design generally well thought through as to intervention, theory of change, outcomes, and impact; they have brought a certain discipline to project planning and evaluation.
- Rigorous, adequately powered RCTs have a greater level of reliability (internal validity) compared to other research methods.
- RCTs work best in clear-cut situations where it is feasible to answer questions about attribution and causality and the intended impacts of the intervention are clear and measurable.
- RCTs are based on the scientific belief that changes in knowledge will lead to better development results.
- There are different methods of randomization that allow for customization to the situation.
- In theory, large numbers of RCTs could provide answers to the same question in a variety of circumstances, thus increasing the external validity of the findings.
- Development RCTs have moved academic work back out to the field and have given many young researchers invaluable field and project management experience.
- Philanthropic funders are attracted to RCTs since it allows one to go directly to the field level, bypassing government bureaucracies.

Sources: Hariton and Locascio (2018), Gaille (2020), White et al. (2014); Bedecarrats, Guerin, and Roubaud (2020), Ogden (2016)

Box 7.3   Limitations of Randomized Controlled Trials in Development Work

- RCTs are not helpful where poverty is more the result of macro-policies and the prevailing political settlement as opposed to technical knowledge about what works.
- RCTs do not work well in situations of uncertainty, where design is still ongoing or where implementation flexibility is needed.
- RCTs are relatively costly and time-consuming, with complex logistics, raising the possibility that they could be "crowding out" other valuable data gathering and analytical methods.
- RCTs generally require a large sample to be statistically valid in measuring impact.
- The quality of RCTs can suffer from attrition (participants dropping out of either the control or treatment group), "contamination" (similar interventions being carried out in the control area or participants crossing over from one group to the other), and lack of compliance with the process. Also, randomization does not guarantee that the treatment group and the control group will be similar without additional controls.
- Doing RCTs in the field frequently involves compromises and deviations from the strict protocol, which can detract from the reliability of the findings.
- Ethical concerns have been raised about RCTs because of their experimental nature and the fact that the control group does not receive the intervention. Some of these concerns can be mitigated by ensuring that if the desired benefits materialize, the control group will also receive the intervention, albeit at a later stage. However, the principles of "informed content" and "do no harm" have not always been respected and/or have jeopardized the internal validity of the experiment.
- RCTs are not comprehensive evaluations because they can only evaluate the short-term impact of interventions with simple causal chains.
- RCTs cannot analyze the mechanisms and processes of how impact occurs. They measure impact but cannot tell how or why it occurred without complementary data and analysis using other methods.
- Randomization is not the only form of experimentation; trial and error, along with other forms of experimentation, can produce useful insights more quickly in given circumstances.

- Producing comparable RCTs in different environments allowing for generalizable conclusions is, in practice, extremely difficult to achieve and may not be the most effective method. Unless there is a robust series of similar trials in different environments, external validity, or the applicability of the results of RCTs to other settings, will always be in doubt.
- RCTs generally study the impact of interventions at the individual level, but change also happens at more aggregate levels as individuals and groups interact with each other. Evidence and analysis leading to big reforms and policy changes are still needed.

Sources: Hariton and Locascio (2018), Gaille (2020), White et al. (2014), Bedecarrats et al. (2020), Deaton (2020), Picciotto (2020), Ogden (2016)

Thousands of experimental and quasi-experimental impact evaluations have taken place over the last 20 years. What have these RCTS yielded in terms of development knowledge?

First, a great deal of site-specific, project-specific design and implementation knowledge has been gained. RCTs are an important tool for understanding which delivery methods or types of interventions work best in a particular setting. Second, they have brought increased discipline to the field of development evaluation; it is no longer acceptable to produce a "snapshot", single-point-in-time impression and call it a serious evaluation. Third, RCTs have mostly spelled an end to evaluations that attribute all changes to the project. RCTs, by having a control group, allow for the recognition and discounting of changes that happen independently of the project. This has influenced other methodologies as well. Fourth, in a limited number of cases, where similar RCTs have been conducted in a variety of country settings, J-PAL and IPA have been able to come to a somewhat robust (albeit still contested) conclusion about the effectiveness of certain types of interventions. This has been the case with micro-finance, where seven RCTs in six countries found little or no poverty reduction impact from small group lending (Banerjee, Karlan, & Zinman, 2015). The second case disseminated by J-PAL and IPA has been the "graduation approach" for interventions that help the ultra-poor. The approach originated in Bangladesh with BRAC, one of the largest and most successful NGOs in the world. RCTs conducted in six different country settings found promising evidence that an intensive package of assistance providing a productive asset, training, and cash over a relatively short period of time (less than two years) could help families break out of extreme poverty (Banerjee et al., 2015).

To summarize, micro-level evaluation has yielded some valuable insights and knowledge. However, as Picciotto noted:

> Finding out whether an intervention works is not the same as examining whether it was the right intervention, figuring out why it performed the way it did or whether its goals were worth pursuing in the first place.
>
> (2020, p. 276)

Moreover, it is unclear whether and how knowledge generated from most RCTs will yield any changes. Without understanding how policy is formulated and implemented – the governance and aid relationship pieces – it is hard to see how the data from RCTs can help bring about the type of significant, albeit small, changes needed and achieve impact.

In summary, the knowledge about how specific policies affect outcomes at both the macro and micro levels is growing and becoming more robust. There are some indications that aid at the aggregate level and specific aid interventions at the project level can be effective in promoting growth and poverty reduction. Yet, it is less certain why this happens in some cases and not in others. How policies are formulated, how decisions are made, and how aid relationships function are essential pieces of this puzzle.

Policymakers to Policies – Governance

There are many fields that have studied how policymakers make decisions. In the development context, political science, economics (especially institutional and behavioral), and public policy are absorbed with this question, with psychology, anthropology, and sociology also playing a role. There is an enormous amount of scholarship. Not surprisingly, there are few clear answers and much controversy as noted previously. Important historical analyses have attempted to show that variations in economic growth and development have been brought about by differences in institutions and governance in the broadest sense (Acemoglu & Robinson, 2012; Fukuyama, 2011, 2014). However, the exact nature of the relationship between governance and economic growth is still an open question.

Among development theorists, there are those who believe that economic growth has a larger impact on governance than the impact of governance on economic growth. There are also those who strongly believe the direction of causality runs in the other direction. Supported by cross-country empirical analysis and specific case studies, the evidence is contradictory and probably signifies that the relationship runs in both directions. The important fact here is that there *is* a relationship (Durlauf, 2020). While many studies deal with broader concepts of institutions and governance, the relationship validates the importance of development policymakers, since they are shaped by the prevailing institutions, and, in turn, help shape future policies and institutions, including those related to economic growth.

There also have been many studies about whether the type of political regime within which policymakers operate makes a difference. There has been questioning as to whether democracy is a help or a hindrance for economic development. Democracy presents a conundrum: economic development needs decisive, committed leadership, while democracy is a system of government designed to weaken the power of an autocrat. Economic development needs fast decision-making, while democracy can be a slow and painful process. Fragile states need to strengthen their "state power" (control over territory, ability to provide basic services for all, recognition by the population). Democracy may come into direct contradiction with the strengthening of the state, with competition resulting in increased societal tensions and cleavages (Fukuyama, 2007). So while there is a clear popular yearning for democracy among many throughout the world, it may not always provide the ideal conditions for a policymaker to take decisive, "development-friendly" actions.

In contrast, the concept of the "developmental state" became broadly popular in the 2000s. First introduced by Chalmers Johnson in relation to Japan in the post-war period, more recently it has come to be associated with the East Asian model of strong, state-led macroeconomic planning, where the principal objective of rapid economic growth is pursued in tandem by the government and the private sector (Chambers, 1982; Onis, 1991). While a developmental state can be either democratic or autocratic, the examples of China, Viet Nam, Singapore, and more recently, Rwanda have led some to conclude that autocratic regimes may have an advantage in their ability and commitment to consistently pursue economic development (Wilkins, 2011).

Not surprisingly, the results of cross-country studies have been contradictory and inconclusive as to the effect of regime type on economic growth. A meta-analysis in the 2000s concluded that there were no positive or negative direct effects of democracy on growth. It also concluded that there were some positive indirect effects through impacts on the level of economic freedom, inflation, and political stability (Doucouliagos & Ulubasoglu, 2008). Yet, some autocratic developmental states, such as the ones mentioned previously, have been remarkably stable with good macroeconomic management.

What does this mean for a policymaker in a developing country and how policies, including those related to aid, are developed? First, as noted earlier, the type of political regime does not appear to be a decisive factor. Policymakers, whatever the regime type, must be able to acquire, absorb, and use technical information competently. They need to be aware of their own situation and career goals. Importantly, they must reconcile the views of various stakeholders, including foreign aid agencies, and be cognizant of the overall political and economic environment (Grindle & Thomas, 1989).

In low-capacity environments, technical information will either be insufficient or insufficiently used. In both democratic and autocratic regimes, stakeholders may be insufficiently considered, resulting in political and economic miscalculations. Political instability, such as that found in fragile and conflict states, really ties the hands of policymakers since the sustainability of any policy is seriously in doubt. It also influences the behavior of policymakers since both their policies and careers are likely to have short horizons. Political stability allows policymakers the luxury of not only being reactive to the problems and crises of the moment, but also of being proactive in planning for the future.

Despite the abundance of case studies, anecdotes, modeling, cross-country empirical investigations, and meta-analysis, the impact of governance, and particularly the role of policymakers in relation to economic development and aid decisions, is murky at best. Some of the modeling has been helpful in distinguishing various types of regimes and their propensity for successful reform and economic growth – breaking down autocracies and electoral "democracies" by the type of political settlement (dominant versus competitive) and institutions (personalized versus impersonalized) (Levy, 2014). Nonetheless, when trying to use the typologies to help formulate a governance action plan in a specific country setting, much ambiguity and uncertainty remain.

Part of the reason for this lies in the chasm between social science disciplines and the divide between practitioners and professors. Bringing a multi-disciplinary approach to the existing evidence would be helpful, with a greater emphasis on melding theory with practice. Much more needs to be learned. Przeworski, the eminent political scientist, concluded an essay on democracy and authoritarianism with the following:

> The progress, in both quality and quantity, of research during the past half century has been phenomenal. But there are so many things we still do not know or understand. The issue of central political importance – the ways in which money infiltrates politics, the mechanisms and the effects of competition by interest groups for political influence – is still just one big puzzle, with little systematic evidence outside the United States. . . . The entire field of political economy of development has hurled itself against a brick wall: cross-country regressions, of which I have done thousands, fail to reject almost any of the many brilliant theories, while micro studies, include field experiments, always raise questions of external validity.
>
> (Przeworski, 2016, p. 10)

Donors to Policymakers – Aid Relationships

The nature of aid relationships is an understudied area in a field dominated by economists. The evidence that exists is mainly in the form of context-specific studies, anecdotes, first-person accounts, and survey results.[2] Overwhelmingly, but not unanimously, they describe the relationship between donors and recipient governments as uneasy if not adversarial, fraught with knowledge gaps, misunderstandings, and diverging interests. In the 2000s, several European authors attempted to see the relationships from the recipient's viewpoint (see for example, Whitfield, 2009; Eyben, 2006), and the World Bank published a collection of candid first-person accounts written by World Bank country directors that described both contentious and trusting relationships with recipient government officials (Gill & Pugatch, 2005). The title of that collection, *At the Frontlines of Development: Reflections From the World Bank*, no doubt was meant to refer to the "war" on poverty, but it unwittingly may also have captured some of the strife surrounding aid relationships.

Localization and Decolonialization

In the last decade or so, increased attention has been paid to *localization* and *decolonialization*. While the terms have been used more in the humanitarian aid context, both have a direct bearing on aid relationships more generally. *Localization* refers to transfer of responsibility for implementation of aid projects to local staff and organizations. In developmental aid, most donors have been working with and through recipient governments at the national and local levels, but this is not universally the case. For example, the United States, the largest aid donor, has been struggling over the last years to increase its use of local institutions. Much of its aid goes to large contractors of US origin. Other donors use home country or international NGOs to implement projects. More recently, there has been a push to channel more aid through local institutions, both public and non-profit. International contractors and NGOs have been encouraged to partner with local agencies, and in some cases, have established local subsidiaries with local boards.

Those international donors who have been working closely with governments for decades have expanded their employment of local higher-level staff and have transferred more responsibilities to their field offices. The employment of local staff, however, has been subject to criticism over the years since many donors pay more and/or provide more job security and have lured qualified staff away from the public sector (Knack & Rahman, 2007). Also, some local institutions and NGOs have complained that localization is a "smokescreen" for an elaborate system of subcontracting that gives them responsibility without authority (Shift the

Power, 2017). They maintain that it also creates competition for scarce funds between home-grown NGOs and international NGOs that have created local subsidiaries to demonstrate localization (#ShiftThePower, 2020). Moreover, many find the very term *localization* offensive because its origin and meaning express the perspective of non-locals (Robillard, Atim, & Maxwell, 2021).

Decolonization goes further than localization. Decolonization originally meant handing over the instruments of government from the colonial power to indigenous group or groups. Today it has come to mean a long-term transformation, with divestiture of mindsets, political and bureaucratic norms and practices, and cultural and linguistic traits derived from colonial power (Smith, 1999). The decolonization of aid, in turn, has taken on several specific meanings:

> The idea of decolonizing aid can take many forms in action: from localized leadership in programs on the ground to increased funding. But fundamentally, decolonization means decision-making is in the hands of the people directly impacted by aid and development programs.
>
> (Byatnal, 2021)

As some local NGOs have pointed out, the decolonization of aid discussion is Western-centric and seems yet another sign of a "white savior complex" where the Global North is continuing to be paternalistic and calling the shots. As they point out, independence was hard fought and hard won, and colonial influences are only part of the many ingredients that make up today's developing nations. After all, they are no longer colonies (Khan, 2021).

Ownership

Many of the discussions surrounding localization and decolonization appear distinctly theoretical, given the trajectory of the aid effectiveness agenda and its central tenet of ownership. From the decade before the 2005 Paris Declaration and beyond, recipient "ownership" has been seen as the key to the success of development efforts supported by aid. However, in practice, the term has had various meanings when applied to aid. As seen in Chapter 5, objectives compatible with national development plans have become a proxy for promoting ownership in some donor performance assessments. Others have interpreted ownership to mean that the recipient country agrees with a specific proposal made by a donor. A more robust definition of ownership would mean that development goals, strategies, policies, project formulation, and implementation are those of the recipients – with or without donor approval. In any event, whatever the form of ownership, it is also possible that isomorphic mimicry is going on, where recipients essentially espouse or adopt a policy or program knowing that is what the donor wants. In those cases, sustainability is in doubt. As one example, Keijzer and Black cite a case in Malawi where weak government commitment and ownership contributed substantially to the failure to implement and enforce harmonized allowances for NGOs, even after the guidelines had been endorsed by the Office of the President and the Cabinet. The guidelines were developed by the donors, with the government consulted only in a later stage (Keijzer & Black, 2020, p. 7; Ngwira & Mayhew, 2020, p. 11).

There have also been contradictions, or at least friction, between the donors' push for results-based management and short-term evidence of results and the time needed for governments to assume full ownership and achieve sustainable impact. This may also be the case for vertical global programs in health and other sectors where recipient governments generally have been absent from the critical agenda- and goal-setting stages, although they have been brought in at the implementation stage (Chasek & Rajamani, 2003; Pomerantz, 2014).

It is also unclear how ownership and partnership relate to each other in practice. If full ownership is the objective, what is the nature of the partnership, and why is it still seemingly so contentious? Partnership can be seen as a retreat from full ownership. As one article succinctly put it: "Although ownership remains a guiding principle and requirement, the ownership era may have passed its peak" (Hasselskog & Schierenbeck, 2017, p. 324). There are multiple reasons for this. First, with less of an emphasis on good governance, donors are wary of promoting full ownership by unsavory or authoritarian governments even though they are still providing aid to those countries. There is continuing uncertainty about including country stakeholders outside the government under the umbrella of ownership. With an authoritarian government, the definition of ownership is likely to be quite narrow, with the exclusion of civil society. Moreover, the role of civil society in electoral democracies is also ambiguous. Do CSOs and NGOs have a separate role to play apart from their ability to influence legislators and other government officials? Are they "owners" too? Finally, emerging donors, especially those from the Global South, tend to characterize their aid programs as respectful of sovereignty and providing mutual benefit. They do not identify with the ownership discussion.

New Players and New Dynamics

Changes in recipients, with the presence of more middle-income countries and unstable fragile states, as well as the addition of new donors, have changed aid relationships since the turn of the century. Middle-income countries, having more capacity and somewhat more fiscal space, at least in theory, should be better equipped than low-income and fragile states to break out of principal-agent type relationships and achieve more contractual, business-like arrangements.

In reality, their negotiating power has been diminished by climate change and reoccurring natural disasters, the global pandemic, and the growing accumulation of debt from the public and, more notably, the private sector. For fragile states, especially those in conflict or immediately post-conflict, much of the aid flows through alternate channels, such as NGOs or contractors, rather than the government itself. This continues through the present time despite pleas from fragile states, and international agreements such as the New Deal for Engagement in Fragile States agreed in 2011, to build capacity through using country systems and channeling aid through governments (International Dialogue on Peacebuilding and Statebuilding, 2011; Katoka & Kwon, 2021).

The increase in the number of donors has made a difference in aid relationships, although perhaps not as much as originally presumed to be the case. With more donors, many recipients perceive they have more choice among donors, and some have received more aid because of incremental funding by China and other non-OECD-DAC donors. The choice may still be quite limited, however, since not all donors wish to finance the same things or have the same conditions (Swedlund, 2017). While some recipients emphasize that the emerging donors have less conditionality, nearly all projects have some project-related conditionality. Also, many aid relationships carry within them an unspoken (but sometimes quite clear) obligation to provide support for donors in international arenas. China and other non-DAC donors provide assistance under the umbrella of "South-South Cooperation" rather than aid. However, many of the studies cited in this book show that while differences exist, there are many similarities among bilateral donors when grouped into DAC and non-DAC donors. Moreover, when non-DAC bilateral donors are studied individually, there is also a great deal of heterogeneity in how they provide aid. Both call into question whether there is a truly different Southern aid model (Tapscott, Jing, & Puppim de Olivera, 2019; Lauria & Fumagalli, 2019).

Nonetheless, the presence of new actors, especially those not from OECD-DAC countries, brings with it new opportunities for alliances and rivalries among donors. For recipients, it brings added complexity, with the possibility of winding up with individual aid relationships that are vastly different from each other. Because of those differences, recipient governments can gain more negotiating leverage because of the possibility of alternative funding sources. In practice, the number of donors, donor preferences by country and sector, individual personalities, and varying recipient government ability to manage aid mean that policymaker-donor relationships vary substantially from country to country and need careful study at the country level.

The preceding discussion shows the diversity of aid relationships between donors and governments and how those relationships are characterized by intertwined myths, aspirations, and evidence. When it comes to aid relationships, progress has been made in opening the lid of the "black box", but there is much more that needs to be learned to fully open the box. The same is true for the evidence related to technical knowledge and decision-making by policymakers. Much of the attention so far has been paid to evidence about "what works" in development projects. This has been useful, but it is clearly insufficient when it comes to evaluating and, more importantly, increasing aid effectiveness. Those working in the manner of "working with the grain", PDIA (problem-driven iterative adaptation), and "doing development differently" have begun to learn more about policymaking for development and aid and about how governance functions in low and middle-income countries (Levy, 2014; Andrews et al., 2017; Wild, Andrews, Pett, & Dempster, 2016). That knowledge, along with more emphasis on aid relationships, will take the cover completely off the black box and illuminate its contents, leading to both improved aid effectiveness and development results. The next chapters look at some of the efforts underway and actions that *could* be taken to improve aid effectiveness.

Notes

1 The definition of a "black box": "a usually complicated electronic device whose internal mechanism is usually hidden from or mysterious to the user; *broadly:* anything that has mysterious or unknown internal functions or mechanisms" (Merriam-Webster, n.d.).
2 Some of the relevant survey results can be found in Chapter 5.

Bibliography

Abdul Latif Jameel Poverty Action Lab. (2022). *About us*. Retrieved from J-PAL website: www.povertyactionlab.org/about-j-pal

Acemoglu, D., & Robinson, J. A. (2012). *Why nations fail*. New York: Crown Publishers.

Acemoglu, D., & Robinson, J. A. (2019). *The narrow corridor*. New York: Penguin Press.

Andrews, M., Pritchett, L., & Woolcock, M. (2017). *Building state capacity: Evidence, analysis, action*. Oxford: Oxford University Press.

Anonymous. (1994, December 10). Down the rathole. *The Economist*, p. 69.

Banerjee, A., Duflo, E., Goldberg, N., Karlan, D., Osei, R., Pariente, W., . . . Udry, C. (2015). A multifaceted program causes lasting progress for the very poor: Evidence from six countries. *Science, 348*(6236), 1–16.

Banerjee, A., Karlan, D., & Zinman, J. (2015). Six randomized evaluations of microcredit: Introduction and further steps. *American Economic Journal: Applied Economics, 7*(1), 1–21.

Bedecarrats, F., Guerin, I., & Roubaud, F. (2020). Editors' introduction: Controversies around RCTs in development: Epistemology, ethics, and politics. In F. Bedecarrats, I. Guerin, & F. Roubaud (Eds.), *Randomized control trials in the field of development: A critical perspective* (pp. 1–28). Oxford: Oxford University Press.

Boone, P. (1994). *The impact of foreign aid on savings and growth.* London: CEP Working Paper 677, London School of Economics.

Bourguignon, F., & Sundberg, M. (2007). Aid effectiveness: Opening the black box. *American Economics Review, 97*(2), 316–321.

Burnside, C., & Dollar, D. (1997). *Aid, policies, and growth.* Washington, DC: World Bank.

Burnside, C., & Dollar, D. (2000). Aid, policies, and growth. *American Economic Review, 90*(4), 847–868.

Byatnal, A. (2021, August 24). *Deep dive: Decolonizing aid – from rhetoric to action.* Retrieved from Devex Newswire: www.devex.com/news/deep-dive-decolonizing-aid-from-rhetoric-to-action-100646

Chambers, J. (1982). *MITI and the Japanese miracle: The growth of industrial policy, 1925–1975.* Palo Alto: Stanford University Press.

Chasek, P., & Rajamani, L. (2003). Steps towards enhanced parity: Negotiating capacity and strategy of developing countries. In I. Kaul, P. Conceicao, K. Le Goulven, & R. U. Mendoza (Eds.), *Providing global public goods, managing globalization* (pp. 245–262). Oxford: Oxford University Press.

Clemens, M. A., Radelet, S., Bhavnani, R. R., & Bazzi, S. (2012). Counting chickens when they hatch: Timing and the effects of aid on growth. *The Economic Journal, 122*(561), 590–617.

Commission on Growth and Development. (2008). *The growth report: Strategies for sustained growth and inclusive development.* Washington, DC: World Bank.

Deaton, A. (2020). Introduction: Randomization in the tropics revisited, a theme and eleven variations. In F. Bedecarrats, I. Guerin, & F. Roubaud (Eds.), *Randomized control trials in the field of development: A critical perspective* (pp. 29–46). Oxford: Oxford University Press.

Dijkstra, G. (2021). Not such a good bargain for (the evidence on) budget support. *Development Policy Review, 39,* 1031–1035.

Doucouliagos, H., & Paldam, M. (2008). Aid effectiveness on growth: A meta study. *European Journal of Political Economy, 24,* 1–24.

Doucouliagos, H., & Paldam, M. (2011). The ineffectiveness of development aid on growth: An update. *European Journal of Political Economy, 27,* 399–404.

Doucouliagos, H., & Paldam, M. (2013, April). The robust result in meta-analysis of aid effectiveness: A response to Mekasha and Tarp. *Journal of Development Studies, 49*(4), 584–587.

Doucouliagos, H., & Ulubasoglu, M. A. (2008). Democracy and economic growth: A meta-analysis. *American Journal of Political Science, 52*(1), 61–83.

Durlauf, S. N. (2020). Institutions, development, and growth: Where does evidence stand? In J.-M. Baland (Ed.), *The handbook of economic development and institutions* (pp. 189–217). Princeton: Princeton University Press.

Easterly, W., Levine, R., & Roodman, D. (2004). Aid, policies, and growth: Comment. *American Economic Review, 94*(3), 774–780.

Eyben, R. (2006). *Relationships for aid.* London: Routledge.

Fukuyama, F. (2007). Liberalism versus state-building. *Journal of Democracy, 18*(3), 10–13.

Fukuyama, F. (2011). *The origins of political order.* New York: Farrar, Straus and Giroux.

Fukuyama, F. (2014). *Political order and political decay.* New York: Farrar, Straus and Giroux.

Gaille, L. (2020, March 2). *14 advantages and disadvantages of a randomized controlled trial.* Retrieved from Ittana Personal Finance Blog: https://vittana. org/14-advantages-and-disadvantages-of-a-randomized-controlled-trial

Gill, I. S., & Pugatch, T. (2005). *At the frontlines of development: Reflections from the World Bank.* Washington, DC: The World Bank.

Grindle, M. S., & Thomas, J. W. (1989). Policy makers, policy choices and policy outcomes: The political economy of reform in developing countries. *Policy Sciences, 22*, 213–248.

Hansen, H., & Tarp, F. (2000). Aid effectiveness disputed. *Journal of International Development,* 375–398.

Hariton, E., & Locascio, J. J. (2018). Randomised controlled trials – the gold standard for effectiveness research. *BJOG, 125*(13), 1716.

Hasselskog, M., & Schierenbeck, I. (2017). The ownership paradox: Continuity and change. *Forum for Development Studies, 44*(3), 323–333.

International Dialogue on Peacebuilding and Statebuilding. (2011). *The new deal.* Retrieved from International Dialogue on Peacebuilding and Statebuilding: www.pbsbdialogue.org/en/new-deal/about-new-deal/

Katoka, B., & Kwon, H.-J. (2021, November). A paradox of new deal and foreign aid for fragile states in sub-Saharan Africa. *Global Policy, 12*(5), 639–652.

Keijzer, N., & Black, D. (2020). Ownership in a post-aid effectiveness era: Comparative perspectives. *Development Policy Review, 38*, O1–O12.

Khan, T. (2021, January 15). *Decolonisation is a comfortable buzzword for the aid sector.* Retrieved from Open Democracy: www.opendemocracy.net/en/ decolonisation-comfortable-buzzword-aid-sector/

Knack, S., & Rahman, A. (2007, May). Donor fragmentation and bureaucratic quality in aid recipients. *Journal of Development Economics, 83*(1), 176–197.

Lauria, V., & Fumagalli, C. (2019, October–December). BRICS, the southern model, and the evolving landscape of development assistance: Toward a new taxonomy. *Public Administration and Development, 39*(4–5), 215–230.

Levy, B. (2014). *Working with the Grain: Integrating governance and growth in development strategies.* Oxford: Oxford University Press.

Martens, B., Mummert, U., Murrell, P., & Seabright, P. (2002). *The institutional economics of foreign aid.* Cambridge: Cambridge University Press.

Mekasha, T. J., & Tarp, F. (2013). Aid and growth: What meta-analysis reveals. *Journal of Development Studies, 49*(4), 564–583.

Mekasha, T. J., & Tarp, F. (2019). A meta-analysis of aid effectiveness: Revisiting the evidence. *Politics and Governance, 7*(2), 5–28.

Merriam-Webster. (n.d.). *Black box.* Retrieved from Merriam-Webster.com: www. merriam-webster.com/dictionary/black%20box

Mosley, P. (1996). Aid-effectiveness: The micro-macro paradox. *IDS Bulletin*, *17*(2), 22–27.

Ngwira, C., & Mayhew, S. (2020). Donor-driven harmonised payment of allowances policy and NGOs community engagement in Malawi. *Development in Practice*, *30*(1), 3–14.

OECD DAC Network on Development Evaluation. (n.d.). *Evaluating development co-operation: Summary of key norms and standards* (2nd ed.). Paris: OECD.

Ogden, T. N. (2016). *Experimental conversations: Perspectives on randomized trials in development economics.* Cambridge, MA: MIT Press.

Onis, Z. (1991, October). Review: The logic of the developmental state. *Comparative Politics*, *24*(1), 109–126.

Paul, E. (2006). A survey of the theoretical literature on foreign aid. *Asian-Pacific Economic Literature*, *20*(1), 1–17.

Picciotto, R. (2020). Are the "randomistas" evaluators? In F. Bedecarrats, I. Guerin, & F. Roubaud (Eds.), *Randomized control trials in the field of development: A critical perspective* (pp. 256–279). Oxford: Oxford University Press.

Pomerantz, P. (2004). *Aid effectiveness in Africa: Developing trust between donors and governments.* Lanham, MD: Lexington Books.

Pomerantz, P. (2014). Global programs, aid effectiveness, and poverty reduction. In M. Ndulo & N. Van de Walle (Eds.), *Problems, promises, and paradoxes of aid: Africa's experience* (pp. 75–102). Cambridge: Cambridge Scholars Publishing.

Przeworski, A. (2016). Democracy: A never-ending quest. *Annual Review of Political Science*, *19*, 1–12.

Rajan, R., & Subramanian, A. (2005). *Aid and growth: What does the cross-country evidence really show.* Washington, DC: IMF.

Robillard, S., Atim, T., & Maxwell, D. (2021). *Localization: A "landscape" report, report to USAID.* Boston, MA: Feinstein International Center, Tufts University.

Rodrik, D. (2006). Goodbye Washington consensus, hello Washington confusion? A review of the World Bank's economic growth in the 1990s: Learning from a decade of reform. *Journal of Economic Literature*, 973–987.

Rodrik, D., Subramanian, A., & Trebbi, F. (2004). Institutions rule: The primacy of institutions over geography and integration in economic development. *Journal of Economic Growth*, *9*(2), 131–165.

Sachs, J. D. (2003). Institutions matter, but not for everything. *Finance and Development*, *40*(2), 38–41.

Shift the Power. (2017). *Localisation of aid: Are INGOs walking the talk?* Retrieved from Relief Web: https://reliefweb.int/sites/reliefweb.int/files/resources/WTT_FINAL.pdf

#ShiftThePower. (2020, March 8). *An open letter to International NGOs who are looking to 'localise' their operations.* Retrieved from Open Democracy: www.opendemocracy.net/en/transformation/an-open-letter-to-international-ngos-who-are-looking-to-localise-their-operations/

Smith, L. T. (1999). *Decolonizing methodologies: Research and indigenous peoples.* London: Zed Books.

Swedlund, H. J. (2017). Is China eroding the bargaining power of traditional donors in Africa? *International Affairs*, *93*(2), 389–408.

Swedlund, H. J., & Lierl, M. (2019). The rise and fall of budget support: Ownership, bargaining and donor commitment problems in foreign aid. *Development Policy Review*, 050–069.

Tapscott, C., Jing, Y., & Puppim de Olivera, J. A. (2019). BRICS and international development assistance: Towards divergence or convergence in development assistance amongst North and South donors? *Public Administration and Development*, 39(4–6), 167–173.

White, H., Sabanwal, S., & de Hoop, T. (2014). *Randomized controlled trials (RCTs), Methodological briefs: Impact evaluation 7*. Florence: UNICEF Office of Research.

Whitfield, L. E. (2009). *The politics of aid: African strategies for dealing with donors*. Oxford: Oxford University Press.

Wild, L., Andrews, M., Pett, J., & Dempster, H. (2016, December 16). *Doing development differently: Who we are, what we're doing and what we're learning*. Retrieved from ODI: https://odi.org/en/publications/doing-development-differently-who-we-are-what-were-doing-and-what-were-learning/

Wilkins, S. (2011). Can bad governance be good for development. *Survival*, 53(1), 61–76.

Willoughby, C. (2003). First experiments in operations evaluation: Roots, hopes, and gaps. In P. G. Grasso, S. S. Wasty, & R. V. Weaving (Eds.), *World Bank operations evaluation department: The first 30 years* (pp. 3–13). Washington, DC: The World Bank.

World Bank. (2022). *Work Bank Group – Balanced scorecards*. Retrieved from World Bank website: https://scorecard.worldbank.org/en/scorecard/tier3

Yanguas, P. (2018). *Why we lie about aid*. London: Zed Books.

8 The Rocky Road Towards Aid Effectiveness

The high-level movement that began in the late 1990s and early 2000s to improve aid effectiveness has been overshadowed by a series of events. These events include the wars in Afghanistan, Syria, and Ukraine; the multi-year waves of the COVID-19 pandemic and the associated economic disruptions; the security threats linked to Al-Qaeda and the Islamic State in parts of Africa; the growing debt levels and defaults among low and middle-income countries; and the severe weather and environmental changes linked to climate change. The expectation was that the years prior to 2030 would be devoted to accelerating progress on poverty reduction and prosperity for all. Unfortunately, this has not been the case.

Earlier in the century, when many economies were growing at a robust pace, there was talk that aid was likely to be phased out for all but the most highly vulnerable and fragile states. More than two decades after the start of the new century, it is becoming clear that aid may be more important than ever, not only to fund efforts in fragile states, but to help low and middle-income countries better withstand adverse events and to fund global public goods essential not only to those countries but to high-income countries as well. While the high-level attention to aid effectiveness may have died down, the need to improve aid effectiveness remains both critical and urgent.

This chapter will review high-level efforts, focusing on what has happened after the last High-Level Aid Effectiveness Meeting in Busan in 2011. It will then go on to outline some of the innovations that have taken place in aid modalities and financing and look at trending topics. It will explore whether aid agencies are doing business differently today, including increased adaptation to context and appropriate staffing at the local levels. Finally, it will return briefly to the question of aid relationships. By the end, it will be clear that there is still a robust agenda for improving aid and aid effectiveness.

DOI: 10.4324/9781003265320-10

High-Level Efforts After Busan

Busan was the largest high-level aid meeting, with over 3,000 participants from recipient and donor governments, CSOs/NGOs, international organizations, and the private sector. The aid effectiveness movement changed considerably after Busan. Notably, OECD-DAC agreed to wind down its Working Party on Aid Effectiveness, which had evolved from a small donors-only effort to a much larger forum involving donor and recipient countries, international and civil society organizations, and private sector representatives. It did so because the agreement was to focus on development effectiveness as opposed to aid effectiveness. For this purpose, a new organization, the Global Partnership for Effective Development Cooperation (GPEDC) was to be created with the United Nations Development Program (UNDP) and OECD-DAC acting as the joint secretariat. GPEDC was created to promote and monitor progress towards the four shared principles agreed at Busan:

- Ownership of development priorities by developing countries
- Focus on results
- Inclusive development partnerships
- Transparency and accountability to each other

The Busan document was drafted with the help of non-traditional donors and contained the phrase "shared principles and differential commitments", highlighting the fact that South-South Cooperation providers (non-traditional donors) viewed their programs and operations differently from those of the OECD-DAC donors (Fourth High Level Forum on Aid Effectiveness, 2011). As mentioned earlier, the outcome document was silent on the topic of donor harmonization and cooperation, which was subsequently dropped from the aid and development effectiveness agenda.

GPEDC began operating in 2012, and it was deliberately positioned as an inclusive partnership that would welcome everyone, including NGOs and non-traditional donors such as China, India, and Brazil. The addition of the UNDP to the secretariat was meant to signal that the OECD-DAC donors would no longer dominate since the GPEDC was designed to be a multi-stakeholder partnership (Taggart, 2022). CSOs and participating donors welcomed the broader representation, but problems lay ahead.

Although the non-traditional donors had signed the Busan declaration, China and India were absent from the first high-level meeting of the partnership in Mexico City. There was considerable reluctance to join in what they still perceived as a traditional donor initiative. The first monitoring framework for GPEDC evaluated compliance with ten commitments: five for aid providers, three for recipients, and two for both. The provider commitments were "conceived by and for traditional donors", and the non-traditional donors did not agree to being evaluated by those criteria (Bracho, 2021, p. 370). At the same time, despite some efforts, they failed to provide alternative criteria. There was also suspicion that traditional donors were welcoming non-traditional partners to "share" more of the heavy aid burden with them. Finally, non-traditional providers were afraid that their views and experiences would not receive adequate attention: the strength of research institutes located in DAC countries could mean that the traditional donors would also dominate the knowledge exchange (Li, 2017). After the absence of China and India from the Mexico City meeting, they and several other non-traditional donors have not participated in GPEDC activities.

The governance structure of the partnership was meant to reflect the wider participation that has only partially materialized. There are four co-chairs, representing "partner countries" (recipients), "development partners" (donors), "dual characteristic countries" (non-traditional donors), and "non-executive constituencies" (e.g., civil society, trade unions, philanthropic organizations, and the private sector), the last added after the 2016 Nairobi meeting. It also has a 25-person steering committee that meets biannually (Global Partnership for Effective Development Cooperation, n.d.). While the creation of GPEDC clearly signals the widening circle of aid providers, recipients, and other stakeholders in the effectiveness dialog, the criticism remains that OECD-DAC donors still dominate the circle. On the other hand, there is acknowledgement that traditional aid has played an important role in many countries, including South Korea and China, and that it has been responsible for a broad range of examples and lessons that are critical for successful development (including what not to do). Since Mexico, GPEDC has had a second high-level meeting in 2016 in Nairobi and a first senior-level meeting in New York in 2019. It had a third high-level meeting referred to as a summit in Geneva in December 2022. According to the GPEDC website, the goals for the summit were:

- **A joint commitment** for more ACTION
- **A new set of toolkits and practices** for better IMPLEMENTATION
- **A renewed way of monitoring** for more EVIDENCE
- **A revitalized way of working** for a better GLOBAL PARTNERSHIP

> (Global Partnership for Effective Development
> Cooperation, 2022; emphases in the orginal)

After the approval of the Sustainable Development Goals (SDGs) in 2015, GPEDC sought to position itself as a key support in at least three strategic priorities and nine action areas of the 2030 agenda (Global Partnership for Effective Development Co-operation, n.d.). It is unclear whether GPEDC can regain a central role among all stakeholders and, more importantly, become a respected source for effective development policies and practices.

Meanwhile, OECD-DAC has continued to debate and issue new policies and guidelines for traditional donors and others that follow DAC guidelines as summarized in Chapter 4. As development aid has become more integrated into foreign policy, it becomes more difficult to discern the fundamental purpose of assistance that lies at the heart of the ODA concept. OECD-DAC also continues to develop the TOSSD concept to measure a broader range of official support for development.

The Impact of the SDGs

The SDGs were approved by the UN General Assembly in 2015, following a protracted debate on what the goals should be. They were meant to be follow-up goals to the Millennium Development Goals (MDGs) and to the discussions held at the United Nations Conference on Sustainable Development in Rio de Janeiro in 2012. The SDGs are comprised of 17 goals, 169 targets, and 231 unique indicators[1] (United Nations, 2022a) (Box 8.1).

Box 8.1   The Sustainable Development Goals

Goal 1: End poverty in all its forms everywhere

Goal 2: End hunger, achieve food security and improved nutrition and promote sustainable agriculture

Goal 3: Ensure healthy lives and promote well-being for all at all ages

Goal 4: Ensure inclusive and equitable quality education and promote lifelong learning opportunities for all

Goal 5: Achieve gender quality and empower all women and girls

Goal 6: Ensure availability and sustainable management of water and sanitation for all

Goal 7: Ensure access to affordable, reliable, sustainable, and modern energy for all

Goal 8: Promote sustained, inclusive and sustainable economic growth, full and productive employment, and decent work for all

Goal 9: Build resilient infrastructure, promote inclusive and sustainable industrialization and foster innovation

Goal 10: Reduce inequality within and among countries

Goal 11: Make cities and human settlements inclusive, safe, resilient, and sustainable

Goal 12: Ensure sustainable consumption and production patterns

Goal 13: Take urgent action to combat climate change and its impacts

Goal 14: Conserve and sustainably use the oceans, seas, and marine resources for sustainable development

Goal 15: Protect, restore and promote sustainable use of terrestrial ecosystems, sustainably manage forests, combat desertification, and halt and reverse land degradation and halt biodiversity loss

Goal 16: Promote peaceful and inclusive societies for sustainable development, provide access to justice for all and build effective, accountable, and inclusive institutions at all levels

Goal 17: Strengthen the means of implementation and revitalize the global partnership for sustainable development

Source: United Nations, 2015, p. 14

The SDGs were, for the most part, enthusiastically received, representing for the first time a set of agreed goals that applied to all nations and not just low and middle-income countries. The SDGs are were also the first set of comprehensive goals, covering social, economic, political, and environmental aspects. Many had felt that the MDGs, with their heavy concentration on social aspects, had been too narrow, and ironically both over-ambitious and not ambitious enough, depending on the country. With the advent of the SDGs, there were critiques that they were overly broad, aspirational, and without clear priorities. William Easterly's concerns were shared by many development practitioners.

Unlike the MDGs, the SDGs are so encyclopedic that everything is top priority, which means nothing is a priority: . . . Beyond the unactionable, unquantifiable targets for the SDGs, there are also the unattainable ones: "ending poverty in all its forms and dimensions", "universal health coverage", "ending all . . . preventable deaths [related to newborn, child, and maternal mortality] before 2030", "[end] all forms of discrimination against all women and girls everywhere", and "achieve full and productive employment and decent work for all women and men". Again, these could have been great as ideals – I share such ideals with great enthusiasm. But the SDGs are not put forth as ideals but as "targets" for the year 2030.

(Easterly, 2015)

Lant Pritchett made the positive point that since aid should be based in each case on an agreement on country priorities, the SDGs, unlike the MDGs, did not lock countries into a specific development agenda (Pritchett, 2015). However, the SDGs do little to guide donor behavior or reinforce Pritchett's point: donors can claim that what they are doing is in line with one or more of the SDGs and therefore is legitimate, even when not conforming to a country's top priorities. The broad nature of the SDGs may also provide "cover" to countries that do not possess a coherent development strategy since it is possible to associate many actions with specific goals and targets and claim that the strategy is driven by the SDGs.

The SDGs have generated a considerable amount of new monitoring activity. As one small part of this, the United Nations reported that as of mid-2022, 188 countries had submitted 305 Voluntary National Reviews (VNRs). VNRs are described as "regular and inclusive reviews of progress at the national and sub-national levels, which are country-led and country-driven" and "expected to serve as a basis for the regular reviews by the high-level political forum (HLPF)" (United Nations, 2015, para. 79, 2022c). The effort to gather the requisite information to monitor progress towards the goals is significant, with the United Nations producing an annual progress report based on many different sources including the VNRs. The annual report includes an SDG Index and Dashboard providing data on progress.

One of the issues the SDGs has brought to the forefront is the need for more reliable, consistent statistical data, especially from low and lower-middle-income countries. Undoubtedly, the SDGs will have a salutary effect on data availability related to development actions. At the same time, it is valid to question whether and how much the new monitoring requirements for both countries and donor agencies are contributing to development knowledge and effectiveness.

The SDGs were meant to spearhead a concerted 15-year push to improve people's well-being everywhere. The potential impact of the SDGs has been overtaken by events. The coronavirus pandemic, along with war in Ukraine and severe weather events linked to climate change, have resulted in increased misery for millions. Inflation and higher food prices negatively impacted many countries. While the estimates vary by source, the UN estimates that global extreme poverty increased in 2020 for the first time in 20 years, bringing well over 100 million people back into extreme poverty (United Nations, 2022b, p. 2). While some recovery was projected for 2021, the World Bank estimates that by the end of 2022, there will be some 75 to 95 million more people living in extreme poverty compared to pre-pandemic levels (Gerszon Mahler et al., 2022). In addition to increased poverty, the pandemic interrupted schooling for many children worldwide and increased domestic violence and other burdens on women. At the macro level, the added expenditures for the pandemic, coupled with rising prices and declines in foreign direct investment and exports, left many low and middle-income countries with significantly increased debt burdens and pushed a number of countries into debt distress (United Nations, 2022b).

Undoubtedly, aid has a major role to play in helping low and middle-income countries recover from the multiple blows that they have faced in the 2020s and reinvigorate their efforts towards the SDGs. For that, aid will need to become more efficient and effective, as well as finding new ways of mobilizing financial resources.

New Aid Modalities

One of the most promising avenues towards aid effectiveness in the last years has been the development of new aid modalities and new financing mechanisms. This section, by no means exhaustive, highlights some of the innovations that hold the promise of making aid more effective and available.

New Project Types and Flexible Disbursement Mechanisms

In the last two decades, cash has become more respectable as a development modality. Cash transfers, both conditional and unconditional, have become popular in both humanitarian and developmental settings. Cash transfers allow beneficiaries to have a choice instead of rigidly controlling the inputs they receive. During the pandemic, cash transfers were critical in helping poor people maintain their consumption. According to one source, in 2020 cash transfer amounts nearly doubled, with 214 countries and territories planning or implementing over 400 cash transfer programs (Matin, 2022). Some 16 percent of the world's population, 1.3 billion people, received at least one COVID-19-related cash payment between 2020 and 2021. In low-income countries, however, cash transfers reached only an average of 4.5 percent of the population (Chowdhury et al., 2022).

As more evidence is gathered, there are many debates surrounding cash transfers. These debates include the merits of conditional versus unconditional cash transfers and the circumstances in which each should ideally be used (see, for example, Ozler, 2020; Baird, McIntosh, & Ozler, 2019; Hagen-Zanker et al., 2016). Conditional cash transfers are better suited to inducing behavioral change, while unconditional cash transfers are important for social protection, ensuring that vulnerable populations have the safety net they need (Ozler, 2020). Other aspects under discussion are delivery modes (e.g., how payments are made and to whom), size of payments, and the importance of combining payments with other types of interventions. In particular, the latter aspect, referred to alternately as the graduation approach, the inclusion approach, or "cash-plus", has shown substantial promise in lifting people out of extreme poverty (Matin, 2022). While there is still much to be learned about cash transfers, there is little question that the programs alleviate extreme poverty in the near term. The big question remains as to whether cash transfers are valuable in stopping the cycle of intergenerational poverty. More will be known about this as the programs mature and there is sufficient time to conduct medium- and long-term impact evaluations. Cash transfer programs are likely to remain an important part of the toolkit enhancing aid effectiveness.

Aid in the form of cash has also been useful as a concept at the macro level in recent years. While bilateral donor enthusiasm for budget support has waned over the last years, multilateral organizations have continued to provide budget support through mechanisms that provide financing in exchange for either advance actions or commitments to act on policy reform. While recipients don't necessarily like the conditions, they do like the funding that is not earmarked for specific projects. There are also some relatively new mechanisms that provide "cash on delivery" or what the World Bank terms "program for results", as briefly discussed in Chapter 4. With this type of aid, funds are disbursed when the recipients reach certain concrete targets or results. This is in contrast to the classic model, where funds are disbursed for inputs rather than outputs. With "cash" modalities, there is more flexibility in how to spend the cash when received, something recipient governments signal as important. Although obviously not without conditions, the newer mechanisms also provide a greater degree of freedom in the ways in which recipient governments choose to obtain results. It is also a way of lessening risk for the donor agencies. While the newer types of funding mechanisms have grown and budget support has been particularly important during the pandemic, the standard investment project is still the most prevalent form of financing, even for two of the largest funders of budget support, the World Bank and the European Union (World Bank, 2022, p. 6; European Commission, 2021, p. 43). There is plenty of room for future growth in budget support and results financing.

New Finance and Financing Vehicles

The SDGs, along with the pandemic and climate change, have underlined the need for a substantial increase in development finance. In response, there has been a concerted effort to mobilize resources from new sources and to use new mechanisms. There is not enough space here for an exhaustive treatment, and new initiatives are continually surfacing, but the following gives an idea of the types of innovative financing that have emerged in response to the tremendous need for additional resources.

Domestic Resource Mobilization

Low and middle-income countries are expected to step up their tax collection efforts. In addition to the need to sustain public expenditures and invest in development, it is generally thought that taxation creates an expectation and increases citizens' willingness and ability to hold their government accountable for how the money is spent. While increased accountability may be associated with taxation in high-income economies and certain developing countries, there is little evidence that this is actually the case in most developing countries (Tsai, Toral, Read, & Lipovsek, 2018). In any event, the coronavirus pandemic both increased the urgency for funds and hampered the ability of many governments to increase tax revenues. Low-income countries are frequently caught in a vicious circle. The government cannot raise taxes or enforce existing tax laws unless the public sees improved services and infrastructure. But without additional funds, the government cannot afford the changes needed to perform better. Aid could and should have an important role to play, but so far aid's ability to leverage sustainable improvements in public services has not fulfilled this promise, especially in low-income countries.

Private Sector Financing

Using public funds to attract increased private sector investment in developing countries received renewed emphasis in the last decade. The idea was to move from "Billions [the size of ODA] to Trillions [mostly private sector finance]". This was to be done in a variety of ways, including engaging in joint public-private partnerships for infrastucture; promoting local capital markets; supporting private domestic banking; providing equity, guarantees, and loans to the private sector for discrete investment projects; and investing in regional and global public goods (Africa Development Bank et al., 2015). The COVID-19 pandemic and ensuing economic disruptions have been particularly harmful in developing countries. Investment collapsed in 2020 and only partially recovered in 2021. In terms of foreign direct investment, 2021 saw a recovery, but developing economies, and the least-developed countries in particular, saw a limited recovery, growing only 30 percent and 19 percent respectively from the very low levels of 2020 (United Nations Conference for Trade and Development, 2022). Meanwhile, high-income countries have had a series of financial and economic difficulties as well. While the private sector remains a central and growing part of development finance, as discussed in Chapter 4, public sector finance is still the main source of investment in low-income countries and an important element in middle-income countries.

Public Sector Borrowing and Debt Relief

In recent years, middle-income countries have turned increasingly to borrowing on international capital markets to finance expenditures and investment. They have also accepted loans on both concessional and non-concessional terms from non-traditional sources, including China and India. Signs of a new debt crisis were visible before the COVID-19 pandemic (Gill & Karakulah, 2018). However, with the economic disruptions caused by both the pandemic and the Ukraine war, indebtedness increased rapidly, particularly in Africa. Although there was a debt service suspension by official creditors during much of 2020 and 2021, by end-2022, the situation was grim. Higher prices, especially for oil and wheat, slow growth, and higher interest rates and tighter credit were a recipe for debt crises in a number of countries. The head of the IMF said that 60 percent of low-income countries were in or near "debt distress", where debt payments represent half the size of a country's GNI (Wiseman, 2022). Debt service payments in middle-income countries were also at a 30-year high (Estevao, 2022).

Moreover, the characteristics of today's debt crisis are different from those that led to debt restructuring and the HIPC debt relief initiative in the 1990s and 2000s. At the time, most low-income debt was held by official bilateral Paris Club members and multilateral creditors.[2] In the 2020s, most of the debt is held by commercial creditors, both domestic and foreign, and non-Paris Club members such as China. In 2022, it was estimated that just under 10 percent of debt-service payments for low-income countries would go to Paris Club creditors. In addition, unlike in the 1990s, a significant portion of the debt has variable interest rates, which means that payments rise with inflation and higher interest rates (Estevao, 2022). Debt relief is back again on the agenda of development finance discussions and is likely to become once again a sizeable component of aid.

Philanthropy

As noted in Chapter 3, philanthropy has grown to become an important source of development finance, particularly in certain sectors such as health. OECD now receives data from 42 foundations providing development finance. In 2019, these foundations provided 9 billion dollars, mostly in grant form. While foundations are unlikely to become a dominant force in development finance, their independence allows them to take risks and pilot innovative ideas. Additional growth in philanthropic finance can be expected over the coming years: OECD estimates that there has been about a 43 percent increase in foundation spending for development from 2013 to 2019 (based on data from OECD, 2021 and OECD, n.d.).

New Sources of Finance

While ODA continues its modest expansion, new financial sources or mechanisms are being developed. The United Kingdom launched the first social impact bond in 2010. While most social impact bonds are found in high-income countries, as of May 2022, 22 *social impact* and *development impact bonds* were financing programs in 15 low and middle-income countries (Gustafsson-Wright, Bogglid-Jones, Nwabunnia, & Osborne, 2022). Essentially, an impact bond is a contract in which private investors (sometimes foundations or development finance institutions) provide financing for social and development programs with the understanding that specific results will be achieved. If the results are achieved, public sector agencies (sometimes with donor funds) pay back investors the principal and a return on their investment. If results are not achieved, the investor loses the money (Center for Global Development, n.d.).

Impact bonds are a way of financing innovative programs that may be too risky for donors and governments to finance upfront without a guarantee of success. The risk is transferred to the private investor, but there is close monitoring because of the investor's incentive to ensure that performance issues are satisfactorily addressed. In theory, the idea is to provide a partnership between the private investor and the public sector to achieve a desired set of results, using the expertise of both. In practice it is possible to have a development impact bond that circumvents the recipient country's government using private funders, private or NGO implementation agencies, and donor funds for the payout. As with most development programs, there is no guarantee that beneficiaries will be included in design and implementation decisions.

Impact bonds in developing countries have been used mainly for employment and livelihood programs and health, although investments in education, social welfare, agriculture, and the environment have also been made. So far, impact bonds have played only a minor role in development. Both the number of beneficiaries and amount of upfront finance have been relatively small: about US$460 million in upfront capital has been invested so far in all countries, including the 204 programs in high-income countries. Consequently, the average funding amount and number of beneficiaries in each operation is usually quite modest. Given the number of partners, the time and resources needed to set up a program financed by a DIB are generally quite extensive. In short, development and social impact bonds are most likely limited vehicles to be used in certain circumstances where risks are substantial. Nonetheless, they provide another example of results-based financing. Also, they can bring in new funders or provide an exit strategy for a donor seeking to transition programs from grants to government funding (Gustafsson-Wright et al., 2022; Gustafsson-Wright & Osborne, 2022). Box 8.2 provides two examples of development impact bonds.

Box 8.2   Two Examples of Development Impact Bonds (DIB)

Quality Education India DIB

The Quality Education India DIB, started in 2018, is the world's largest education DIB, valued at US$11.2 million (US$9.2 million in outcome finding). It was scheduled to last for four years. It focuses on improving learning outcomes in language and math for 200,000 primary school children from government and low-fee private schools in Delhi, Gujarat, Maharashtra, and Utter Pradesh. It involves UK, US, global, and Indian funding and implementation partners from the public, private, and not-for-profit sectors. It builds on a previous pilot, DIB Educate Girls, that achieved 160 percent of its target outcomes.

The risk investor provides working capital upfront to enable the implementing partners to deliver results. The risk investor will recover its initial investment and earn a return only if the target outcomes are reached. As with all DIBs, the learning outcomes are agreed upfront and independently verified. The outcome funders only pay for successful results. Outcome funders release funds in proportion to outcomes achieved. If targets are not achieved, the outcome funders do not pay.

The implementing partners are Indian foundations and NGOs: Kaivalya, Gyan Shala, Society for All Round Development and Education Initiatives, and Pratham Infotech Foundation. The risk investor is UBS Optimus Foundation, headquartered in Switzerland. The outcome funders are the Michael and Susan Dell Foundation and the British Asian Trust (BAT), which convenes the smaller funders (Comic Relief, British Telecom, the Mittal Foundation, and the Ellison Foundation). BAT also coordinates a technical assistance grant from FCDO. The performance manager is Dalberg Consultants, and the outcome evaluator is CGI (formerly Gray Matters India). Technical and knowledge advisors include Tata Trust, Government Outcomes Lab, and Brookings. There are also legal partners and an advisory board.

Learning improvements were measured for each student through a standardized test at the beginning and end of each year. Second-year results indicated that children were learning twice as fast as their peers in comparable schools. The COVID-19 pandemic disrupted operations as schools were closed for a while and migrant children returned to their home villages, but operations subsequently resumed.

Sources: Ecorys (2021), Quality of Education India (2020), Quality of Education India (2022)

***

Village Enterprise Development DIB

The Village Enterprise Development DIB was launched in late 2017 and ran to the end of 2020. Funding was US$5.32 million (including US$4.28 million in outcome funding). The program focused on applying a simplified graduation approach model to extremely poor families in rural Kenya and Uganda. It built on a similar program using normal aid funding. It formulated Business Savings Groups based on 30 individuals and ten businesses, provided business training and seed funds for start-up businesses (livestock, retail, crops, etc.), and mentored the participants for one year.

The implementing partner (service provider) was Village Enterprise. The risk investors were a group of nine investors: Delta Fund, Bridges Impact Foundation, King Philanthropies, Laidir Foundation, Skees Family Foundation, Silicon Valley Social Venture Fund – SV2, Excelsior Impact Fund, and Impact Assets. The outcome funders were: FCDO, USAID, and an anonymous donor. Project management support and process evaluation were done by Instiglio, and the trustee of the outcome fund was the Global Development Incubator.

Outcomes in 241 villages were measured through consumption and assets as proxies for household income and compared to a control group of 241 villages. Over 14,000 first-time entrepreneurs were trained, and 4,766 businesses were started. The RCT conducted by IDInsight showed positive increases in household consumption (6.3 percent) and assets (5.8 percent) compared to the control group and a benefit-cost ratio of 140 percent. The projected increase in lifetime household income was US$21 million. The evaluation recommended the maximum payout to the investors. While most of the participants reported negative effects from the COVID-19 pandemic, the DIB still exceeded its targets.

Sources: Village Enterprise (2022), Ecorys (2020), Jimenez Gallardo, Kananu, Lazicky, and Njogu-Ndongwe (2021)

The idea of using bonds sold to the private sector to finance development is not new. The International Finance Facility for Immunization (IFFIm) was founded in 2006 to finance immunizations in low and middle-income countries. Essentially, it issues bonds that are sold on international capital markets allowing GAVI (the Vaccine Alliance) to obtain additional finance and immediately take advantage of multi-year commitments from donors, knowing in later years that donor funds can be used to repay investors. Unlike social or development bonds, IFFIm's mechanism is purely financial; there are no targets for payouts, and investors are not involved in monitoring performance. Both GAVI and IFFIm have played a role in the coronavirus pandemic by emitting vaccine bonds. The bonds provided the means for COVAX, the COVID-19 Vaccines Global Access initiative, to immediately purchase and distribute vaccines while donors spread out their financial commitments over future years (International Financing Facility for Immunization, 2022; GAVI the Vaccine Alliance, 2022).

The World Bank (IBRD) has traditionally financed its lending operations in middle-income countries by selling bonds on the international capital market. In contrast, until 2018, IDA, its credit and grant facility for low-income countries, was financed mostly by donor contributions, as well as IDA repayments and grants from IBRD income. The World Bank began selling *IDA bonds* in 2018. This has allowed IDA to substantially increase its credit and grant commitments annually by several billion dollars even while some IDA donors have cut back on their contributions. In the fiscal year ending June 30, 2021, IDA was able to provide US$36 billion in new financing, with US$37 billion in the following year. This is significant not only because of the quantity of aid, but because IDA, despite sharing many common issues with the aid community, is considered one of the more effective donor agencies (International Development Association, 2022, p. 2; World Bank, 2022, p. 15; Independent Commission for Aid Impact, 2022; Standard & Poor, 2022; Mitchell, Calleja, & Hughes, 2021).

One of the most significant new financing options is the *IMF's Resilience and Sustainability Trust*, a new source of long-term financing for low-income and vulnerable middle-income countries. Approved in April 2022, it became operational in late 2022. The trust focuses on helping countries meet longer-term structural challenges generally related to global public goods, such as climate change and pandemic preparedness. In 2021, the IMF approved a US$650 billion equivalent SDR allocation to its member countries to boost global liquidity. The allocations were made to countries in proportion to their existing quotas (International Monetary Fund, 2021). Funding for the new trust initially comes from countries with strong external positions who voluntarily channel part of their SDR allocation to the trust for lending to low and middle-income countries. The loans have appealing terms: a 20-year maturity and a 10-and-a-half-year grace period. The interest rates are attractive, only slightly above the low SDR interest rate, with the most concessional terms provided to the poorest countries. The trust aims to have total resources of about US$42 billion, and loans to countries would not exceed 150 percent of a country's quota or one billion SDRs, whichever is lower.[3] To be eligible, countries would need a package of "high-quality policy reforms", a concurrent IMF-supported program (with or without financing), and debt levels judged to be sustainable (International Monetary Fund, 2022a, 2022b).

Even with all the activity surrounding new aid modalities and new financing options, the needs of low and middle-income countries far exceed available finance. While this has always been the case, the COVID-19 pandemic, the war in Ukraine, and the resulting economic disruptions have made the needs more intense and the gap wider between the "haves" and the "have nots". So, more than ever, there is a need to ensure that every aid dollar is well spent, both for efficiency's sake and to attract additional resources.

Trending Topics

Digital Transformation

In addition to innovations in financial mechanisms and sources, the last decade has seen changes in what donors perceive as priorities. First, looking through the lens of OECD's Development Co-operation Reports and the World Bank's World Development Reports, there has been a clear emphasis on digital transformation and the role of data in development. This is a topic that has emerged as important for both the process and substance of development, one that underpins other efforts. The computer and the Internet, and more recently, big data and artificial intelligence, have enormous power and change the limits of human possibilities. Fintech, edtech, agritech, and healthtech, to name only a few, are using technology (and frequently digital technology) to change products and services *and* the way they are delivered to the world's poor and disadvantaged. Technology has the potential to bring about both increased efficiency and improved effectiveness of development interventions.

Resilience and Recovery

Resilience and recovery are other major themes influenced by the multiple crises generated by war, the COVID-19 pandemic, and finance and trade disruptions. These have all led to economic and social hardship throughout much of the world, especially in low and middle-income countries. Improving disaster readiness, ensuring food security, and dealing with the debt crisis are not new topics in development. However, the early 2020s saw a confluence of events that has underlined the needs in these areas once again. Conflict and fragility in a significant number of countries have meant that donors have needed to place more emphasis on emergency assistance and crisis management. Whether related to disease prevention, emergency food aid, maintaining peace, or financial assistance, the agenda confronting the donors has meant that decisions have to be accelerated and assistance provided in less-than-ideal circumstances. Meeting these types of challenges will determine whether resilience and recovery are merely "buzzwords" or a paradigm shift that changes business as usual in the aid industry.

Climate, Environment, Global Health, and Gender

Climate change and environment, global health, and gender are cross-cutting themes that show the continuing interconnectedness of today's world while also highlighting the large disparities that exist among nations. Global programs are prominent in these areas, and the aid that donors allocate to these programs, as opposed to individual countries, is growing (World Bank, 2021a). The amount of incremental resources flowing to these themes is an open question. According to OECD, environmental support is increasing, while "support to gender equality and women's empowerment is stalling" (OECD, 2020, p. 390). Global health continues to enjoy a relatively high level of funding, although there are shortfalls for emergencies and basic health care, for example. There has always been a tendency to re-label ongoing and planned actions in line with the latest priorities, so questions remain as to the extent of actual support for these themes. Box 8.3 provides an example of the difficulties in using the existing data to gauge support. In addition, when the funding flows through global programs, there is a risk that agenda-setting and program choices will be more in line with donor preferences instead of those of the recipients. However, there is a growing consensus that these areas are critical for successful development and will likely enjoy increasing support over the next decades.

Box 8.3   Interrogating the Data on Relative Funding Priorities: An Example

Development data is difficult to obtain and frequently imperfect. Even when data sources are "tried and true" and efforts have been made to publish reliable figures with good explanations and definitions, legitimate questions remain.

Here is one example:
According to OECD, in 2020:

- Bilateral aid in support of **gender** activities totaled some US$59.5 billion. Some US$6 billon had gender as its principal objective, while US$53.5 billon had gender as a "significant objective".

- Bilateral aid in support of **global environment** activities totaled some US$38.5 billion. Some US$14.6 billion had global environment activities as its principal objective, while US$23.9 billion had global environment as a "significant objective".
- Bilateral aid in support of **health** totaled some US$11.6 billion.

Which of the three themes received the most support from bilateral donors? Not an easy question to answer.

OECD identifies health clearly as a subsector, while gender and global environment are cross-cutting and are "flagged" as either significant or principal objectives in many sectoral activities. While at first glance it appears that gender enjoys the most support, activities related to global environment and health likely receive more direct support, and health could, in fact, receive the most clearly targeted support. Admittedly, this is a subjective view with some skepticism as to how the special topic flags are assigned in practice. Another limitation is that this only reflects data from OECD-DAC donors.

Clearly, there is a need to review aid data carefully and use it with humility and many caveats to support conclusions.

Source: Data from OECD (2022), OECD Statistics

Governance and Corruption

Finally, there are the topics of governance and more narrowly, corruption. Although ever present, there is a sense that these are not trending topics. "Good governance" in the sense of good stewardship of aid monies is still sought through support for public financial management and legal and regulatory reform. Nonetheless, the diversity of regime types in low and middle-income countries and the emergence of donors from non-democratic countries have made donors cautious about taking on issues that are viewed as strictly political or impinging on national sovereignty. Donors have acted when faced with egregious cases of corruption, and it is still a major issue. However, the rhetoric surrounding corruption has been tamped down. First, at least some developing countries have been able to grow despite the presence of considerable corruption. Bangladesh and Vietnam, along with many Latin American countries, fall into this category. Second, health and environmental emergencies have meant that funds needed to be provided rapidly and without some of the usual "checks and balances". While not ideal, donors in practice have concluded that the implicit trade-off and risks are acceptable even as they do what they can to prevent corruption and misuse of funds. Third, the donors' growing emphasis on assisting fragile and conflict states puts them at odds with steering clear of serious corruption. More fundamentally, there is now a growing understanding of corruption as a long-term societal issue that is not amenable to "quick fixes" or donor ultimatums. It is an issue that must be tackled in a variety of ways primarily by a committed government.

New Ways of Doing Business?

Understanding the Local Context

The need to understand the local context for development has long been recognized (Chambers, 1983). How much the local context is being considered in the design and implementation of aid-financed projects is an open question. First, practice varies among donors. For example, an ODI study found that OECD donors and multilateral development banks were more likely to identify and monitor the overall context than emerging bilateral providers (Sharp & Wild, 2021, p. 6). Second, while project context may be reviewed during design, time constraints and bureaucratic bottlenecks often make it difficult to make alterations during implementation because of changed circumstances. The same study confirmed that all aid providers were weaker in identifying success and risk factors and adapting to context during implementation (as opposed to design), although multilateral development banks were the strongest in this regard (p. 6). Third, and perhaps most fundamentally, there is a question as to how much aid officials understand about the context. Besides the inevitable data gaps and economic uncertainties, there are complex sociological and political factors that many development practitioners are not equipped to analyze. Misunderstandings about beneficiaries' behaviors and preferences, as well as unforeseen or unrecognized political and policy barriers, have caused many development projects to fail.

As noted earlier, there are calls from several quarters to change how development projects are designed and function, making them more flexible and adaptive to changing circumstances, since change and uncertainty are facts of life in the developing country context. There is also at least some recognition that development itself is a complex process, a "wicked problem" in economic terms (among others, Ramalingam, 2013, Honig, 2018). Those types of problems are not amenable to simple fixes and blueprint solutions. Instead, experimentation – trial and error, with built-in flexibility – on a continuing basis is called for.

There is also a sense that results-based management has not always been helpful in this regard. Clear objectives, tied to coherent strategies and associated inputs, targets, outputs, and outcomes, have led to *less* flexibility in practice, with targets and outputs taking on a life of their own in many instances. It has also given rise to complicated monitoring procedures and a focus on quantifiable results that are easily measured (Yanguas, 2018, especially pp. 44–70). On the other hand, there is concern among some donors that adaptive management may be just an excuse for not rigorously thinking through the results chain in a project intervention (Sharp & Wild, 2021, p. 5). To counterbalance this and acknowledge that rigor and flexibility are not opposing concepts, in 2019, OECD came out with a new set of OECD DAC Guiding Principles: Managing for Sustainable Development Results (OECD, 2019). As shown in Box 8.4, there are six principles; the second principle is focused specifically on adapting to context.

Box 8.4   OECD's 2019 Guiding Principles: Managing for Sustainable Development Results

1   Support sustainable development goals and desired change
2   Adapt to context
3   Enhance country ownership, mutual accountability, and transparency
4   Maximize the use of results information for learning and decision-making
5   Foster a culture of results and learning
6   Develop a results system that is manageable and reliable

Source: OECD (2019)

OECD's rationale for developing the principles begins by saying that results-based management has become increasingly complex over the last two decades because of the SDGs, targeting those left behind, the need for multiple partnerships, and rapid technological advances, among other factors. It then goes on to say the following:

> Development co-operation providers have developed various, often mixed, approaches to address this complexity and navigate volatile and uncertain environments. . . . Most providers are also driven by the pressing need to be accountable to their domestic constituencies. They therefore focus reporting on outputs and short-term outcomes, often relying on sets of standard, aggregate indicators. This may come at the expense of using results information for learning, adapting and

achieving long-term outcomes. In partner countries, this may also make it more difficult to align to national results frameworks and to incentivize bottom-up, context-sensitive approaches.

(OECD, 2019, p. 2)

Principle 2 urges development organizations to balance between internal requirements and local empowerment and to focus on achieving long-term outcomes rather than only on short-term deliverables. It calls for a sound understanding of the local environment and advocates for "iterative (rather than linear)" approaches to deal with complexity (OECD, 2019, p. 8). Dan Honig calls the iterative approach "navigation by judgment" as opposed to top-down management that relies on extensive monitoring of quantifiable targets and tight control (Honig, 2018). The need for OECD to issue these guiding principles speaks to a clear recognition that more flexibility and less ex-ante control are required from many of the leading donors.

Local Staffing and Local Staff

The last 20 years have seen two types of de-concentration of aid agencies: first, a transfer of headquarters staff to the recipient countries, and the second, the hiring of local staff (staff who already reside in the recipient country) in place of staff hired internationally or in the donor country. While this is not true of all aid agencies, both are the general trend. The numbers of local staff are impressive, well over 500,000 considering only the largest aid agencies and international NGOs (Koch & Schulpen, 2018, p. 240).[4]

The biggest argument in favor of both local offices and local staff has been the ability of aid agencies to gather more information, understand the local environment, and interact with the government and other stakeholders on a regular and frequent basis. The arguments questioning the moves are generally focused on value for money, authority and technical expertise, and communication bottlenecks with headquarters. While examining the arguments, there are two big questions associated with this trend. The first is whether de-concentration has led to actual decentralization, with more authority in the field, rapid decision-making, and flexibility by donors. The second is to ask what impact this has had on recipient "ownership", donor-recipient relationships, and on project success.

The answers are far from simple and clear. The answers differ not only by donor agency, but sometimes by individuals and recipient countries. First, where staff are located varies widely. UN agencies such as UNDP and UNICEF, the German aid agency GIZ, and international NGOs are heavily decentralized. Others, including the Swedish aid agency, SIDA, the IMF, and the Islamic Development Bank have most staff at their headquarters. The World Bank and USAID are somewhere in the middle, with concentrations of staff both in the field and at headquarters (Nunberg, 2017, p. 10; Edwards, 2019). The employment of local staff also varies. International development NGOs tend to be staffed primarily with country nationals, with smaller numbers in a headquarters location. Most of the aid agencies that have local offices have mainly local staff in those offices, often supervised by headquarters staff posted to the office for a tour of duty. The tendency to hire local staff has accelerated over the years (Koch & Schulpen, 2018, p. 240).

Local staff have been invaluable in helping aid agencies build better relationships with recipient governments. Local staff have deep cultural, personal, and professional ties to government counterparts and can improve communication and understanding between donors and recipients even in tense situations (Sundberg, 2020). Local donor staff hold appointments that pay much better than positions in government. This has been beneficial for maintaining access to the knowledge and expertise of skilled local staff, especially those who have been foreign trained and could secure employment outside of the country. For those who are reluctant to leave their country, it has allowed them to continue working in their area of expertise and to further develop professionally. It has also helped improve the living conditions and prospects of both their immediate and extended families (Koch & Schulpen, 2018). At the same time, the wage differential has created tensions with government staff who may have similar qualifications and has left donors open to the frequent charge of "poaching" the best staff from the government and contributing to wage and housing inflation.

There are also tensions with internationally recruited donor staff since local staff earn far less, even when doing essentially the same kind of work. There is a presumption that international staff have greater expertise in development and shoulder more of the responsibility. Obviously, this is not always the case. Also, many local staff are on annual or multi-year contracts. While this provides flexibility for cost-conscious aid agencies, it hinders the ability of local staff to be fully integrated into the agency or to be critical of policy choices or working conditions, even after many years of continuous employment.

Local donor staff are also frequently caught in "delicate" situations. While dependent on local staff, many aid agencies do not fully trust their dedication and allegiance to the agency, especially in controversial matters concerning the recipient country government or other important country stakeholders. Some agencies limit the access to information that is provided to local staff or exclude them from important internal meetings. At the same time, local staff can be viewed as "changing sides" by their country counterparts and envied for their better working conditions. Many local donor staff are still able to establish close working relationships with government and NGO staff who may feel more comfortable and have more trust in local donor staff with whom they share professional, cultural, linguistic, and sometimes personal ties.

Both sides may also use local donor staff as a reliable conduit of information. Some local donor staff intentionally use their international colleagues to deliver hard or unfavorable messages, and many donor agency heads likewise shield local staff from delivering bad news so that their relationships are not undermined (Sundberg, 2020). However, this can have its own problems: the government may question how much authority or decision-making power the local donor representatives have and disregard what they say. There may also be a tendency, or even encouragement, for local donor staff to go beyond their formal role and actually do, or at least informally manage, the government's work. This may be an acceptable solution in practical terms, but the long-term implications for country ownership and sustainability are worrisome. Because of all these complications, every local donor staff member is engaged in a balancing act where much depends on their prior connections, technical expertise, and interpersonal skills.

The trend towards using local staff has clearly grown and is expected to continue even in situations where agenda-setting and much of the decision-making still belongs at an agency's headquarters or with internationally recruited staff. Putting staff in the field or hiring more local staff does not automatically add up to more real decentralization, speed, or flexibility. Nor does it guarantee more country ownership, better relationships, and project success, especially if the staff, either international or local, are engaged in micromanaging or there is little flexibility on the part of the donor. Honig finds evidence that navigation by judgment (more flexibility and delegation on the part of the aid agency) has a strong, positive relationship with project success, especially where project success is not easily verifiable and there is substantial environmental uncertainty (Honig, 2018). He notes, however, that for aid agencies without a tendency to navigate by judgment, a country field office or the hiring of local staff is unlikely to help: "The case studies further underline that having a physical office in-country is not sufficient for an IDO [international development organization] to gain the benefits of soft information . . . or responding to context" (Honig, 2018, p. 149). The incentives for staff are simply not there.

So while local donor offices and the employment of local staff are likely to continue, this is not a trend that will be helpful in all circumstances. Much depends on the aid agency's authorizing environment and consequent management style, as well as the capabilities of both international and local staff. Just putting more staff in the field or hiring more locals is not a guarantee of development impact.

Aid Relationships

Recent developments – GPEDC, the SDGs, new sources of financing and project modalities, new priority topics and challenges, changes in aid business practices and staffing – are slowly changing the face of aid. With these changes, the aid effectiveness paradigm of the early 2000s, based on recipient "ownership" and deepening trust between donors and recipients, has changed as well. Although ownership is still part of the development discourse, partnership has largely taken its place. While in the beginning, developing country recipients were referred to as partners of the donors, in more recent official documents, it is now the donors who are the development partners of the recipient countries. Sometimes, everyone is referred to as a partner. Also, in many recent documents, the terms *aid* and *development assistance* have been replaced by *development cooperation*. It seems that the rhetoric at least is trying to narrow the perceived power inequality between donors and recipients. The rhetoric may not match the reality, however (Hasselskog, 2022).

As noted earlier in this book, both *ownership* and *partnership* can be vague terms. Partnership certainly does not convey full ownership to the recipient. The monitoring indicators for country ownership under GPEDC are about the existence of national development plans and strategies and the improvement of country systems. They are not about a country's ability to decide how aid resources are to be spent. While donors are urged to provide aid in line with national strategies and the SDGs, those broad documents allow donors to continue to exercise a substantial control over aid, and as GPEDC noted, donor alignment with country priorities and results monitoring frameworks has declined since 2016 (OECD/UNDP, 2019, p. 14). Donors have also, at times and primarily at the country level, opened up a discussion on the nature of the country's ownership of priorities. Is it strictly the executive branch or the government as a whole? Is ownership also inclusive of other important country stakeholders including NGOs, women, and the private sector? Talking about inherently political issues as part of the discussion is perhaps not so surprising (Hasselskog, 2022). Through policy-based operations, sector investment programs, and MDG and SDG monitoring, donors have essentially bought a seat at the table to discuss internal policy matters. As aid has become more entwined with foreign policy objectives and the need to provide global public goods, the space for recipient country ownership seems to have narrowed.

With that narrowing of the ownership space and the growing importance of issues of global concern (peace and security, environment, health, gender) to aid donors, the likelihood for trusting aid relationships has also diminished. While there have been some encouraging developments such as increased use of cash transfers, there are several clouds on the horizon. GPEDC's lack of prominence, the use of aid modalities such as "cash on delivery", the over-emphasis on verifiable results when resolving complex problems, and the significant build-up of local donor staff all signal a trust deficit. Combined with the sheer number of national and international crises the donors and recipients face, there is neither the time nor the psychological and political space to create confidence, engage in true dialog, and build the trust needed to change the nature of what continues to be a largely contentious and less-than-honest relationship. Unfortunately, the nature of aid relationships continues to be one of the most important barriers to aid effectiveness. There has been some progress down the road to aid effectiveness in recent years, but the stones in the road continue to make the journey a difficult one.

Notes

1 Indicators are reviewed annually and comprehensively every five years. Because of revisions in 2020, many websites have not fully kept up with the revisions. The UN Statistical Commission is officially in charge of any revisions in the indicators.
2 "The Paris Club is an informal group of official creditors whose role is to find coordinated and sustainable solutions to the payment difficulties experienced by debtor countries." Some 22 countries are permanent Paris Club members: Australia, Austria, Belgium, Brazil, Canada, Denmark, Finland, France, Germany, Ireland, Israel, Italy, Japan, Korea, Netherlands, Norway, Russian Federation, Spain, Sweden, Switzerland, United Kingdom, and United States of America (Paris Club, n.d.).
3 1 billion SDRs are equivalent to US1.33 billion (December 1, 2022).
4 Their data is from 2014 and 2015; the totals have grown.

Bibliography

Africa Development Bank, Asian Development Bank, European Bank for Reconstruction and Development, European Investment Bank, Inter-American Development Bank, International Monetary Fund, World Bank Group. (2015). *From billions to trillions: Transforming development finance*. Washington, DC: Development Committee Discussion Note.

Baird, S., McIntosh, C., & Ozler, B. (2019, September). When the money runs out: Do cash transfers have sustained effects on human capital accumulation? *Journal of Development Economics, 140*, 169–185.

Bracho, G. (2021). Failing to share the burden: Traditional donors, southern providers, and the twilight of the GPEDC and the post-war aid system. In S. Chaturvedi, H. Janus, S. Klingebiel, L. Xiaoyun, A. de Mello e Souza, Elizabeth Sidiropoulos, & D. Wehrmann (Eds.), *The Palgrave handbook of development cooperation for achieving the 2030 agenda: Contested collaboration* (pp. 367–392). Cham: Palgrave Macmillan.

Center for Global Development. (n.d.). *Investing in social outcomes: Development impact bonds*. Retrieved from Center for Global Development website: www.cgdev.org/page/investing-social-outcomes-development-impact-bonds-0

Chambers, R. (1983). *Rural development: Putting the last first*. London: Longman.

Chowdhury, A., Lawson, C., Kellison, E., Chia, H. S., Kharas, H., Fuller, J., . . . Dercon, S. (2022, February 17). *Accelerating digital cash transfers to the world's poorest*. Retrieved from Brooking Future Development blog: www.brookings.edu/blog/future-development/2022/02/17/accelerating-digital-cash-transfers-to-the-worlds-poorest/

Easterly, W. (2015, September 28). *The SDGs should stand for senseless, dreamy, garbled*. Retrieved from Foreign Policy website: https://foreignpolicy.com/2015/09/28/the-sdgs-are-utopian-and-worthless-mdgs-development-rise-of-the-rest/

Ecorys. (2020). *Village enterprise development impact bond: A case study*. FCDO.

Ecorys. (2021). *Quality education India development impact bond*. FCDO.

Edwards, S. (2019, October 25). *In decentralization push, World Bank to relocate hundreds of DC staffers*. Retrieved from DEVEX: www.devex.com/news/in-decentralization-push-world-bank-to-relocate-hundreds-of-dc-staffers-95875

Estevao, M. (2022, March 18). *Are we ready for the coming spate of debt crises?* Retrieved from World Bank Voices Blog: https://blogs.worldbank.org/voices/are-we-ready-coming-spate-debt-crises

European Commission. (2021). *Budget support: Trends and results 2021*. Brussels: EC.

Fourth High Level Forum on Aid Effectiveness. (2011). *Busan partnership for effective development co-operation*. Busan, Korea.

GAVI the Vaccine Alliance. (2022). *COVAX*. Retrieved from GAVI website: www.gavi.org/covax-facility#:~:text=COVAX%20is%20the%20vaccines%20pillar,treatments%2C%20and%20vaccines

Gerszon Mahler, D., Yonzan, N., Hill, R., Lakner, C., Wu, H., & Yoshida, N. (2022, April 13). *Pandemic, prices and poverty*. Retrieved from Data Blog World Bank: https://blogs.worldbank.org/opendata/pandemic-prices-and-poverty

Gill, I., & Karakulah, K. (2018, April 6). *Sounding the alarm on Africa's debt*. Retrieved from Future Development Blog, Brookings: www.brookings.edu/blog/future-development/2018/04/06/sounding-the-alarm-on-africas-debt/

Global Partnership for Effective Development Cooperation. (2022). *Effective development co-operation summit*. Retrieved from GPEDC website: www.effectivecooperation.org/hlm3

Global Partnership for Effective Development Co-operation. (n.d.). *GPEDC at a glance*. Retrieved from GPEDC website: www.effectivecooperation.org/content/gpedc-glance

Gustafsson-Wright, E., Bogglid-Jones, I., Nwabunnia, O., & Osborne, S. (2022, May 13). *Social and development impact bonds by the numbers: May 2022 snapshot*. Retrieved from Brookings: www.brookings.edu/research/social-and-development-impact-bonds-by-the-numbers/

Gustafsson-Wright, E., & Osborne, S. (2022, January 6). *A review of the global impact bonds market in 2021 and what to expect in 2022*. Retrieved from Brookings: https://www.brookings.edu/blog/education-plus-development/2022/01/06/a-review-of-the-global-impact-bonds-market-in-2021-and-what-to-expect-in-2022/

Hagen-Zanker, J., Bastagli, F., Harman, L., Barca, V., Sturge, G., & Schmidt, T. (2016). *Understanding the impact of cash transfers: The evidence – Briefing*. London: ODI.

Hasselskog, M. (2022). What happened to the focus on the aid relationship in the ownership discussion? *World Development*, 1–13.

Honig, D. (2018). *Navigation by judgment: Why and when top-down management of foreign aid doesn't work.* Oxford: Oxford University Press.

Independent Commission for Aid Impact. (2022). *The UK's support to the World Bank's international development association.* London: ICAI.

International Development Association. (2022). *Management's discussion & analysis and financial statements.* Washington, DC: World Bank.

International Financing Facility for Immunization (IFFIm). (2022). *About IFFIm.* Retrieved from IFFIm website: https://iffim.org/about-iffim

International Monetary Fund. (2021, August 2). *IMF governors approve a historic US$650 billion SDR allocation of special drawing rights.* Retrieved from IMF website: www.imf.org/en/News/Articles/2021/07/30/pr21235-imf-governors-approve-a-historic-us-650-billion-sdr-allocation-of-special-drawing-rights

International Monetary Fund. (2022a, April 18). *Factsheet: Resilience and sustainability facility (RSF).* Retrieved from IMF website: www.imf.org/en/About/Factsheets/Sheets/2022/resilience-and-sustainability-facility-rsf

International Monetary Fund. (2022b, April 18). *IMF executive board approves establishment of the resilience and sustainability trust.* Retrieved from IMF website: www.imf.org/en/News/Articles/2022/04/18/pr22119-imf-executive-board-approves-establishment-of-the-rst

Jimenez Gallardo, M. A., Kananu, W., Lazicky, C., & Njogu-Ndongwe, F. (2021). *Village enterprise development impact bond evaluation findings.* Retrieved from IDInsight: https://www.idinsight.org/publication/village-enterprise-development-impact-bond-evaluation-findings/

Koch, D.-J., & Schulpen, L. (2018). An exploration of individual-level wage effects of foreign aid in developing countries. *Evaluation and Program Planning, 68,* 233–242.

Li, X. (2017). *Should China join the GPEDC? The prospects for China and the global partnership for effective development co-operation.* Bonn: DIE – German Development Institute.

Matin, I. (2022, January 5). *What 'Cash Plus' Programs Teach Us About Fighting Extreme Poverty.* Retrieved from Stanford Social Innovation Review: https://ssir.org/articles/entry/what_cash_plus_programs_teach_us_about_fighting_extreme_poverty

Mitchell, I., Calleja, R., & Hughes, S. (2021). *The quality of official development assistance.* Washington, DC: Center for Global Development.

Nunberg, B. (2017). *Improving human resource management in development agencies.* London: ODI.

OECD. (2019). *Managing for sustainable development results: OECD DAC guiding principles.* Paris: OECD.

OECD. (2020). *Development co-operation report 2020: Learning from crises building resilience.* Paris: OECD.

OECD. (2021). *OECD statistics on private philanthropy for development.* Retrieved from OECD website: www.oecd.org/dac/Private-Philanthropy-for-Development-Flyer-2018-19.pdf

OECD. (2022). *OECD statistics database.* Retrieved from OECD website: https://stats.oecd.org

OECD. (n.d.). *The role of philanthropy in financing for development.* Retrieved from OECD website: www.oecd.org/dac/financing-sustainable-development/development-finance-standards/beyond-oda-foundations.htm

OECD/UNDP. (2019). *Making development co-operation more effective: 2019 progress report*. Paris: OECD Publishing.

Ozler, B. (2020, February 6). *How should we design cash transfer programs?* Retrieved from Let's Talk Development World Bank blog: https://blogs.worldbank.org/developmenttalk/how-should-we-design-cash-transfer-programs

Paris Club. (n.d.). Retrieved from Paris Club website: https://clubdeparis.org/en

Pritchett, L. (2015, October 20). *The new global goals spell the end of kinky development*. Retrieved from Center for Global Development website: www.cgdev.org/blog/new-global-goals-spell-end-kinky-development

Quality of Education India. (2020, August 27). *Press release: Year 2 results*. Retrieved from Quality of Education India DIB website: https://qualityeducationindiadib.com/2020/11/11/year-2-results/

Quality of Education India. (2022). *Quality of education India*. Retrieved from Quality of Education India DIB website: https://qualityeducationindiadib.com/

Ramalingam, B. (2013). *Aid on the edge of chaos*. Oxford: Oxford University Press.

Sharp, S., & Wild, L. (2021). *Opportunities and challenges for DAC members in 'adapting to context'*. London: ODI.

Standard and Poor. (2022, February 25). *Ratings direct: International development association*. Retrieved from World Bank Treasury website: https://treasury.worldbank.org/en/about/unit/treasury/ida/ratings-reports

Sundberg, M. (2020, October). Building trust, gaining truth: The relational work of national staff in foreign aid agencies. *Current Anthropology, 61*(5), 562–582.

Taggart, J. (2022). A decade since Busan: Towards legitimacy or a "new tyranny" of global development partnership? *Journal of Development Studies*, 1–19.

Tsai, L. L., Toral, G., Read, B., & Lipovsek, V. (2018). *Taxation and accountability in developing countries: Does taxation motivate citizens to hold government accountable? If so, how is taxation increased and tax evasion decreased?* Washington, DC: Transparency and Accountability Initiative.

United Nations. (2015). *Transforming our world: The 2030 agenda for sustainable development*. New York: UN.

United Nations. (2022a). *SDG indicators*. Retrieved from UNStats website: https:unstats.un.org/sdgs/ndicators/indicators-list

United Nations. (2022b). *The sustainable development goals report 2021*. New York: United Nations.

United Nations. (2022c). *Voluntary national reviews*. Retrieved from Sustainable Development Knowledge Platform: https://sustainabledevelopment.un.org/vnrs/

United Nations. (n.d.). *Sustainable development goals*. Retrieved from United Nations website: www.un.org/en/sustainable-development-goals

United Nations Conference for Trade and Development. (2022, January 19). *Global foreign direct investment rebounded strongly in 2021, but the recovery is highly uneven*. Retrieved from UNCTAD website: https://unctad.org/news/global-foreign-direct-investment-rebounded-strongly-2021-recovery-highly-uneven

Village Enterprise. (2022). *Development impact bond*. Retrieved from Village Enterprise website: https://villagecenterprise.org/what-we-do/development-impact-bond/

Wiseman, P. (2022, April 20). *IMF, World Bank chiefs warn of debt squeeze in poor nations*. Retrieved from AP News website: https://apnews.com/article/covid-health-business-world-bank-international-monetary-fund-71aa7e9c225e973e-c16a962fe6d53773

World Bank. (2021a). *A changing landscape: Trends in official financial flows and the aid architecture*. Washington, DC: World Bank.

World Bank. (2021b). *Annual report 2021: From crisis to green, resilient and inclusive recovery*. Washington, DC: World Bank.

World Bank. (2022). *2021 development policy financing retrospective: Facing crisis, fostering recovery*. Washington, DC: World Bank.

Yanguas, P. (2018). *Why we lie about aid: Development and the messy politics of change*. London: Zed.

9 Summing Up and Looking Ahead

It is not an easy task to end a book on foreign aid. This book has no grand conclusions; the subject matter is too complex. Instead, this final chapter will recap some of the insights that have emerged and then turn to what might happen in the future with aid. Words of caution and humility are warranted. While there are lessons, there are always exceptions. While there are trends, a "black swan" event like the COVID-19 pandemic can send the future in an opposite direction. The more one knows, the more one questions.

Summing Up

Aid in the Age of Pragmatism

Although linked to a dark past (colonialism, along with slavery and oppression), foreign aid in the early years of the 1960s and 1970s was imbued with a spirit of optimism and a belief in the soundness of Western values. Aid, similar to what the Marshall Plan did to Europe, was supposed to help newly independent nations develop. Even during the Cold War years, when aid decisions were driven by political strategy, the backdrop was a battle of big ideals: democracy versus communism. In any event, aid was not successful in pulling many nations out of poverty. In the 1980s and 1990s, the US and other Western nations used aid to stem economic crises and entrench market economics to a greater or lesser degree, with differing views on the role of government and NGOs depending on each donor's structures and experience (Dietrich, 2021). The 1990s, at least in Africa and Latin America, were a time of pessimism amid declining aid budgets and poor economic performance. This ushered in an age of renewal, with increasing amounts of aid, a push for aid effectiveness and "ownership" by recipients. There was renewed excitement, especially since several Asian countries, most notably China, had turned into success stories. The 2000s saw the entrance of many new players, the non-traditional or emerging donors and foundations, bringing more diversity

DOI: 10.4324/9781003265320-11

in both aid policies and practices. Enthusiasm welled up again in the first half of the 2010s despite the global financial crisis in 2008–2009. Significant gains were made in reducing extreme poverty and improving health outcomes. To succeed the Millennium Development Goals, the UN General Assembly endorsed the Sustainable Development Goals in 2015. The headline goal was to eliminate extreme poverty by 2030 and "to leave no one behind".

By 2020, storm clouds gathered once again. Insufficient action on climate change increased the rhythm and severity of environmental disasters and disruptions, with low-income countries suffering the most. A pandemic swept through the world and turned the attention of many donor countries inward even while it was clear that global solutions were needed. War in Europe and ensuing food and fuel shortages slammed developing countries, and inflation and other economic woes occupied the US and Western Europe. The need to provide vaccines kept aid totals increasing, but idealism was clearly on the wane. Poverty in low and middle-income countries increased, and a debt crisis once again loomed despite the debt relief of the early 2000s.

The situation today is that most donors now see aid as part of their diplomatic toolbox: they keep a close check on their aid bureaucracies or fold them into their foreign affairs ministries. Donors also want to make sure that aid is centered on their priorities and are less concerned about recipient ownership. Some focus on fragile states to avoid the threat of violence or its expansion. The results agenda also means focusing on interventions that are relatively easy to measure so that tangible progress can be shown to donor constituencies. An increase in local staff keeps costs down while expanding donor knowledge and contacts with recipients to help shape projects and policies. In short, a new pragmatism is afoot in the donor community. This also applies to south-south cooperation and emerging donors. For China, mutual benefit continues as its guiding principle. Others have made it clear that their aid interventions are tied to their own interests, be those religion, commercial pursuits, or security.

Aid Is Here to Stay

Thoughts that aid is or should be a dying industry have proven to be premature (Gill, 2018; Moyo, 2009). In the aggregate, aid has been eclipsed by other forms of development finance and by private sector flows to developing countries. However, in low-income countries and fragile and conflict-affected states, aid is still an essential lifeline and frequently the largest source of external finance. Also, as seen during financial crises and pandemics, aid steps in to become an important tool for providing extra finance even for middle-income countries.

As climate emergencies and other disasters occur, humanitarian aid is indispensable and can be expected to remain so for the forseeable future.

Of course, there will be changes, as there have been in the past, in the rules of the game and the things that aid finances. The changes perhaps will not be as dramatic as some would expect because there are tendencies pulling in different directions. There are those who want aid to essentially leverage greater private sector investment, which would benefit primarily resource-rich and/or middle-income countries attractive to the private sector. This is in direct contrast to those who see aid as helping the poorest by concentrating on low-income and fragile states. There are those who want aid to be redirected towards primarily global public goods and global programs, while others are proponents of country-based aid and tackling country-specific problems first. There are those who would limit aid to humanitarian and emergency needs only, while others argue that aid is best used to assist in policy changes, structural reform, and medium-term development needs such as basic infrastructure. There are those who argue that aid amounts will decline sharply because of pressing domestic needs in donor countries and the ever present donor fatigue and skepticism in some quarters. In contrast, others point to the expansion of needs and the entrance of new donors, a sign that aid will increase. All these different tensions, ironically, provide a certain unexpected stability for aid, despite periodic upheavals in some donor countries.

No Magic Bullets

Despite the increasing number of aid providers, more aid, and the innovative design of aid projects such as cash transfers, "cash on delivery", or the graduation approach, there are no magic bullets in the arsenal of aid that will resolve development bottlenecks or reduce poverty universally. Context deeply matters. History, resource endowments, population diversity, culture, and politics are a few of the big headlines that can affect how development interventions work. Some trends are discernible, but aid and development are likely to continue based on a "trial and error" approach. Randomized controlled trials are just one specialized tool for this. Most experimentation and adaptation will take place on the ground without "scientific" monitoring and measurement. What is needed, then, is not more certainty about design, but more flexibility during implementation. This includes ensuring that aid can be rapidly redeployed when needed and that both recipient and donor managers have the skills, and importantly, the permission to highlight problems and make changes in a timely fashion. Progress on the issues of timeliness and flexibility has been mixed at best. Delays and rigidities diminish aid's potential for impact.

The Rhetoric and the Reality

The rhetoric of aid continues to be one of helping poor nations and the need for low and middle-income countries to "own" the interventions financed by aid. The word *partnership* has become common in the aid lexicon for many kinds of relationships. Partnership is a different concept than sole ownership. There are many kinds of "partners", e.g., silent partners, managing partners, junior partners; the use of the word *partnership* does not imply or confer a certain kind of power in the relationship. It does not mean that donors have relinquished the ability to set agendas and determine where their funds will be spent. In good aid relationships, there is extensive upstream discussion and the setting of mutually agreed-upon objectives for funding. In others, donors tell their "partners" where they want to put their funds. The "partner" may not agree with the priority or the specifics, but also knows that the funds are needed. National development strategies, which are generally very broad, can easily become distorted by the preferences of donors and the availability of aid.

Where does the reality lie today? Unquestionably, there is less flexing of donor "muscle" than in the past, and there are serious efforts by some donors to faithfully align with national development strategies. However, there are also donors (e.g., global funds, private foundations, some emerging donors) who have specific mandates and/or mechanisms and are interested in funding interventions that conform closely to their interests. The retreat from bilateral budget support, the growing use of earmarked trust funds to steer the activities of multilateral development banks (the bilateral-multilateral funding discussed in Chapter 4), the growth of global funds even for activities that are not global public goods (e.g., education, urban development), all speak to a desire for donors to have control over what gets funded. In short, the rhetoric – whether centered on ownership or even on partnership – does not match the reality.

Good aid relationships, with honest and open communication, transparency, and intercultural understanding are possible and could help aid become more effective. Local donor staff could play an important role here. But those relationships, besides needing good will, take time to develop, time that simply does not exist in today's fragmented aid scene. Governments are overwhelmed by the depth and scope of the problems facing them today. There is little time for the informality and the conversations that need to take place to cement understandings and develop trust. If anything, aid relationships have become more formal, given the avalanche of tasks on both sides. Consequently, opportunities are being missed to increase understanding of each other's position and facilitate fast and reliable interaction that is action-oriented and can make development interventions more effective.

An End to Harmonization?

One of the biggest changes since the Paris Declaration of Aid Effectiveness has been that the harmonization of aid among donors has receded. Whether through conviction, i.e., competition and choice are good, or pragmatism, i.e., non-OECD donors are not prepared to collaborate closely with traditional donors, the emphasis on harmonization has diminished. Yet, the lack of harmonization is costly, given the duplications, gaps, increases in transaction costs, and general inefficiencies it brings. Moreover, it is difficult to see how aid can be fully aligned with recipient preferences and national development strategies without a considerable degree of harmonization.

One of the issues in the past with harmonization was that it tended to be the work of donors rather than the work of recipients. Some recipient governments were concerned, perhaps with some justification, that harmonization could also facilitate donors "ganging up" when things were not going well. For harmonization to truly exist, it needs to be an exercise that is led by recipient governments with clear guidance to donors. Transparent discussions and negotiations are required. This may not suit every donor, but there is a critical mass of donors who would welcome the initiative. Nonetheless, it is precisely in those countries where harmonization is most needed that this task is the most challenging because of the number and diversity of donors. Many recipient governments understand the difficulties and simply choose to avoid the aggravation and perceived risk involved. Others have not yet built up the capacity or confidence to take the lead. However, along with ensuring coherent national development strategies and sound public financial management systems, this is an essential task for recipient governments who want to exercise ownership over their aid programs.

The related tasks of aid alignment and harmonization have become easier in recent years due to the advent of technology with the capability to track complex aid programs on the ground. Whether technology can help to overcome the hesitations that are shared by some recipients and donors towards a more tightly managed aid system remains an open question. For recipients and donors with less of a development mindset, a laissez-faire system is more suitable to their interests.

Tension Between Global and National Priorities

The tensions between global and national priorities are growing stronger, particularly as global problems related to disease, conflict, climate, and environment surge. Optimists point to the many cases where the priorities are compatible, e.g., fighting COVID-19, climate-smart agriculture with higher yields and less environmental damage. Yet, on some issues, including those related to energy, trade, finance, and biodiversity, the priorities of recipient nations are seldom aligned to global priorities and policies mainly set by donor countries (even when agreed to in principle by others in international fora). Some recipient countries also are concerned that global priorities will "crowd out" national priorities because aid will increasingly be used for the former. For many low and middle-income countries, economic growth is still unquestionably the first priority. In theory, aid for domestic priorities is an outright donation, while funding for global public goods can be viewed as a compensatory payment in cases where benefits accrue more to others than to the recipient nation or when the priority is global but less urgent nationally. This argues for funding global public goods separately and *incrementally* (Kaul et al., 1999). However, this is theory only, and aid is currently financing a wide variety of interventions, including those related to global public goods.

An increasing emphasis on global public goods may lead to more "aid orphans". These are countries that receive relatively little aid despite high poverty and population levels because they have little impact on global public goods and bads and are not central to the national security concerns of donor countries (Tengstam & Isaksson, 2021; Davies & Klasen, 2019). Moreover, with increased conflict in Europe and elsewhere, more aid may go to support displaced populations and initial migration costs in donor countries, leaving less for recipient country development initiatives. Countries in conflict such as Iraq, Afghanistan, and Ukraine, where the international community is deeply involved, tend to need and receive large amounts of aid, leaving more peaceful countries with less. The tension between global and national priorities will likely play itself out with more attention – and more aid – to the global issues that matter most to donors.

Tensions Between the Global North and the Global South

Friction between aid donors and recipients is not new, nor are the tensions between high-income countries from Europe and North America and those countries collectively referred to as developing countries or in today's language, the Global South. However, when it comes to foreign aid, despite the rhetoric of international cooperation and the global nature of the SDGs, the rift between the Global North and the Global South is growing. Because GPEDC and others have been unable to span that rift, the OECD-DAC continues in its efforts to coordinate and guide aid for some 31 members and others, while the BRICS countries are undertaking similar efforts among themselves and with other developing countries. Emerging donors from the Global South pointedly refuse to call their support aid and establish their own principles. The BRICS in mid-2022 hosted a High-Level Dialog on Global Development as part of the 14th BRICS Summit. At that time, China came out with its first Global Development Report outlining its Global Development Initiative (GDI).

Box 9.1   GPEDC Development Effectiveness Principles and China's Principles From Its Global Development Initiative

GPEDC	CHINA
• Country ownership over the development process	• People-centered core philosophy
	• Development first
	• Innovation-driven development
• A focus on results	• Inclusive development
	• Harmonious coexistence of man and nature
• Inclusive development partnerships	• Multilateralism, openness, and inclusiveness
	• Action-oriented
• Transparency and mutual accountability	• Synergy with existing mechanisms

Source: Center for International Knowledge on Development (2022), Johnson and Brettfeld (2022), Global Partnership for Effective Development Co-operation (n.d.)

Box 9.1 contrasts the Busan/GPEDC aid effectiveness principles with the core principles in the GDI. Some of the core principles of the GDI are in tune with Global North thinking; others are not necessarily. Both refer often to the SDGs. There is a joint emphasis on inclusive partnerships and synergy with existing mechanisms. A focus on results and being action-oriented are related. GPEDC refers to transparency, and the GDI mentions openness. The GDI also mentions the need for "harmonious coexistence between man and nature" (Center for International Knowledge on Development, 2022, p. 32), acknowledging global environmental and climate concerns. At the same time, the CGI emphasizes development first. Referring to China's history, it says that "only by focusing on development can a nation achieve prosperity and strength, and its people live a happy life" (p. 36). The biggest difference in terms of principles is that GPEDC focuses on process while GDI focuses on development. In addition, the GDI spells out eight substantive priorities: poverty reduction, global food security, health, finance for development, green and low-carbon development, industrialization, digitalization, and connectivity. While all of these are in the SDGs and are embraced by the Global North, it is notable how involved the GDI is in the *substance* of development. This is absent in the work of GPEDC, which seems focused on mostly donor-centric themes in the aid relationship.

The tensions between the Global South and the Global North are multi-layered. Strikingly, China's Global Development Report, while covering the broad substance of development, makes little mention of gender disparities except in relation to the digital divide. The same is true for governance. Global governance and its deficits figure prominently, but there is little mention of governance at the national level, a perennial concern, whether voiced or not, of the Global North. While the Global North remains focused on regime type and the need for democratic government, leading countries in the Global South (e.g., China, Russia, Vietnam) have taken alternative paths. There has been a renaissance in nationalism, slowing globalization and exacerbating the tensions between countries. How these tensions will play out in the aid arena remains to be seen.

What the Future Holds

What does the future of aid look like? How will the trends and tensions described in the last chapter and this chapter play out? Because of the continuing rifts between ideals and pragmatism and between policies and actual practice, each of the topics in the following section speculating on aid's future is divided into two parts: what would be desirable and what is likely to happen.

Aid Effectiveness

What Would Be Desirable

Given the need to ensure that low-income countries finally advance out of poverty and the urgency of growing global crises, this is the right time to redouble efforts on aid effectiveness, defined as aid that reduces poverty and improves the welfare and well-being of people. Although there are no magic bullets, there is much accumulated knowledge and good experience. This is a time for "doing development differently" by thoroughly understanding the context, having flexibility, developing patience, and showing the ability to receive and incorporate feedback at all levels. This applies equally to governments and donors. Monitoring and measuring results should be mainly for the purpose of learning and corrective action rather than for backward-looking, static accountability. The emphasis needs to be on effective implementation. Reportedly, a farmer once said, "You'll never fatten a steer by spending all your time weighing it."

What Is Likely to Happen

Increasingly, the aid effectiveness agenda seems to be dead. Some of this can be attributed to the growing tensions between the Global North and the Global South, which have not been able to agree and cooperate on this agenda except in the broadest terms. More of the problem lies with the fact that aid is increasingly being guided by foreign affairs ministries with strategic interests for whom development is not necessarily the primary objective. Donor nations, in an age of uncertainty, are protective of their national economies and interested in dampening the effects of migration, terrorists, pandemics, climate change, and financial disruptions at home. So effective aid for them is not about poor country development except when those interests coincide with their strategic agenda. Recipient ownership is basically off the table, replaced by the ambiguous concept of partnership.

Ironically, given this scenario, aid effectiveness may *appear* to improve in the future, as more aid is channeled to middle-income countries, primarily for global public goods. Those countries have greater capacity to use funds and produce "results". In the meantime, most low-income countries will remain stuck where they have been since 1960, on the Least Developed Country list maintained by the UN and OECD.

Aid Amounts

What Is Desirable

Aid amounts have never been near the 0.7 percent of GDP target set many years ago. Aid needs to increase to provide the amount of support needed for low and lower-middle income countries to prosper. This is especially true given the toll that has been exacted by the "polycrisis" – pandemic, food insecurity, climate disasters, rising prices and debt – that has characterized many of these countries in the early 2020s. At the same time, humanitarian and migration costs have also risen because of ongoing conflicts, while efforts related to the environment and global health run the risk of being seriously underfunded. Official aid is only a relatively small part of total development finance. However, it is critically important both as a catalyst for other types of private and public investment and as a funder of last resort. In low-income and fragile states, aid is frequently the largest source of external support. Remittances help families survive, but they do not provide critical public services and infrastructure. A meaningful increase in aid implies a substantial increase in aid budgets almost across the board from both OECD-DAC donors and non-traditional donors.

What Is Likely to Happen

As mentioned previously, there are opposing views and forces that result in a certain stability in aid amounts. Increases are likely to be gradual and driven by growing humanitarian needs. Competition between the leaders of the

Global South and the Global North may help to keep aid budgets robust in many countries. Aid will also be used, along with other parts of national budgets, to provide global public goods on an increasing scale. However, recurring global financial crises that bring disruptions to advanced economies, as well as political preferences, could result in aid reductions from time to time in specific countries, as seen, for example, in Australia and Great Britain in the early 2020s. Consequently, while aid budgets could well increase, low and lower-middle income countries are unlikely to see large increases in aid to fund their national development strategies.

The Composition of Aid

What Would Be Desirable

Traditional aid has been heavily weighted towards the social sectors, balanced to a certain extent by some non-traditional donors who have generally favored economic and production-oriented sectors such as infrastructure. In the future, it would be desirable to keep a balance with a tilt towards economic and productive sectors to favor rapid and sustainable economic growth and job creation. The ideal balance, however, should vary from country to country based on recipient priorities and the realities of the political and social situation.

Low-income countries should receive most of the aid, with less aid focused on middle-income countries. Middle-income countries should be encouraged to use the aid they receive to leverage more private sector investment, including guarantees and development finance operations. The focus of aid in low-income countries should continue to be on providing basic public goods and services. For the lowest-income countries and those with exceptionally high debt burdens, aid should overwhelmingly be on a grant basis. That should happen only in cases where the recipient country agrees to be fully accountable for how that aid is spent.

In terms of the mixture between country-based programs and global programs, it would be advisable for the overall shift to be gradual from the former to the latter. Global programs should be reserved for those issues like environment and disease control that need to be tackled on a global, rather than national, basis. If the shift is too rapid towards global programs, many low-income countries are likely to see a premature decline in aid receipts. Global programs could have a positive effect on middle-income countries by providing concessional transitional finance while more traditional aid is channeled mainly to low-income and lower middle-income countries.

Ideally, more aid should be given the form of budget support, both general and sector specific. The pace with which this happens should be consistent with the progress made in establishing sound recipient country systems for procurement, managing, monitoring, and auditing. Projects would not be managed by consultants, contractors, or aid agencies, but by recipient governments utilizing help where needed. Technical assistance would be limited to those cases where the recipient government has taken the initiative and specialized, short-term knowledge is indispensable or the government has a realistic plan for building the capacity to replace the technical assistance.

What Is Likely to Happen

Some balance will be achieved just because of donor preferences and some donors who are willing to fund gaps. However, given pandemics and natural disasters, the balance is likely to remain tipped towards social sectors for traditional aid donors. Also, in the next few years, humanitarian aid, because of more frequent emergencies and conflicts, is likely to rise. The combination of pandemics, food insecurity, and economic disruptions will also result in another wave of debt relief, as countries struggle to cope.

While aid to low-income countries may marginally increase, aid to middle-income countries and aid provided in support of global public goods will remain predominant, much like the situation today. If there continues to be an increase in conflict and natural disasters requiring donor support in more developed parts of the world, there may be a decrease in aid to low-income countries, especially in sub-Saharan Africa. While middle-income countries will try to use aid to leverage private sector investment, this will depend on the overall stability of the world economic order and how well those countries have managed the crises of the early 2020s. Although there will be encouragement for grant funding, multilateral banks and some prominent donors are likely to continue to use loans with varying degrees of concessionality in their aid programs. Even confronted with moral hazard because of successive rounds of debt relief, some aid providers argue that having to pay back aid monies encourages accountability while loan repayments take some pressure off their aid budgets.

Global programs are likely to grow in number and importance. As discussed, they are a way for donors to control what gets financed while not having to administer the aid directly. Global programs will expand with the need for reinforcing global public goods. Similar to what is happening today, the programs will also be used to attract more attention to areas considered priority by donors. The attraction of global programs will be that goals can be established at the global level and directed explicitly towards specific issues. In an age of pragmatism, being able to show results on a grand scale will be important. Country-based aid will also continue, and non-traditional donors are likely to increase in relative importance at that level. How more traditional donors respond to that development will depend on their perception of the strategic importance of the recipient country. More "aid darlings" and "aid orphans" are a distinct possibility.

Although favored by recipients, budget support is unlikely to re-emerge as a popular form of aid, although the World Bank, the IMF, and the EU, three important donors, will continue to provide policy-based budget support. Project aid will remain the predominant vehicle of support, and recipient nations will argue for bigger projects that cover sub-sectors or larger geographical areas. Over time, as some countries grow and strengthen their public administrations, some recipient nations will exercise more control over their aid budgets and take the lead in trying to harmonize donor support, especially in sectors where there are many donors and small projects. There will also be some progress made on what the US calls localization, relying more on local contractors and local NGOs in project implementation. This, however, is unlikely to result in increased implementation responsibilities for low-income countries, especially fragile states. Both traditional and non-traditional donors will remain leery of turning over funds and authority to low-income states with weak governance, especially those with a lack of capacity and a propensity for corruption. Ownership, and even partnership, will remain muted concepts at best.

Who Will Give Aid

What Would Be Desirable

As is the case today in medium-income countries, support for development in low-income countries would come from many different public and private sources. Private foundations, NGOs who raise funds from the public, faith-based NGOs, international agencies, and official bilateral sources would take the lead on aid. All would partner with the recipient country government and follow government strategy, plans, and procedures. Their project and programs would be subject to recipient government supervision. Over the next decade, these sources would transition to strictly financing agencies as opposed to implementation agencies. With the recipient government's agreement, NGOs who receive bilateral aid would continue to implement projects but would report directly to the recipient government. All aid would be captured in the recipient government's budget, with any recurrent cost obligations clearly specified so the recipient would be aware of and agree to related future expenditures.

In fragile and extremely low-capacity countries, aid agencies – public, private, and not-for-profit – would pursue a two-track strategy over a longer period. Humanitarian aid would continue to be administered and implemented outside of the government. Developmental aid would start slowly, mostly administered outside government, at first focusing mostly on capacity and governance. Projects financed by aid would transition over time to be implemented by the recipient government as capacity and governance improve.

Private foundations and non-traditional donors would provide more aid. This would be incremental to and not a substitute for the aid provided by traditional donors and multilateral agencies and banks. Bilateral and multilateral official sources would still provide much of the aid to low-income countries, but multilateral sources would become more important relative to bilateral ones. This would help keep the focus on development, rather than on the strategic priorities of any one donor. Also, in cases where one donor, public or private, dominates in a subsector, a sector or a country, care would be taken to ensure that the donor does not become the determining voice in related policy. This is particularly important in the case of private funders providing public goods.

Ideally, over time, there would be increasing convergence in the way that aid agencies operate and interact with recipient governments. Recipient governments would have a clearer picture of all the aid provided and could work to better align aid with their priorities.

What Is Likely to Happen

What is happening today is likely to continue. While there will be more "localization", i.e., use of local government agencies and NGOs, many bilateral donors will be reluctant to strictly follow recipient government plans and procedures and will not allow recipients to have control over their aid. Similarly, donors will contract NGOs directly when they are mistrustful of the capabilities of the recipient government. Both the donors and the NGOs will be reluctant to hand control over to recipient governments in those instances. This is particularly true in fragile and low-capacity states. Most aid will continue to be administered outside the government system. Also, given the need to show concrete results, most donors do not have the expertise nor patience to pursue a two-track strategy, where capacity and governance issues, including corruption, are pursued gradually over a long period of time. While, increasingly, aid amounts are being put "on budget", it is still unlikely that aid amounts and development interventions will be sized appropriately to consider the government's real capacity to implement activities and finance recurrent expenditures.

Private foundations and non-traditional donors will provide more aid, although they are unlikely to come close to the amounts provided by traditional donors and multilateral agencies. Instead of bilateral donors providing more aid to multilaterals directly, there will continue to an increase in multi-bi aid, which spares donors the costs of direct administration while preserving their ability to influence what gets financed. For the same reason, global programs will continue to be popular even when they are not strictly needed because of the nature of their interventions.

The picture that emerges is one of continued aid fragmentation that will go on until recipient countries can adroitly manage their aid. Most low-income countries still see being honest with official and even private donors as fraught with risk. They fear that raising objections could damage the relationship and result in lower amounts of aid. Instead, most recipient countries talk about lessening aid dependency. However, given the turbulence of the early 2020s, the system, especially for low-income countries without natural resources, is not amenable to rapid change.

Final Thoughts

As outlined in this chapter, the future of aid is decidedly mixed. Aid will continue because official bilateral donors have come to see aid as an important foreign policy tool. Aid is also useful because of the exigencies created by climate change, conflict, pandemics, and poverty. New project designs, efforts to at least "partner" with recipient countries, the diversity of donors, and the growing capabilities of recipient governments are positive developments that will permit overall aid to modestly increase. At the same time, the strategic interests of donors could differ from the most pressing needs of recipients, and the need for global public goods could well overshadow the basic developmental needs of low-income and fragile countries. The distance between rich countries and very poor countries could well increase. Progress has been slow in donors relinquishing or even sharing decision-making with respect to their aid, and impatience has created a results agenda favoring results that are quick to emerge and easy to count but that may not be sustainable. Tensions between the Global North and the Global South are building as well, while the lack of harmonization has adversely effected aid efficiency and, most likely, aid effectiveness.

Although most of this book has spoken about low-income countries or fragile states as opposed to regions, it is important to highlight sub-Saharan Africa. All projections show that in a few years, Africa will be the continent that will be furthest behind, with continuing poverty, disease, conflict, and devastation from climate change. In the past, it has also been fertile ground for proxy wars and competition among Great Powers. Yet, Africa is also the continent that holds the most promise, with entrepreneurial populations, capable youth, new discoveries, natural resources, and a resilience that is hard to fathom at times. It would be abundantly sensible to give special attention to Africa in the next decade. That means trying to push against the tide and ensure that its poorest states have the resources they need to heal and to develop. However, it is not just about the amount of aid, but the need for both donors and recipients to lose the historical legacy of disappointment and cynicism and make strong efforts so that the aid provided is truly effective.

Foreign aid for development is a complex business where uninterrupted linear progress is a myth. It is a daily struggle – for donors, for recipient governments, and for beneficiaries. There are moments of celebration involving true change and moments of disillusion and despair when change is halted or reversed. This will continue to be true in the current "age of pragmatism". That is why it is so important to keep the bigger picture on aid in mind and to understand how it works, to keep opening the "black box". While aid is far from perfect – in both policies and practice – it is neither feasible nor desirable to conceive of a world without aid, especially if the goal is truly to "leave no one behind".

Bibliography

Center for International Knowledge on Development. (2022). *Global development report*. Beijing: Center for International Knowledge on Development.

Davies, R. B., & Klasen, S. (2019). Darlings and orphans: Interactions across donors in international aid. *The Scandinavian Journal of Economics, 121*(1), 243–277.

Dietrich, S. (2021). *States, markets, and foreign aid*. Cambridge: Cambridge University Press.

Gill, I. (2018, January 19). *The end of aid*. Retrieved from Future Development Blog, Brookings website: www.brookings.edu/blog/future-development/2018/01/19/the-end-of-aid/

Global Partnership for Effective Development Co-operation. (n.d.). *The global partnership at a Glance*. Retrieved from GPEDC website: www.effectivecooperation.org/content/gpedc-glance

Johnson, Z., & Brettfeld, C. (2022, July 25). *What is China's GDI? Five takeaways from China's first global development report*. Retrieved from Donor Tracker website: https://donortracker.org/insights/what-chinas-gdi-five-takeaways-chinas-first-global-development-report

Kaul, I., Isabelle, G., & Stern, M. A. (1999). *Global public goods: International cooperation in the 21st century*. New York: Oxford University Press for UNDP.

Moyo, D. (2009). *Dead aid: Why aid is not working and how there is a better way for Africa*. New York: Farrar, Straus and Giroux.

Tengstam, S., & Isaksson, A.-S. (2021). *Kill Your darlings? Do new aid flows help achieve a poverty minimizing allocation of aid?* Stockholm: Research Institute of Industrial Economics.

Index

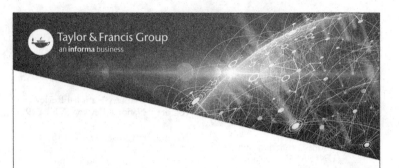

Printed in the United States
by Baker & Taylor Publisher Services